ATTITUDES OF RELIGIONS AND IDEOLOGIES TOWARD THE OUTSIDER

The Other

ATTITUDES OF RELIGIONS AND IDEOLOGIES TOWARD THE OUTSIDER

The Other

Edited by

Leonard Swidler

and

Paul Mojzes

Religions in Dialogue
Volume 1

The Edwin Mellen Press
Lewiston/Queenston/Lampeter

Library of Congress Cataloging-in-Publication Data

This volume has been registered with The Library of Congress.

This is volume 1 in the continuing series
Religions in Dialogue
Volume 1 ISBN 0-88946-270-4
RD Series ISBN 0-88946-379-4

A CIP catalog record for this book
is available from the British Library.

The Edwin Mellen Press
Box 450
Lewiston, New York
USA 14092

The Edwin Mellen Press
Box 67
Queenston, Ontario
CANADA L0S 1L0

Edwin Mellen Press, Ltd
Lampeter, Dyfed, Wales,
UNITED KINGDOM SA48 7DY

Printed in the United States of America

ATTITUDES OF RELIGIONS AND IDEOLOGIES TOWARD THE OUTSIDER

The Other

CONTENTS

INTRODUCTION

Religions as social phenomena, like other social groupings and institutions, tend to draw a circle around their own adherents. Beliefs and practices are usually intended solely for the benefit of the group. If it is believed, however, that they should be universally applicable, a distinction is then made between those who accept and practice them and those who do not. In any case, there is often an awareness of others who do not belong within the circle of one's own religion. In some instances that awareness is implicit with no specific attitudes toward others being fostered among the adherents, whereas the actual response to the outsider may range from hostility, fear, curiosity, indifference to even partial acceptance and cooperation. In other cases explicit attitudes may be deliberately inculcated, moving from extreme good will to extreme ill will.

On the whole the impression is that the relationship of a given religion to "the other" has been a sore point. When we look at the religions stemming from the Near East, the so-called "Abrahamic" religions, until recently their *preponderant* attitude toward others has been exclusivist, i.e., the tendency to view one's own religion as true and others as less than completely true, and therefore to view them with hostility. Religions of the Far East and India have shown greater toleration of religious diversity, but there too "the other," especially if radically different, has presented a problem, which sometimes escalated into armed conflict, the same as among the Abrahamic faiths.

Why is this an important problem? Most obviously because certain attitudes toward the "other" have caused bloody conflicts both in the past and the present. We need only to mention well known conflict areas such as Ireland, Lebanon, Sri Lanka, the Philippines, India and Pakistan.

Even a tolerant religion such as Hinduism is embroiled in armed conflicts with Muslims, Sikhs, and Buddhists, and not so long ago with Christians. Conflicts between Armenians and Azerbeijanis in officially atheist U.S.S.R. still bear marks of the Christian and Muslim traditions of the respective antagonists. The civil war in Afghanistan between a Marxist government and Muslim guerillas takes on distinct religious/ideological coloring. Ideology has also played a role in some of the conflicts among Communist countries.

Short of war, the attitude toward "the other" has often been one of suspicion, contempt, hatred, and bigotry. Examples abound. Have not Christians throughout the centuries perpetuated the "teaching of contempt" toward Jews, which ultimately contributed to the Holocaust? Is it not true that a typical American Christian has had deep-seated fears and suspicions that Muslims are up to no good and has been quick to conclude that all Muslims are extremists *a la* Ayatollah Khomeini or the *Hezbollah*? Have not people of various religious persuasions in Asia been suspicious that Christianity in reality brings colonialism, racism, and the loss of traditional identities and morality?

Anyone genuinely interested in promoting peace on earth cannot overlook religious attitudes toward "the other" as one of the serious causes of conflict in the world. Some have even drawn the – albeit unwarranted – conclusion that religion always causes war and is the major source of hatred. Such people argue that if religion were to disappear there would be peace.

Others point out that many conflicts, economic, political, and national, often "dress up" as religious or ideological conflicts. This latter may well be true, but the disturbing factor is then that religion or ideology allows itself to be used as the sanctioner and justifier and perhaps intensifier of other types of conflict.

Why are we bothering to deal with this issue? Many religious people throughout the world are no longer content simply to look at the deplorable aspects of this abuse of dealing with "the other." They are looking for alternatives.

In order to promote peace and cooperation, dialogue is advocated as a means to work out problems between religious people of various persuasions. Dialogue, while a relatively contemporary approach to the encounter between religions, encourages each partner to make a serious appraisal of its own religious tradition to search objectively for both negative and positive attitudes toward "the other" from the outset of the religion.

When the negative attitudes are studied in their historical contexts, it will often be discovered that the reasons for a negative attitude may have been very specific circumstances—which no longer exist, and therefore it is wrong to perpetuate the attitude, since the source of aggravation has ceased to exist. Or else, one will honestly and self-critically face up to shortcomings of one's religious tradition, pointing out that there is no need to perpetuate the negative attitudes simply because they lasted so long.

The positive attitudes can be recovered, highlighted and promoted. Religious adherents often show genuine joy and satisfaction when they discover elements in their tradition which are appreciative of others and which help liberate them from prejudices and suspicions and when they realize that their inclinations to view the other as friend and not enemy are not necessarily recent in origin.

What better inspiration for cooperation and dialogue than to find out that the founder or a holy scripture or a great saintly figure of the tradition advocated respect, tolerance, or love toward those who are not members of the in-group? How satisfying it is when one discovers that although some adherents of a religion or ideology have regretfully stressed only one dimension of the relationship with "the other," namely, conflict, other more seminal thinkers showed a much more nuanced approach. It is gratifying to rediscover in the riches of one's own tradition the kind of impulses toward dialogue, peace, and cooperation which a contemporary adherent longs for.

A word here should be said about our understanding of religion and ideology. There have been numerous attempts to give a universally acceptable definition of religion. The task, however, seems ill-conceived, for the reality in question is too broad and diverse to be subject to a definition in the technical sense. Literally, to define something means to draw the limits (*fines*) around it, indicating clearly what belongs, and what does not belong. However, the human reality is not susceptible to such a clear-cut distinction in this case. The best we can hope to do is to provide a more or less acceptable "de-scription," that is, a "writing around," the subject that will include everything that scholars clearly include within the term religion and clearly exclude what they do not, and leave sufficient leeway to talk about those fuzzy entities which sort of belong and sort of do not belong. What we offer, then, is a description or "working definition" of religion.

Our "working definition" of religion is: "An explanation of the ultimate meaning of life, and how to live accordingly." In the past most "explanations of the ultimate meaning of life, and how to live accordingly" have entailed a belief in that which goes beyond, which "transcends," humanity and the world, traditionally termed the divine or the transcendent – Theravada Buddhism is a clear exception – and in recent centuries they have been called *religions* in the West. Those most recent "explanations of the ultimate meaning of life and how to live accordingly" which do not include a belief in the transcendent, such as Marxism, have at times been called *ideologies*, as in the World Council of Churches' "Dialogues with Peoples of Living Faiths and Ideologies."

Perhaps the most generic term or phrase in this area is "worldview and way," of which there are two main species: religion and ideology. A "worldview and way" is an "explanation of the ultimate meaning of life, and how to live accordingly." It will always include the "four c's": *creed* (belief-system), *code* (ethical system), *cult* (celebratory-system), and *community-structure* (social system). If the "explanation of the ultimate meaning of life, and how to live accordingly" is based ultimately on something which "goes beyond," "transcends," humanity and the world, *anthropon kai kosmon*, it belongs to the species "religion"; if it does not, but is ultimately "innerwordly" in its explanation, it belongs to the species "ideology."

There is of course something problematic with the term ideology – and also its possible alternatives. "Ideology," despite the fact that it etymologically means something like the systematic study of an idea (as biology is the systematic study of living things), often is understood to have a pejorative denotation. Thus used, an ideology would be a system of thought which like a Procrustean bed forces all data within its structures, even if it means distorting them grossly. However, ideology is also understood in a neutral fashion, meaning simply a systematized body of thought, as for example in a reference to Marxist ideology, which also includes a code for behavior flowing from the theoretical analysis.

"Philosophy" is a possible alternative here to the term ideology in a neutral sense. But it has the disadvantage of including Christian philosophy, Hindu philosophy and other "religious" philosophies. Hence, it could lead to confusion if it were used without a modifying adjective to refer *solely* to a system of thought and action which does not include the notion of the transcendent. The difficulty with using the term "worldview" (*Weltanschauung*) alone instead of "ideology" is that it usually does not denote a spelled-out thought structure, which the term "ideology" does, but rather suggests a general, somewhat vague attitude toward life – and that surely does not describe Marxism, for example. Hence, the neutral, more nearly root etymological, understanding of "ideology" seems to be the least problematic term to use to describe an "explanation of the ultimate meaning of life, and how to live accordingly" which is not based on the transcendent. Moreover, it is a self-description also used by at least some Marxists, and it also has the additional practical advantage of having been part of the official terminology used by the World Council of Churches. Consequently, its usage in this manner will probably gain in consensus and thus further create clarity in communication.

* * *

This book is a collection of essays which stands on its own because of the common focus of all authors on the theme of how their religion or ideology views "the other." However, simultaneously it is also part of a much larger project, of which it is the initial product. The project's acronym is GEO-DAPRI – "Global Education on Dialogue And Peace among Religions and Ideologies."

In response to the United Nations 1981 "Declaration on the Elimination of All Forms of Intolerance Based on Religion and Belief" the Secretariat of the UN held a Seminar on the implementation of that

Declaration in Geneva in 1984. At that Seminar Professor Leonard Swidler of Temple University in Philadelphia and Professor Iwao Munakata of Sophia University in Tokyo submitted a resolution (which was adopted) that the United Nations University in conjunction with other academic institutions undertake to produce a series of texts written by modern scholars from within the world's major religious and ideological traditions in collaboration with sympathetic outside experts which would contribute to religious freedom, understanding, dialogue, and peace among religions and ideologies.

This mandate to the United Nations University was re-enforced by Resolution 40/109 of the General Assembly of the United Nations on February 20, 1986, which in its operative part reads: "Invites the United Nations University and other academic and research institutions to undertake programmes and studies on the encouragement of understanding, tolerance and respect in matters relating to freedom of religion."

The GEO-DAPRI Project was then launched under the sponsorship of the United Nations University, the *Journal of Ecumenical Studies*, and the "Institute for Interreligious, Interideological Dialogue" (IFIID), the latter two being headquartered at Temple University. An Executive Committee was formed, consisting of, in addition to Professor Swidler, Professor Kinhide Mushakoji, Vice-Rector of the United Nations University in Tokyo, Professor Iwao Munakata of Sophia University in Tokyo, and Professor Paul Mojzes of Rosemont College in Pennsylvania. Swidler and Mojzes, being editors of the *Journal of Ecumenical Studies* and directors of the IFIID undertook to lead the project.

A group of 26 international scholars from various religious traditions and ideologies have accepted the invitation to become Major Authors of the project. An initial ten volumes are planned. In addition to an introductory volume there will be volumes on the religions of India the religions of China, Japan and Korea, Buddhism, Judaism, Christianity, Islam, indigenous religions, new religious movements, and ideologies.

Ideologies were included because scholarly findings indicate that in the modern world ideologies often fulfill the role or function of religion in their adherents' lives, and that currently the most organized ideology,

Marxism, in fact plays a quasi-religious role in the lives of scores of millions of people.

The special characteristics of the GEO-DAPRI Project are as follows:

1.   It will stress and foster interreligious, inter-ideological dialogue and the means to peace.

2.   It will consciously link its treatment with the United Nations Universal Declaration of Human Rights (1948) and the United Nations Declaration on the Elimination of All Forms of Intolerance and of Discrimination Based on Religion or Belief (1981).

3.   It will highlight the common elements of the various religions and ideologies, while at the same time noting and appreciating the differentiating elements.

4.   It will be written by critical-thinking "insider" scholars in dialogue with sympathetic "outsider" experts.

5.   It will, in addition to religions, cover ideologies, which for large numbers of people are the functional equivalents of religion.

6.   It will treat fully the role of women in each of the religions and ideologies.

7.   It will employ a substantial number of women scholars among its authors.

Each of the ten volumes, of 500-600 pages length, will contain both narrative and interpretative material written by the Major Authors or Invited Authors as well as samples of classical or relevant texts from that tradition. Subsequently a single-volume version will be produced for use as an introductory textbook in a general university-level course on world religions. At the same time teaching materials for secondary, primary and adult education will be adapted and extrapolated from the initial scholarly work, and translations and adaptations for other language areas and cultures will be undertaken as well.

To launch the GEO-DAPRI Project a conference was held wherein an intensive interaction among the Major Authors in conjunction with scholars from a variety of disciplines and kinds of institutions could come together in order to clarify the purposes and methodology of the Project.

The conference, on the theme "How Believers Account for Other's Beliefs," was held in Minnesota in April 1989. Initiator of the conference was Project Tandem, Inc. a nonsectarian, nonprofit corporation, and the only organization in the world focusing solely on promotion of the 1981 United Nations Declaration. Project Tandem, affiliated with the University of Minnesota, organized a 1986 International Conference, attended by 125 persons from thirty countries and sponsored by the University of Minnesota Law School and the United Nations Association of Minnesota, on ways to promote the Declaration. From these beginnings in Minnesota Project Tandem has organized not only the April 1989 conference of which this book is the record, but also a Second International Conference in Warsaw in May 1989, sponsored by the University of Minnesota College of Liberal Arts, the Institute of State and Law of the Polish Academy of Sciences, the Norwegian Institute of Human Rights, and the World Federation of United Nations Associations.

At the suggestion of Project Tandem and its Director, Michael Roan, three Minnesota academic institutions – Luther Northwestern Theological Seminary in Saint Paul, Saint John's University in Collegeville, and the University of Minnesota in Minneapolis, each hosted the conference on its own turf for an entire day. Several GEO-DAPRI authors spoke at these sessions, but beyond the traditional presentation of papers, the Minnesota institutions organized programs that would suggest to all the GEO-DAPRI authors questions to consider and angles of approach – from the experience and concerns of a theological seminary with a strong confessional identity, a religiously committed college operated by a monastic order, and the largest public secular university in country. A core group of nine Minnesota scholars, three from each institution, met regularly and often with the GEO-DAPRI authors throughout the conference. As was stated in the prospectus: "This is not a conference that would be the same no matter where it was held; the character of the three host institutions is an integral part of the theme and design."

Conference planning took seriously the fact that a framework of a conference is not a neutral setting but plays a determining role in what happens. The Minnesota planning committee wanted 1) to bring the central concern of the United Nations Declaration into focus, 2) to have a common theme for the conference, and 3) to make religious pluralism not just the context of discussion, but in some sense also its substance. To this end GEO-DAPRI authors who would speak at the conference were asked to address the following question:

> *How does the tradition about which I am writing account for the fact that there are many other religious traditions whose adherents are as firmly committed to them as I am to mine?*

This book gathers the papers delivered in response to that question, and concludes with a chapter developed by the Minnesota participants as they reflected together on what they had heard, both in the papers and in the many discussions generated by the conference in their three institutions.

* * *

We wish to express our gratitude to the organizers and sponsors of the conference, particularly to Dean Fred Lukermann of the College of Liberal Arts of the University of Minnesota, who underwrote the larger portion of the expenses for the conference. We wish also to thank Michael Roan of Project Tandem, Inc., and Lori Graven of the Department of Professional Development and Conference Services at the University of Minnesota, who provided invaluable support services. Bishop David Preus and President David Tiede of Luther Northwestern Theological Seminary, and Dr. Patrick Henry, Executive Director of the Institute for Ecumenical and Cultural Research, located at Saint John's Abbey and University, and Dean Dietrich Reinhart, O.S.B., of Saint John's University, rendered substantial service on the planning committee. Dean Lois Cronholm of Temple University supported the conference morally and financially.

The other GEO-DAPRI Major Authors contributed vigorously to the success of the conference and raised many questions which will be helpful in further work on these issues. They were:

Dr. Melanie May (Christianity) from the U.S., Dr. Riffat Hassan (Islam) from Pakistan/U.S., Dr. Nikky Singh (Indian Religions) from India/U.S., Dr. Klaus Klostermaier (Indian Religions) from Austria/Canada, Dr. David Chappell (Buddhism) from Hawaii, Dr. Iwao Munakata (Japanese Religions) from Japan, Dr. Paul Watt (Japanese Religions) from the U.S.,

Dr. Joon Sik Choi (Korean Religions) from South Korea, Dr. John Mbiti (Indigenous Religions) from Kenya/Switzerland, Dr. Franklin Littell (New Religious Movements) from the U.S., Dr. Herbert Richardson (New Religious Movements) from Canada, and Joseph Stoutzenberger (popular-text expert) from the U.S.

Major Authors who were unable to attend the Minnesota conference are: Dr. Eugene Fisher (Judaism) from the U.S., Dr. David Kerr (Islam) from England/U.S., Dr. Taitetsu Unno (Buddhism) from Japan/U.S., Dr. Inez Talamantez (Native American Religions) from the U.S.

TYPES OF ENCOUNTER BETWEEN RELIGIONS

by

Paul Mojzes

Encounter is the most suitable neutral word for describing the meeting between religions when it is desirable not to designate whether the encounter is positive or negative. In real life encounters range from war to merger, namely, from attempted mutual annihilation to synthesis. It is helpful to see these encounters on a continuum:

war	anta- gonism	indif- ference	nego- tiation	dialogue	cooper- ation	synthesis

The continuum should not be interpreted as a possibility of holding only one possible position simultaneously. For instance, it should be possible, indeed, even desirable, to dialogue and cooperate simultaneously. Nor does the continuum represent a desirable movement from war to synthesis through successive stages. Rather the continuum represents the spectrum of options in encounters classified in a range from hostility to voluntary absorption. It should also be noted at the outset that different members within a given religion may and do display a variety of responses to another religion(s), i.e., some may harbor antagonistic feelings or be indifferent, while others may be cooperative or even unify or merge the two views in their lives.

The five options need a further description.

Religious or Ideological War

From the beginning of the human species to the present members of different religious or ideological convictions warred against one another. To them the encounter with another religion meant the need to conquer or be conquered, annihilate or be annihilated. Often the reason for these wars was not purely religious. Political, territorial, economic, racial, ethnic, and other issues played a role alongside, or even more importantly than, religious or ideological ones. But this should not deter us from seeing that the religious component in these conflicts sometimes played a major, or even exclusive, role. More often than not there was no clear delineation between the religious and other spheres of life. Hence, when one felt threatened, e.g., politically or territorially, it was also experienced as a religious threat. Such is the situation in many locales in the contemporary world, as for example, Lebanon, Ireland, India, Sri Lanka, Philippines, and Israel, and also between countries, such as India and Pakistan or Iran and Iraq, or Greece and Turkey. In a number of other places there is at present no open war, but tensions exist stemming from previous wars, which, under appropriate circumstances, could flare up again as a war, e.g., in Yugoslavia and the U.S.S.R.

On the other hand, in a number of instances previous warfare has been resolved successfully and now there is cooperation rather than tension: e.g., between Catholics and Protestants in the Netherlands and Germany.

It is not easy to isolate the reasons for human aggressiveness exploding into violence. Feeling threatened in one's physical existence and values often issues in various forms of hostility, whether defensive or offensive in nature. For many people the deep-seated conviction that they hold the "Absolute and Complete Truth" issued not only in the conviction that they need no other truths, but also that other insights are false and have no right to exist alongside "Truth." It has been noted that religious wars were often more total in nature than those fought for territorial acquisition or plunder. In a helpful analysis John McKenzie pointed out that in sacred war the ancient Israelites, seeking actually to limit the number of wars fought for economic or territorial gains, mandated that in victory they spare no person or thing that belonged to the enemy.[1] Hence, such sacred wars were not only wars fought under the guise of religious motivation, but were in fact perceived as wars in which the entire religious existence of a people seemed to be threatened. This is, for instance, also the nature of Islamic *jihads* (holy wars). The attempted obliteration of all religions in the Soviet Union in the 1930s under Stalin was also carried out under the pretext of saving the Revolution.

A clue to the nature of religion can be gleaned from the frequent resorting to a religious justification of armed conflicts. It is vastly more difficult to persuade or pressure people to fight for the economic gain or political aggrandizement of one's group or leader than it is to motivate people to potentially give their lives and shed the blood of others for a lofty goal. Hence, the frequent "For God and Country" slogans accompanied even rather evidently political and economic conflicts, since people then seem more willing, ardent and inspired to engage a religious or ideological opponent. Indeed, if religion is one's ultimate concern, it should not be surprising that people are willing to live and to die for it. Hence, there is always a greater possibility of fanaticizing the combatants when religion or ideology is in question. One of the paradoxes of human existence is that our loftiest convictions spur us into the most inhumane actions on their behalf.

Religious wars may have several purposes. One, mentioned above, is the holy war bent on total destruction of the rival. Many religions have historically engaged in such wars and others have been obliterated by it. In some instances physical genocide was carried out. More frequently, cultural and religious genocide resulted, in that the identity of the defeated people perished as they were forcefully absorbed into the victorious group. Such was, for instance, the fate of the indigenous religions of the Norse, Slavic, Germanic, Hunic peoples in their encounter with Christians or the fate of the

---

1.   John McKenzie, *Old Testament Without Illusions* (Chicago: Thomas Moore Press).

North African or Iranian religions during the spread of Islam. Though remnants of the defeated religions sometimes make interesting reappearances in later customs and beliefs (e.g., Germanic Christmas trees, Haitian Voodoo, Orthodox Slavic funeral customs, African Muslim traditions), it is clear that war and conquest often ended in the demise of one religion and the victory of another.

Sometimes such wars simply changed the borderline of their geographic locations, without completely annihilating the opponent. Such was the case in the Catholic-Protestant and the Christian-Muslim and Muslim-Hindu wars, and the wars between Taoists, Confucians and Buddhists in ancient China. Successes in such wars and the desire for revenge provided ample justification for the continuance of such wars and aspirations for the future.

There was also the case of more limited wars, e.g., tribal wars in which members of different tribes espouse different primal religions. Here, limiting the power of the rival tribal supernatural protectors may have sufficed to terminate a conflict. Such conflicts did not attempt to spread the religion to other people; on the contrary, religious views and practices were often jealously guarded from outsiders.

It appears that the wars between religions take more sweeping proportions as religious consciousness moves from tribal to universalistic claims. The more comprehensive the claim on behalf of a religion as the religion or ideology suitable for the entire human race, the more likely were the conflicts to evolve into violent confrontations. Thus the frontal conflict between Islam and Christianity and between Marxist Communism and other religions were both protracted and incredibly bloody. The extent of the violence cannot be accounted for only by the improved weapons technology. The absolute universal claim of the historical religions and ideologies is capable of taking hold of followers in such an exclusivist manner that more often than not their confrontations with other religions take on an imperialistic posture.

Religious or Ideological Antagonism

Hostilities between religions and ideologies are not usually expressed in constant warfare. In its milder form the confrontation between religions is not explicitly violent but is expressed in intolerance, hatred, distrust, oppression, persecution, restrictions of human rights, especially religious liberties, contempt, and other forms of near-violent hostility. Such antagonism tends to be mutual and often issues in anathematizing the opponent; "enemy mentality" is spontaneously or methodically inculcated into the followers of the religions. In its milder form it may be blaspheming or disrespect for the opponent or a more deliberate vilifying or demonizing of the opponent.

Such antagonism is merely a milder form of war. Using the image from recent East-West political relations, one may call it a "cold war." The basic purpose is the same, namely, to eradicate and destroy the enemy, though methods short of physical violence may be used. One attempts to destroy the opponent doctrinally or psychologically. Contestation, debates and propaganda may be used to obtain the victory over the opponent. The educational system may be used to fortify the attack; sometimes the antagonism can take quite subtle forms. At times not even the perpetrator may be aware of the degree of antagonism held against other views. The hostility may be masked by a veneer of scholarly objectivity. One may detect the carefully concealed antagonism when one analyzes the arguments and sees that they are not meant to help the opponent improve, but are rather aimed at putting down the opponent, denigrating and ridiculing him. Debates or disputations between religions have been carried out with the intention of defeating the enemy or, at a minimum, obtaining some advantage to oneself and preferably a set-back for the opponent. Sometimes debates were held in order to determine which religion will be followed by a specific group. At other times debates were meant to be a tool of conversion, since it was held that the defeated party in the debate must abandon their position and adopt the winner's.

Antagonism is mostly of a tactical nature due to the impracticality of terminating the existence of the opponent. The long-range strategy is not co-existence but defeat of the enemy. This may be expressed by such long-range aims as "bringing the world to Christ," or "making all mankind submit to the will of Allah," or "building Communism throughout the World" or achieving "unification of humanity" in such manner that pluralism would be eliminated. Needless to say, the desire for a worldwide victory of such basic human values as liberty, justice, love, humanness, or equality, often embodied in notions of the "will of God," "God's rule or sovereignty" need not be seen as instruments of antagonism, unless the group promoting these universal values envisions itself as the sole carrier of such principles.

Indifference

There is a form of living side by side characterized by apathy or indifference and usually more than a little ignorance about the other. While active antagonism may be missing, there is a self-satisfaction which typifies this model which simply has no need of the neighbor. Each community lives by itself, perhaps even side by side. At times apparent harmony prevails, but not infrequently antagonism and distrust fester beneath, only to erupt in open hostility or warfare in a moment of crisis. A casual observer may fail to see the lurking problems which are masked by indifference, for this is what indifference does well – it does not solve problems – it merely prolongs them.

When compared to war and antagonism, indifference may be viewed as an advance. It would seem preferable to the fanatical desire to destroy the other. At least it gives time in which one may work for peace and understanding. But indifference is also a fertile ground for the seeds of distrust and enmity.

The negative aspect of indifference or apathy is that it is destructive not only of the neighbor but also of one's own religious or ideological conviction. Generally things simply do not matter sufficiently to become agitated over some issue. Often it results in cynicism about fundamental values and about the well-being of others. Self-centeredness is the likely result and with it the potential for destructive behavior toward others, which ultimately results in animosity or war. Hence, indifference is actually a form of hidden hostility. Unconcern for others is a form of wishing them away, removing them from our world, no matter how narrowly or broadly that world be defined. On the surface indifference would seem to bode better for peace than antagonism and war, which, of course, are antithetical to peace. But ultimately indifference is no more successful in bringing peace than *Apartheid* is able to bring equality and justice.

Negotiations

An important device used from time immemorial when victory over the enemy was not in sight was to enter into negotiations. Here the two antagonists attempt to obtain that which they were unable to get by means of war, namely, security, peace, and, if possible, advantage. The partners in negotiation are generally uninterested in the others' welfare, but are looking out the best they can for their own interest. This is why it is advisable to negotiate from positions of strength. Unity and conformity in the face of the enemy are often advocated within the ranks because it is feared that internal disunity may be taken advantage of by the competitor. One brings to bear all the cunning, knowledge, and experience in order to outwit and outplay the opponent and create an advantage to oneself. In rare instances negotiations result in mutual advantage. Nearly always they are preferable to war. According to the classical concept of the just war, all other alternatives must have been exhausted before resorting to war. Hence, negotiation is to be seen as a method of both preventing war, and if not successful, then later of leading to war.

Some negotiations are unfriendly; others are relatively friendly. In either case the perception is of leaders or representatives of competing groups attempting to establish favorable terms for their respective groups whose aims are fundamentally conflictual. Despite the presupposition of conflict, negotiation is a far more preferable way of settling disputes and may create an atmosphere in which genuine peace can be created over a longer period of time.

Dialogue

Dialogue is one of the most recent phenomena in the encounter between religions and ideologies, but it has already shown its eminent suitability to promote understanding and peace. There is a fundamental shift in perception of the other in dialogue as compared to the previous alternatives. In dialogue the other is a partner, though possibly very different and perhaps even antagonistic, but a partner nevertheless, in working toward improving conditions.

Dialogue is the methodology of reconciliation between differing positions which fundamentally grants the other the right to be different. It aims at reaching a degree of commonality which would increase the chances that the relationship would evolve in the direction of a durable peace, co-existence (living with each other) and even pro-existence (living for each other). Dialogue does not shy away from differences, though it seeks to underscore shared views and convictions. The reason partners in dialogue do not shy away from differences is that they value variety. The presupposition of dialogue is that the other partner *is* valuable and *has* valuable insights which may be of benefit to both partners and perhaps even to the world at large.

Not every gathering of partners with different convictions results in a dialogue. It is not sufficient to label a meeting a dialogue and assume that in fact a dialogue took place. Often it is parallel monologue or other forms of encounter take place, but not dialogue. For instance, a scholarly conference, does not usually end in dialogue; usually none is even intended. At some gatherings dialogue is intended but not achieved because each partner is interested in being heard and understood, but does not actively listen. If one only relies on preconceived notions of who the partner is and what the partner wants and says, a dialogue has little chance of taking place.

While the Greek root of the word is *dia* (between) and *logos* (word) it would be fallacious to assume that dialogue is just any exchange of words or speeches between people. The *logos* meant here is that word by which one expresses and communicates what is of one's essence to the partner. Seen from this perspective, dialogue is not a prelude to cooperation, not a means to some other goal, but it is a *sui generis* mode of relating which is to be interwoven with cooperation, and which goes far beyond practical cooperation since it consciously seeks purposiveness. One might say that dialogue is the intercourse of two consciousnesses seeking some common goals without sacrificing the partner's uniqueness and separateness. Seeking unity while affirming diversity, may be the slogan of dialogue.

Martin Buber provided some insight into the nature of dialogue by his distinction between I-It and I-Thou relationships. In the I-It relationship the other is an object of the subject's perception and need, something to be used with relatively little concern for the sensibilities of the other. On the other hand the I-Thou relationship recognizes the other to be unique in the manner in which the I is held to be unique. Hence, respect is accorded to the other and one interacts with the other as an equal, voluntarily and eagerly, yet critically and self-critically.

It has been recognized that one may learn the skill of dialoguing just as one may learn the skills of warring, negotiating, or cooperating. There are certainly some conditions which are favorable for a dialogue, while other approaches or attitudes may become serious obstacles. Both editors of the present book have previously published guidelines for conducting successful dialogues: Leonard Swidler's grew over several years' of publication and were more or less finally cast as the "Dialogue Decalogue."[2] Paul Mojzes' originally developed as guidelines to aid the Christian-Marxist dialogue, but they are also generally applicable.[3] Both are here reproduced with minor alterations, despite some overlap rather than attempting to synthesize them since their styles are divergent. Both aim at the same end, namely, the

---

2.   The earliest (shorter) published version of Leonard Swidler's dialogue guidelines appeared as follows: "Ground Rules for Inter-religious Dialogue," *Journal of Ecumenical Studies*, 15,3 (Summer, 1978), pp. 414-415, and were slightly expanded in: "Ground Rules for Inter-religious Dialogue," in Richard W. Rousseau, ed., *Inter-religious Dialogue* (Scranton: Ridge Row, 1981), pp. 9-12. They were subsequently greatly expanded and published as follows: "The Dialogue Decalogue: Ground Rules for Inter-religious Dialogue," *Journal of Ecumenical Studies*, 20, 1 (Winter, 1983), pp. 1-4, and were revised (to include specifically inter-ideological dialogue) and slightly expanded into their present form in September, 1984. The "Dialogue Decalogue" has appeared in at least thirty additional publications in sixteen countries and ten different languages. It also prompted several "parallel" articles, including: Robert Knast, "The Dialogue Decalogue: A Pastoral Commentary," *Journal of Ecumenical Studies*, 21,2 (Spring, 1984), pp. 311-318; Richard A. Freund, "Applications of the 'Dialogue Decalogue' for Latin American Inter-religious Dialogue," *Journal of Ecumenical Studies*, 23, 4 (Fall, 1986), pp. 671-675.

3.   Paul Mojzes, *Christian-Marxist Dialogue in Eastern Europe* (Minneapolis: Augsburg Publishing House, 1981), pp. 213-214; first published in Paul Mojzes, ed., *Varieties of Christian-Marxist Dialogue*, special issue of the *Journal of Ecumenical Studies*, 15, 1 (Winter, 1978), pp. 3 ff.

improvement of communication between and the enriching of the lives of the dialogue partners:

The Dialogue Decalogue

Leonard Swidler

First Commandment: *The primary purpose of dialogue is to learn, that is, to change and grow in the perception and understanding of reality and then to act accordingly.* We come to dialogue so that we ourselves may learn, change, and grow, not so that we may force change on the *other*, our partner, as the old polemic debates hoped to do. On the other hand, because in dialogue both partners come with the intention of learning and changing themselves, each will in fact find the partner has changed. Each partner will also have taught the other - but only because teaching was not the primary purpose of the encounter. Thus the alleged goal of debate, and much more, is accomplished far more effectively by dialogue.[4]

Second Commandment: *Inter-religious, ideological dialogue must be a two-sided project – within each religious or ideological community and between religious or ideological communities.* Because inter-religious, inter-ideological dialogue is corporate, and because its primary goal is for all partners to learn and change themselves, it is necessary that all the participants enter into dialogue not only with their partners across the faith line – the Catholic with the Protestant, for example – but also with their coreligionists, with their fellow Catholics, to share the fruits of the inter-religious dialogue. In this way the whole community can eventually learn and change, together gaining ever more perceptive insights into reality.

Third Commandment: *Each participant must come to the dialogue with complete honesty and sincerity.* It should be made clear in what direction the major and minor thrusts of the tradition move, what the future shifts might be, and even where the participants have difficulties with their own traditions. False fronts have no place in dialogue.

---

4.   Gadamer makes a series of similar points: "If dialogue (*Gespräch*) means allowing the participants to seek a fuller understanding of what is being discussed, then the art of dialogue is the art of questioning by which the solidity of opinion is opened up to new possibilities of meaning. A person who possesses the art of questioning is a person who is able to prevent the suppression of questions by the dominant opinion. A person who possesses this art will himself seek for everything in favor of an opinion. Dialectic consists, not in trying to discover the weakness of what is said, but in bringing out its real strength. Dialogue requires not the art of arguing but the art of thinking whereby what is said is strengthened by reference to the subject matter being discussed." Hans-Georg Gadamer, *Wahrheit und Methode* (Tübingen: J.C.B. Mohr, 1965), p. 349.

Conversely, *each participant must assume the same complete honesty and sincerity in the other partners.* A failure in sincerity will prevent dialogue from happening, but a failure to assume the partner's sincerity will do so as well. In brief: no trust, no dialogue.

Fourth Commandment: *In inter-religious, inter-ideological dialogue we must not compare our ideals with our partner's practice,* but rather our ideals with our partner's ideals, our practice with our partner's practice.

Fifth Commandment: *Each participant must define her or himself.* Only the Jew, for example, can define from the inside what it means to be a Jew; the rest of us can only describe what it looks like from the outside. Moreover, because dialogue is a dynamic medium, as each participant learns, she or he changes and hence continually deepens, expands, and modifies her or his self-definition as a Jew, being careful to remain in constant dialogue with fellow Jews. Thus it is mandatory that each dialogue partner define what it can mean to be an authentic member of that tradition.

Conversely, *the side interpreted must be able to recognize itself in the interpretation.* This is the golden rule of inter-religious, inter-ideological hermeneutics often reiterated by the "apostle of inter-religious dialogue," Raimundo Panikkar. For the sake of clarity, the dialogue participants will naturally attempt to express for themselves what they think is the meaning of the partner's statement; the partner must be able to recognize her or himself in that expression. The advocate of "a world theology," Wilfred Cantwell Smith, would add that the expression must also be verifiable by critical observers not involved.

Sixth Commandment: *Each participant must come to the dialogue with no hard-and-fast assumptions as to where the points of disagreement lie.* Both partners should not only listen to one another with openness and sympathy, but also try to agree as far as is possible while still maintaining integrity with their own tradition; where they absolutely can agree no further without violating their own integrity, precisely there is the real point of disagreement – which most often turns out to be quite different from what was assumed beforehand.

Seventh Commandment: *Dialogue can take place only between equals,* or *"par cum pari"* as Vatican II put it. Both must come to learn from each other. This means, for instance, that between a learned scholar and an uninformed person there can be no authentic, full dialogue but at most a gathering of information as in a sociological interrogation. Or, if a Muslim views Hinduism as inferior, or a Hindu views Islam as inferior, there will be no dialogue. For authentic inter-religious, inter-ideological dialogue between Muslims and

Hindus, both partners must come mainly to learn from each other; only then will they speak "equal with equal," *par cum pari*. This rule also indicates that there can be no such thing as a one-way dialogue. The Jewish-Christian discussions begun in the 1960s, for example, were on the whole only prolegomena to inter-religious dialogue. Understandably and properly, the Jews came to these exchanges only to teach Christians, and the Christians came mainly to learn. But, for authentic inter-religious dialogue between Christians and Jews the Jews must also come to learn; only then will the conversation be *par cum pari*.

Eighth Commandment: *Dialogue can take place only on the basis of mutual trust.* Although inter-religious, inter-ideological dialogue has a kind of "corporate" dimension in that the participants must be involved as members of a religious or ideological community–for instance, as Marxists or Taoists–it is also fundamentally true that only *persons* can enter into dialogue. But a dialogue among persons can be built only on personal trust. Hence it is wise not to tackle the most difficult problems in the beginning, but to seek those issues most likely to provide some common ground and establish a basis of human trust. Then as this personal trust deepens and expands, the more thorny matters can gradually be undertaken. As Lao Tzu has said: *Tu nan yu yi* (Hard work must have its beginnings in the easy).[5] Just as in learning we move from the known to the unknown, in dialogue we proceed from commonly held matters–which given our mutual ignorance resulting from centuries of hostility, will take us quite some time to explore–to matters of disagreement.

Ninth Commandment: *As we enter into inter-religious, inter-ideological dialogue we must learn to be at least minimally self-critical of both ourself and our own religious or ideological tradition.* A lack of such self-criticism implies that our own tradition already has all the correct answers. Such an attitude not only makes dialogue unnecessary, but even impossible, since we enter into dialogue primarily so *we* can learn–which obviously is impossible if our tradition has never made a misstep, if it has all the right answers. To be sure, participants in inter-religious, inter-ideological dialogue must stand within a religious or ideological tradition with integrity and conviction, but their integrity and conviction must include, not exclude, healthy self-criticism. Without it there can be no dialogue–and, indeed, no integrity.

Tenth Commandment: *Each participant eventually must attempt to experience the partner's religion or ideology "from*

5.　　Lao Tzu, *Tao Te Ching*, Chapter 63, quoted in Tang Yi, "Taoism as a Living Philosophy," *Journal of Chinese Philosophy*, 12, 4 (December, 1985), p. 399.

within." A religion or ideology does not merely engage the head, but also the spirit, heart and "whole being"; it has both individual and communal dimensions. John S. Dunne speaks of "passing over" into another's religious or ideological experience and then coming back enlightened, broadened and deepened.[6] As Raimundo Panikkar notes, "To know what a religion says, we must understand what it says, but for this we must somehow believe in what it says."[7] "A Christian" he notes by way of example, "will never fully understand Hinduism if he is not, in one way or another, converted to Hinduism. Nor will a Hindu ever fully understand Christianity unless he, in one way or another, becomes Christian."[8]

Inter-religious, inter-ideological dialogue operates in three areas: the practical, where we collaborate to help humanity; the depth or "spiritual" dimension, where we attempt to experience the partner's religion or ideology "from within"; the cognitive, where we seek understanding and truth. Dialogue also has three phases. In the first phase, which we never completely outgrow, we unlearn misinformation about each other and begin to know each other as we truly are. In phase two we begin to discern values in our partner's tradition and wish to appropriate them into our own. In the Buddhist-Christian dialogue, for example, Christians might learn a greater appreciation of the meditative tradition, and Buddhists might learn a greater appreciation of the prophetic, social justice tradition-both values strongly, though not exclusively, associated with the other's community. If we are serious, persistent and sensitive enough in the dialogue, we may at times enter into phase three. Here we together begin to explore new areas of reality, of meaning, of truth-aspects which neither of us had even been aware of before. We are brought face to face with these new, still unknown dimensions of reality through questions, insights, probings produced in the dialogue. We will experience for ourselves that dialogue patiently pursued can become an instrument of new "re-velation," a further "un-veiling" of reality-on which we must then act.

Between phase one and phases two and three there is a radical difference. No longer do we simply add on another "truth" or value from our partner's tradition. Now as we assimilate it within our own religious self-understanding it transforms our self-understanding proportionately. Since our

---

6.   *Cf.* John S. Dunne, *The Way of All the Earth* (New York: Macmillan, 1972).

7.   Raimundo Panikkar, *The Intra-religious Dialogue* (New York: Paulist Press, 1978), p. 67.

8.   Raimundo Panikkar, *The Unknown Christ in Hinduism* (Maryknoll: Orbis, rev. ed., 1981), p. 43.

dialogue partner is in the same position, we now can witness sincerely to those valuable elements in our own tradition that our partner's tradition may find profitable to assimilate. All this sharing and transformation is done with complete integrity on each side, each partner remaining true to the vital core of his or her own religious tradition. Yet, that vital core will now be perceived and experienced differently under the influence of dialogue. Still if the dialogue is carried on with both integrity and openness, the Jew will remain authentically Jewish or the Christian authentically Christian, not despite the fact that they have been profoundly "Buddhized," but because of it. This is much different from syncretism, which involves amalgamating elements of different religions into some kind of a (con)fused whole with no concern for the integrity of the religions involved.

Guidelines for Dialogue
Paul Mojzes

1. Both partners must have a need for dialogue.

2. Have a preliminary knowledge of your partner and the position with which you are going to dialogue.

3. Have a clear understanding of your own position.

4. Be well informed about the topic being discussed and present it clearly.

5. Set concrete areas of discussion ahead of time.

6. Seek specific issues, which are more promising to discuss than general, abstract issues.

7. Do not stereotype. Be open to the presentation of your partner's viewpoint.

8. Interpret your partner's view in its best light. Look at the whole picture, and do not try to belittle that view.

9. Look at the weaknesses and strengths of both views.

10. Emphasize things you have in common.

11. Listen to what your partner is saying. Strive for a clearer understanding of his or her position. Be continually willing to revise your understanding of the other's views.

12. Have no hidden agendas. There should be no tactical or selfish motives motivating the dialogue.

13. Be open to constructive criticism, and avoid destructive criticism. Be aware of your partner's sensitivities.

14. Be self-critical and honest. This does not mean giving up dignity and self-respect.

15. Do not assume that the conclusions reached are final. There will always be a need for dialogue regarding these views.

16. Accept responsibility for the good and bad your group has done or is still doing.

17. Take into account both the ideals and the realities of each group.

18. Face issues which cause conflict, but emphasize those things upon which you agree. Antagonistic relationship may then give way to cooperation.

19. Challenge one another to be faithful to the search for truth.

20. Make soul-searching and mutual enrichment part of the dialogue. Neither partner's truth is absolute; each needs the other for a more complete picture of truth. Monopoly in truth-claims leads to sluggishness in thinking and the perversion of truth.

21. Do not try to convert your partner, or the dialogue may turn again into a monologue. Differences must be maintained, although they should change from irreconcilable ones to a diversity of approaches for the common good.

22. Work toward accomplishing something for the better. Work at improving the situation.

23. Observe the dialogical nature of the dialogue. Both views should be included in final conclusions, though not necessarily in equal measure. Both partners ought to move to new positions (not necessarily convergent ones) which would not have been possible without the dialogue.

24. Be aware that there are other people involved. The dialogue should be for the benefit of the whole community.

25. Dialogue is impossible if either partner claims to have already solved the problem for all time to come.

26. Dialogue should present a new appreciation for the value of both positions.

27. Dialogue occurs between persons or groups of persons, not between disembodied ideas.

28. Dialogue should enable easier cooperation.

One may distinguish between bilateral and multilateral dialogues:

Bilateral dialogue occurs when representatives of two religious groups engage one another in a dialogical process on one or more topics on either a temporary or sustained basis. There is a large number of such dialogues taking place between various Christian churches, such as the Catholic-Lutheran, Catholic-Reformed, Catholic-Methodist, as well as Christian-Marxist, Hindu-Muslim dialogues, and so forth.

Multilateral dialogue takes place when representatives of three or more groups meet to interact with one another. Thus representatives of Islam, Judaism, and Christianity may meet to discuss issues of common concern, or Catholic-Orthodox-Protestant trialogue may take place, or else a larger number of representatives of various religions may get together to engage one another in dialogue. As may be expected, the larger the number of participants and the more diverse their backgrounds, the more difficult it will be to carry out a successful dialogue simply because it is difficult to keep the focus and pay equal attention to all views expressed.

There are some who expect, sometimes fearfully and sometimes triumphalistically, that dialogue will lead to complete convergence so that finally instead of two distinct partners there will be only one united position. In rare instances this does occur, sometimes even deliberately as, for instance, when two churches enter dialogue with the clear intention of merging. If the intention was held consciously and freely by both partners, there is nothing wrong with dialogue ending in convergence.

But generally this is neither the intended nor desired result. Convergence is not the final goal of the vast majority of the dialogues, though partial and gradual movement closer to one another will occur if both partners desire it. It is a positive result of dialogue if at the end of the dialogue the gap between the two has been narrowed – not so much the gap of identity but the gap of misunderstanding and distrust. When that happens even the self-image of each partner is bound to be altered as one attains a more adequate first-hand experience with "the other."

Cooperation Between Religions and Ideologies

One may distinguish between cooperation in a narrower and a broader sense. In a narrower sense, cooperation is a practical venture of limited scope and duration intended to promote a specific goal, such as helping the victims of a flood, building a school, rescuing a child, etc. In a broader sense, cooperation is an ideal to be sought and cultivated so that two religions might benefit individually and mutually from working together, and, perchance, also help others in the wider community.

Cooperation in the narrower sense is an expression of limited tolerance, but may have in it seeds of enmity and confrontation. It may occur in times of crisis, when both partners are confronted by a greater common enemy or threat. One frequently hears a plea by contemporary religious leaders that it is the time to put aside animosities between religions and to start to cooperate in the face of a common enemy, such as materialism, atheism, secularism or such. At other times factions of various religious traditions may find that they have more in common with a similarly oriented faction from another religion than with a differently oriented faction within their own religious traditions and they may decide to cooperate across religious lines. For instance, liberal Christians may find it relatively easy to get along with Reform Jews or moderate Muslims than either of these groups is able to get along with their more conservative or orthodox branches. Similarly, more traditionalist religionists may have a greater appreciation of other traditionalists than of reformers in their own circle.

Sometimes cooperation is promoted as a practical alternative to dialogue. There are those who believe that discussion of theoretical issues is a waste of time, as if nothing can be accomplished to bring two views closer to one another. Instead, cooperation is offered as an alternative to dialogue. In the early stages of the Christian ecumenical movement at the beginning of the twentieth century there were those who felt that in the doctrinal realm there was not much hope for making progress, but that certainly Christian churches could successfully cooperate on a number of issues, and they formed the "Life and Work" movement, which originally distinguished itself from the "Faith and Order" movement, which paid attention to doctrinal and polity questions. Ultimately it became obvious that attention needs to be given to both of those concerns and, indeed, they coalesced and formed the World Council of Churches in Amsterdam in 1948.

From the experience of the World Council of Churches and from the various national councils of churches within the Christian community it became obvious that cooperation in the broader sense of the word is possible and necessary on a wide and permanent scale. Already in 1911 at the International Missionary Conference in Jerusalem a number of Christian churches concluded that instead of competing with each other they ought to cooperate. The agreement to cooperate brought about modern ecumenism and religious dialogue first among a limited number of churches and then an ever increasing number of churches so that by the end of the 20th century there are not many Christian churches which are not involved in one manner or another in dialogue and cooperation. The cooperation was extended to non-Christian religions, primarily Judaism (for instance the National Conference of Christians and Jews in the U.S.A.), and then other religions (e.g., International Council of Religions for peace, the initiative of the Moscow Patriarchate of the Russian Orthodox Church of organizing international interfaith conference for defense of peace, or the projects of the Unification Church, etc.).

Currently the need for cooperation across religious lines is widely recognized as useful and needed. More and more cooperative networks are emerging with narrower or wider goals both on the local level (e.g., in sections of London nearly all religious groups may cooperate on promoting mutual understanding and elimination of prejudice; in New York they cooperate in the creation of better housing for the poor, etc.) and on the national and international levels. Some cooperative religious ventures have been successful in various forms of humanitarian aid and relief work, combating racism, improving educational and medical facilities, teaching agricultural and construction skills, and in various other ways benefiting a large number of people irrespective of their religious or non-religious affiliation. It is with satisfaction that one observes formerly hostile religious groups working together so well in solving some of humanity's burning problems. One might say that what one religion is not able to do alone, several together may accomplish, or even, what one religion might do well, several together may accomplish even better. In the global society of today there is an increasing awareness of the need for and efficacy of inter-religious cooperation.

Synthesis and/or Union

The last alternative is for two entities to gravitate so powerfully toward each other that they end up becoming a single entity. The differences which existed are either downplayed or overcome or else somehow contained and managed successfully within the newly unified entity. A number of religious traditions have shown a syncretic ability to absorb or include within themselves other traditions. One may note that Hinduism has been able to include insights from Buddhism so that a Hindu may define herself or himself as a follower of the Lord Buddha and yet remain a Hindu. The revelatory experience of Guru Nanak, while authentically new, did preserve, what Guru Nanak believed to be the best elements of both Hinduism and Islam in the Sikh religion. Popular variations of Roman Catholicism in Latin America, such as Santeria, which is practiced mostly in the Caribbean, may include elements of African and Indian primal religions. Note also Caribbean Voodoo, various Cargo cults in Africa and Asia and the more recent indigenized Independent African churches which contain a large mixture of native primal religions and Christianity in its Protestant or Catholic form.

Within the Protestant Christian tradition in the twentieth century came a powerful movement not merely toward unity but toward church merger or union. Many local churches of different denominations formed a single Community church. Entire denominations have merged with the new denomination either retaining the name of one of the former denominations or else selecting a new one.

Often the mergers take place within a denominational family. This was the case when first three Methodist bodies, the Methodist Episcopal Church, the Methodist Episcopal Church South and the Methodist Protestant Church merged in 1939 to form The Methodist Church. Later in 1960s the Methodist Church merged with another Methodistic body, the Evangelical United Brethren to form the United Methodist Church. This happened on a worldwide scale, though in other parts of the world the Church is named the Methodist Evangelical Church, or similarly. Like processes took place among the Presbyterian and Lutheran Churches in the U.S.A. At times the denominations which form a union select an entirely other name. Thus when the Congregational and the Evangelical and Reformed Churches united they formed the United Church of Christ.

Sometimes the union includes more radically different denominations. In India the Church of South India and later the Church of North India united Congregational, Presbyterian, Methodist, Lutheran, and other churches into a single denomination and likewise in Canada the United Church of Canada included the Presbyterian, Methodist, Congregational, and other churches in its membership. The Consultation on Church Union is at present involving in a unifying process nine major Protestant churches in the U.S.A., potentially leading to the single largest merger of churches in history. The National Council of Churches of Christ in the U.S.A. has adopted in the second half of the 1980s a formula called "communion of communions" which is believed to involve a greater degree of unity than simply a cooperation of communions. Some of the new religions, such as the Unification Church, display even greater ambitions of unifying many, if not all religions.

It should be pointed out that such moves toward unification often raise concern and opposition by some groups within the existing bodies, which occasionally lead to breakaways and the formation of new, independent religious institutions. Thus some Presbyterian and Congregational churches disapproved of the unions of their denominations with others and they broke off from the main body and established their separate churches, often rather ill-disposed toward ecumenism.

There are other forms of synthesis which do not result in the merger of institutions but do bring about the unifying of various views within the individual person. Thus there are people who synthesize Christian and Marxist convictions and become Christian-Marxists. In Japan and China there are large scale syntheses. In China there are many followers of the "three ways," namely, people who simultaneously follow many precepts of Buddhism, Confucianism, and Taoism. In Japan one frequently finds people who follow both Buddhism and Shinto and this is so widespread that frequently within a Shinto shrine complex one finds a Buddhist temple and vice versa. Ryobo or Mixed Shinto was an attempt to provide a formal linkage between Buddhist and Shinto pantheons and beliefs. The great nineteenth-century Hindu saint, Ramakrishna, believed that in his own religious experiences he was able to follow the paths of Hinduism, Buddhism, Christianity and Islam, and allegedly all paths ended in the same ultimate religious experience, leading him to the conviction that all religious paths lead to the same summit. The Hindu Brahmo Samaj movement synthesized some Hindu and Western religious approaches. Perhaps even more frequent is the incorporation of ancient traditional beliefs into a historic religion, as was the case of Tibetan Bon, with Mahayana (and Vajrayama) Buddhism resulting in contemporary Tibetan Buddhism.

Sometimes people within a religious tradition have aspirations for the complete union of all branches of their respective traditions into a single unified institution. Among Christians there are those who long for one united Christian Church which would embrace all, or nearly all, Christians. Muslims often make the claim that Islam is one, despite the division into Sunnis and Shi'as. Many Hindus talk of Hinduism as if it were a single religion rather than a family of religions.

Finally, there are some – not many – who long for a single religion of the future which would unify all humankind into its fold. As they see it, this may be one of the existing religions or ideologies or it may be a yet to emerge religion or ideology. They long for a unified world and believe that a religious system is needed for the underpinning of such a unified humanity.

Intolerance or Tolerance

The United Nations Universal Declaration of Human Rights in Article 2 states:

> Everyone is entitled to all the rights and freedoms set forth in this Declaration, without distinction of any kind such as race, color, sex, language, religion, political or other opinion, national or social origin, property, birth or other status.

Article 18 states:

> Everyone has the right to freedom of thought, conscience and religion; this right includes freedom to change his religion or belief, and freedom, either alone or in community with others and in public or private, to manifest his religion or belief in teaching, practice, worship and observance.

These articles represent the basis of religious liberty and tolerance, and were further amplified (after a protracted political struggle) by the 1981

United Nations Declaration on the Elimination of All Forms of Intolerance and of Discrimination based on Religion or Belief. Particularly pertinent parts are here cited:

Considering that the Universal Declaration of Human Rights and the International Covenants on Human Rights proclaim the principles of non-discrimination and equality before the law and the right to freedom of thought, conscience, religion and belief...

Considering that religion or belief, for anyone who professes either, is one of the fundamental elements in his conception of life and that freedom of religion or belief should be fully respected and guaranteed,

Considering that it is essential to promote understanding, tolerance and respect in matters relating to freedom of religion and belief...

Convinced that freedom of religion and belief should also contribute to the attainment of the goals of world peace, social justice and friendship among peoples...

Article 1

1. Everyone shall have the right to freedom of thought, conscience and religion. This right shall include freedom to have a religion or whatever belief of his choice, and freedom, either individually or in community with others and in public or private, to manifest his religion or belief in worship, observance, practice and teaching.

2. No one shall be subject to coercion which would impair his freedom to have a religion or belief of his choice...

Article 2

1. No one shall be subject to discrimination by any State, institution, group of persons, or person on the grounds of religion or other beliefs.

2. For the purposes of the present Declaration, the expression "intolerance and discrimination based on religion or belief" means any distinction, exclusion, restriction or preference based on religion or belief...

Article 3

Discrimination between human beings on grounds of religion or belief constitutes an affront to human dignity...

Article 4

1. All States shall take effective measures to prevent and eliminate discrimination on the grounds of religion or belief in

the recognition, exercise and enjoyment of human rights and fundamental freedoms in all fields...

Article 6

...the right to freedom of thought, conscience, religion or belief shall include, *inter alia*, the following freedoms:

(*a*) To worship or assemble in connection with a religion or belief, and to establish and maintain places for these purposes;

(*b*) To establish and maintain appropriate charitable or humanitarian institutions...

(*d*) To write, issue and disseminate relevant publications in these areas;

(*e*) To teach a religion or belief in places suitable for these purposes...

(*g*) To train, appoint, elect or designate by succession appropriate leaders called for by the requirements and standards of any religion or belief...

(*i*) To establish and maintain communications with individuals and communities in matters of religion and belief at the national and international levels.

Article 7

The rights and freedoms set forth in the present Declaration shall be accorded in national legislation in such a manner that everyone shall be able to avail himself of such rights and freedoms in practice.

Article 8

Nothing in the present Declaration shall be construed as restricting or derogating from any right defined in the Universal Declaration of Human Rights and the International Covenants on Human Rights [this article was especially important in the face of the militant Islamicist resistance to including a statement of the right to change one's religion or belief – it *is* in article 18 of the Universal Declaration (see above)].

If one looks again at the chart of the spectrum from war to synthesis it becomes clear that the first two positions, namely, war and antagonism, are undeniably forms of intolerance. The third and fourth positions of indifference and negotiation already contain seeds of tolerance though intolerance may still be present in large doses. Dialogue, cooperation and synthesis are typically tolerant, though occasional outbursts of intolerance may still occur. Thus, the question of intolerance or tolerance is not without some ambiguities. Despite these ambiguities it is possible to implement attitudes of tolerance by promoting understanding, open mindedness, curiosity about others, increased contacts, development of trust, joint endeavors, and other peace-making activities.

Tolerance in itself is not the highest mode of interaction between different religions. One may speak of mere toleration of others. For instance, enlightened rulers such as Joseph II of Hapsburg Austria, who favored Roman Catholicism, issued an Edict of Toleration which was an enormous step forward in protecting some of the rights of Protestants and Jews in his Empire, but it did not bring equality and it did not include all religions in his realm (e.g., the Churches of the Czech Brethren had to declare themselves either Lutheran or Reformed in order to be tolerated or else they would not have benefited from the Edict).

In this sense tolerance may not bring equality before the law or insure full religious liberty, but it is a definite advance over persecution and suppression. When viewed from this perspective, tolerance is usually seen as a concession or privilege from above, rather than an inherent value. If it is offered from above, it may be withdrawn from above.

There is another, more positive notion of tolerance, which means that members of different religions are able to live alongside each other in peace without interfering in the free practice of each others religious observances. Toleration in this sense is what is promoted by the United Nations Declaration.

However, we venture to affirm not only this important principle of tolerance, but also wish to promote understanding and appreciation of many values espoused by the various religious and ideological traditions and to promote the dialogue between them so that increasing cooperation and positive interactions will take place for mutual benefit and the larger peace of the human community.

WHAT IS DIALOGUE?

by

Leonard Swidler

I. The Meaning of Dialogue

Today when we speak of dialogue between religions or ideologies we mean something quite definite, namely, a two-way communication between persons; one-way lecturing or speaking is obviously not meant by it. However, there are many different kinds of two-way communication: e.g., fighting, wrangling, debating, etc. Clearly none of these are meant by dialogue. On the other extreme is the communication between persons who hold precisely the same views on a particular subject. We also do not mean this when we use the term dialogue; rather, we might call that something like encouragement, reinforcement – but certainly not dialogue. Now, if we look at these two opposite kinds of two-way communication which are *not* meant by the word dialogue, we can learn quite precisely what we do in fact mean when we use the term dialogue.

Looking at the last example first – the principle underlying "reinforcement," etc., is the assumption that both sides have a total grasp on the truth of the subject and hence simply need to be supported in their commitment to it. Since this example, and the principle underlying it, are excluded from the meaning of dialogue, clearly dialogue must include the notion that neither side has a total grasp of the truth of the subject, but that both need to seek further.

The principle underlying "debating," etc. in the second example is the assumption that one side has all the truth concerning the subject and that the other side needs to be informed or persuaded of it. Since that example also, and its principle, are excluded from the meaning of dialogue, this clearly implies that dialogue means that no one side has a monopoly on the truth on the subject, but both need to seek further.

It may turn out in some instances, of course, that after a more or less extensive dialogue it is learned that the two sides in fact agree completely on the subject discussed. Naturally, such a discovery does not mean that the encounter was a non-dialogue, but rather that the dialogue was the means of learning the new truth that both sides agreed on the subject; to continue from that point on, however, to speak only about the area of agreement would then be to move from dialogue to reinforcement.

Hence, to express at least the initial part of the meaning of dialogue positively: Dialogue is a two-way communication between persons who hold significantly differing views on a subject, with the purpose of learning more truth about the subject from the other.

This analysis may seem obvious to some, and, hence, superfluous. But I believe not. Dialogue has become a faddish term, and is sometimes, like charity, used to cover a multitude of sins. Sometimes, for example, it is used by those who are quite convinced that they have all the truth on a subject, but feel that in today's climate with "dialogue" in vogue a less aggressive style will be more effective in communicating to the ignorant the truth that they already possess in full. Therefore, while their encounters with others still rely on the older non-dialogue principle – that they have all the truth on a subject – their less importuning approach will now be *called* "dialogue." This type of use would appear to be merely an opportunistic manipulation of the term dialogue.

Maybe some of those people, however, truly believe that they are engaging in dialogue when they employ such a "soft sell" approach and encourage their interlocutors to also express their own views on the subject – even though it is known ahead of time, of course, that they are false – for such a "dialogue" may well make the ignorant person more open to receiving the truth which the one side knows it already has. In that situation, the "truth-holders" simply had a basic misunderstanding of the term dialogue and mistakenly termed their "convert-making" dialogue. Therefore, the above clarification is important.

We are, of course, in this context speaking about a particular kind of dialogue, namely, inter-religious dialogue in the broadest sense, that is, dialogue on religious subject by persons who understand themselves to be in different religious traditions and communities. If religion is understood as an "explanation of the ultimate meaning of life and how to live accordingly," then that would include all such systems even though they customarily would not be called religions, but rather, ideologies, such as, atheistic Humanism and Marxism; hence it is more accurate to speak of both inter-religious and inter-ideological dialogue.

II. Why Dialogue Arose

One can, of course, justifiably point to a number of recent developments that have contributed to the rise of dialogue – e.g., growth in mass education, communications and travel, a world economy, threatening global destruction – nevertheless, a major underlying cause is a paradigm-shift in the West in how we perceive and describe the world. A paradigm is simply the model, the cluster of assumptions, on whose basis phenomena are perceived and explained: for example, the geocentric paradigm for explaining the movements of the planets; a shift to another paradigm – as to the heliocentric – will have a major impact. Such a paradigm-shift has occurred and is still occurring in the Western understanding of truth statements which has made dialogue not only possible, but even necessary.

Whereas the understanding of truth in the West was largely absolute, static, monologic or exclusive up to the last century, it has subsequently become deabsolutized, dynamic and dialogic – in a word: relational. This relatively "new" view of truth came about in at least six different but closely related ways.

0) Until the nineteenth century in Europe truth, that is, a statement about reality, was conceived in an absolute, static, exclusivistic either-or manner. It was believed that if a statement was true at one time, it was always true, and not only in the sense of statements about empirical facts

but also in the sense of statements about the meaning of things. Such is a *classicist* or *absolutist* view of truth.

    1)   Then, in the nineteenth century scholars came to perceive all statements about the truth of the meaning of something as being partially products of their historical circumstances; only by placing truth statements in their historical situations, their historical *Sitz im Leben*, could they be properly understood: A text could be understood only in context. Therefore, all statements about the meaning of things were seen to be deabsolutized in terms of time. Such is a *historical* view of truth.

    2)   Later on it was noted that we ask questions so as to obtain knowledge, truth, according to which we want to live; this is a *praxis* or *intentional* view of truth, that is, a statement has to be understood in relationship to the action-oriented intention of the thinker.

    3)   Early in the twentieth century Karl Mannheim developed what he called the sociology of knowledge, which points out that every statement about the truth of the meaning of something was perspectival, for all reality is perceived, and spoken of, from the cultural, class, sexual, and so forth perspective of the perceiver. Such is a *perspectival* view of truth.

    4)   A number of thinkers, and most especially Ludwig Wittgenstein, have discovered something of the limitations of human language: Every description of reality is necessarily only partial for although reality can be seen from an almost limitless number of perspectives, human language can express things from only one perspective at once. This partial and limited quality of all language is necessarily greatly intensified when one attempts to speak of the transcendent, which by definition "goes-beyond." Such is a *language-limited* view of truth.

    5)   The contemporary discipline of hermeneutics stresses that all knowledge is interpreted knowledge. This means that in all knowledge *I* come to know something; the object comes into me in a certain way, namely, through the lens that I use to perceive it. As Thomas Aquinas wrote, "Things known are in the knower according to the mode of the knower." (*Summa Theologiae*, II/II, Q. 1, a. 2) Such is an *interpretative* view of truth.

    6)   Further yet, reality can "speak" to me only with the language that I give it; the "answers" that I receive back from reality will always be in

the language, the thought categories, of the questions I put to it. If and when the answers I receive are sometimes confused and unsatisfying, then I probably need to learn to speak a more appropriate language when I put questions to reality. For example, if I ask the question, "How heavy is green?" of course I will receive a nonsense answer. Or, if I ask questions about living things in mechanical categories, I will receive confusing and unsatisfying answers. I will likewise receive confusing and unsatisfying answers to questions about human sexuality if I use categories that are solely physical-biological: witness the absurdity of the answer that birth control is forbidden by the natural law – the question falsely assumes that the nature of humanity is merely physical-biological. Such an understanding of truth is a *dialogic* understanding.

In brief, our understanding of truth and reality has been undergoing a radical shift. The new paradigm which is being born understands all statements about reality, especially about the meaning of things, to be historical, praxial or intentional, perspectival, language-limited or partial, interpretive, and dialogic. Our understanding of truth statements, in short, has become "deabsolutized" – it has become "relational," that is, all statements about reality are now seen to be *related* to the historical context, praxis intentionality, perspective, etc. of the speaker, and in that sense no longer "absolute." Therefore, if my perception and description of the world is true only in a limited sense, that is, only as seen from my place in the world, then if I wish to expand my grasp of reality I need to learn from others what they know of reality that they can perceive from their place in the world that I cannot see from mine. That, however, can happen only through dialogue.

III. Who Should Dialogue

One important question is, who can, who should, engage in inter-religious, inter-ideological dialogue? There is clearly a fundamental communal aspect to such a dialogue. For example, if a person is not either a Lutheran or a Jew, she/he could not engage in a specifically Lutheran-Jewish dialogue. Likewise, persons not belonging to any religious, or ideological, community could not, of course, engage in inter-religious, inter-ideological dialogue. They might well engage in meaningful religious, ideological dialogue, but it simply would not be inter-religious, inter-ideological, between religions, or ideologies.

Who, then, would qualify as a member of a religious community? If the question is of the official representation of a community at a dialogue, then the clear answer is those who are appointed by the appropriate official body in that community: the Congregation, Bet Din, Roshi, Bishop, Central Committee or whatever. However, if it is not a case of official representation, then general reputation usually is looked to. Some persons' qualifications, however, can be challenged by elements within a community, even very important official elements. The Vatican Congregation for the Doctrine of the Faith, for example, has declared that Professors Hans Küng and Charles Curran were no longer to be considered Catholic theologians. In both these cases, however, hundreds of Catholic theologians subsequently stated publicly in writing that both those professors were indeed still Catholic theologians.

In the end, however, it seems best to follow the principle that each person should decide for her or himself whether or not they are members of a religious community. Extraordinary cases may at rare times present initial anomalies, but they inevitably will resolve themselves. Furthermore, it is important to be aware that, especially in the initial stages of any inter-religious, inter-ideological dialogue, it is very likely that the literally eccentric members of religious, ideological communities will be the ones who will have the interest and ability to enter into dialogue; the more centrist persons will do so only after the dialogue has been proved safe for the mainline, official elements.

Likewise it is important to note that inter-religious, inter-ideological dialogue is not something to be limited to official representatives of communities. Actually the great majority of the vast amount of such dialogue that has occurred throughout the world, particularly in the past three decades, has not been carried on by official representatives, although that too has been happening with increasing frequency.

What is needed then is 1) an openness to learn from the other, 2) knowledge of one's own tradition, and 3) a similarly disposed and knowledgeable dialogue partner from the other tradition. This can happen on almost any level of knowledge and education. The key is the openness to learn from the other. Naturally no one's knowledge of her/his own tradition can ever be complete; each person must continually learn more about it. One merely needs to realize that one's knowledge is in fact limited and know where to turn to gain the information needed. It is also important, however, that the dialogue partners be more or less equal in knowledge of their own traditions, etc. The larger the asymmetry is, the less the communication will be two-way, that is, dialogic.

Hence, it is important that inter-religious, inter-ideological dialogue *not* be limited to official representatives or even to the experts in the various traditions, although they both have their irreplaceable roles to play in the dialogue. Dialogue, rather, should involve every level of the religious, ideological communities, all the way down to the "persons in the pews." Only in this way will the religious, ideological communities learn from each other and come to understand each other as they truly are.

The Catholic bishops of the world expressed this insight very clearly and vigorously at Vatican II when they "exhorted *all the Catholic faithful* to recognize the signs of the times and to take an active and intelligent part in the work of ecumenism [dialogue among the Christian churches, and in an extended understanding, dialogue among the religions and ideologies, as is made clear by other Vatican II documents and the establishment of permanent Vatican Secretariats for dialogue with Non-Christians and with Non-Believers]." Not being content with this exhortation, the bishops went on to say that, "in ecumenical work, [all] Catholics must...make the *first approaches* toward them [non-Catholics]." In case there were some opaque minds or recalcitrant wills out there, the bishops once more made it ringingly clear that ecumenism [inter-religious, inter-ideological dialogue] "involves the whole Church, faithful and clergy alike. It extends to everyone, according to the talent of each" (Vatican II, *Decree on Ecumenism*, 4, 5). Certainly this insight is not to be limited to the 800,000,000 Catholics in the world – and the further hundreds of millions they directly or indirectly influence – massive and important as that group may be.

However, what about the challenge of those who charge that "dialogists" are really elitists because they define dialogue in such a "liberal" manner that only like-minded "liberals" can join in? I will argue below in more detail that only those who have a "deabsolutized" understanding of truth will in fact be able to enter into dialogue. Put in other words, only those who understand all truth statements, that is, all statements about reality, to be always limited in a variety of ways, and in that sense not absolute, can enter into dialogue. This, however, is no elitist discrimination against "absolutists," or fundamentalists, by not allowing them to engage in dialogue. Such a charge would simply be another case of not understanding what dialogue is: a two-way communication so that both sides can learn. If one partner grants that it has something to learn from the other, that admission presupposes that the first partner has only a limited – a deabsolutized – grasp of truth concerning the subject. If one partner thinks that it has an absolute grasp of the truth concerning the subject, it obviously believes that it has nothing to learn from the other, and hence the encounter will not be a dialogue but some kind of attempt at one-way teaching or a debate. Thus the partner with the absolutized view of truth will not only not be able to engage in dialogue, it will very much not want to – unless it falls into the category either of harboring the earlier described misunderstanding of the meaning of dialogue, or the intention of an opportunistic manipulation of the term.

IV. Kinds of Dialogue

In the question of what constitutes inter-religious, inter-ideological dialogue, it is important to notice that we normally mean a two-way communication in ideas and words. At times, however, we give the term an extended meaning of joint action or collaboration and joint prayer or sharing of the spiritual or depth dimension of our tradition. While the intellectual and verbal communication is indeed the primary meaning of dialogue, if the results therefrom do not spill over into the other two areas of action and spirituality, it will have proved sterile. Beyond that, it can lead toward a kind of schizophrenia and even hypocrisy.

On the positive side, serious involvement in joint action and/or spirituality will tend to challenge the previously-held intellectual positions and lead to dialogue in the cognitive field. Catholic and Protestant clergy, for example, who found themselves together in concentration camp Dachau because of joint resistance to one or other Nazi anti-human action began to ask each other why they did what they did and through dialogue were surprised to learn that they held many more positions in common than positions that separated them; in fact these encounters and others like them fostered the Una Sancta Movement in Germany, which in turn was the engine that moved the Catholic Church in the Second Vatican Council (1962-65) officially to embrace ecumenism and inter-religious dialogue after many centuries of vigorous official rejection.

Because religion is not something just of the "head" and the "hands," but also of the "heart"–of the whole human being-our encounter with our partner must also eventually include the depth or spiritual dimension. This spiritual or depth dimension engages our emotions, our imagination, our intuitive consciousness. If we do not come to know each other in this deepest dimension of our selves our dialogue will remain relatively superficial. The technique, called by John Dunne "crossing over," can be of help here. Through it we focus on a central image, metaphor, from our partner's spiritual life and let it work on our imagination, our emotions, evoking whatever responses it may, leading us to different feelings. We then return to our own inner world enriched, expanded, with a deeper sympathy for, and sensitivity to, our partner's inner world. Within the context of this expanded inner dimension we will be prompted to look thereafter for new cognitive articulations adequate to reflect it, and we will be prompted to express our new awareness and understanding of our partner's religious reality in appropriate action.

Encountering our partner on merely one or two levels will indeed be authentic dialogue, but, given the integrative and comprehensive nature of religion and ideology, it is only natural that we be led from dialogue on one level to the others. Only with dialogue in this full fashion on all three levels will our inter-religious, inter-ideological dialogue be complete.

V. Goals of Dialogue

The general goal of dialogue is for each side to learn, and to change accordingly. Naturally, if each side comes to the encounter primarily to learn from the other, then the other side must teach, and thus both learning and teaching occurs. We know, however, that if each side comes to the encounter primarily to teach, both sides will tend to close up, and as a result neither teaching nor learning takes place.

We naturally gradually learn more and more about our partners in the dialogue and in the process shuck off the misinformation about them we may have had. However, we also learn something more, something even closer to home. Our dialogue partner likewise becomes for us something of a mirror in which we perceive our selves in ways we could not otherwise do. In the very process of responding to the questions of our partners we look into our inner selves and into our traditions in ways that we perhaps never would otherwise, and thus come to know ourselves as we could not have outside of the dialogue.

In addition, in listening to our partners' descriptions of their perceptions of us we learn much about "how we are in the world." Because no one is simply in her or himself, but is always in relationship to others, "how we are in the world," how we relate to and impact on others, is in fact part of our reality, is part of us. As an example, it is only by being in dialogue with another culture that we really come to know our own: I became aware of my particular American culture, for example, only as I lived in Europe for a number of years. I became conscious of American culture as such with its similarities to and differences from the European only in the mirror of my dialogue partner of European culture.

This expanded knowledge of our selves and of the other that we gain in the dialogue cannot of course remain ineffective in our lives. As our self-understanding and understanding of those persons and things around us change, so too must our attitude toward our selves and others change, and thus our behavior as well. Once again, to the extent that this inner and outer change, this transformation, does not take place, to that extent we tend toward schizophrenia and hypocrisy. Whether one wants to speak of dialogue and then of the subsequent transformation as "beyond dialogue," as John Cobb does in his book *Beyond Dialogue*, or speak of transformation as an integral part of the continuing dialogue process, as Klaus Klostermeier does (*Journal of Ecumenical Studies*, 21, 4 [Fall, 1984], pp. 755-759), need not detain us here. What is important to see, however, is that the chain dialogue-knowledge-change must not be broken. If the final link, change, falls away, the authenticity of the second, knowledge, and the first, dialogue are called into question. To repeat: the goal of dialogue is that "each side to learn, and change accordingly."

There are likewise communal goals in inter-religious, inter-ideological dialogue. Some of them will be special to the situation of the particular dialogue partners. Several Christian churches, for example, may enter into dialogue with the goal of structural union in mind. Such union goals, however, will be something particular to religious communities *within* one religion, that is, within Christianity, within Buddhism, within Islam, etc. Dialogue *between* different religions and ideologies, however, will not have this structural union goal. Rather, it will seek first of all to know the dialogue partners as accurately as possible and try to understand them as sympathetically as possible. Dialogue will seek to learn what the partners' commonalities and what their differences are.

There is a simple technique to learn where the authentic commonalities and differences are between two religions or ideologies: Attempt to agree with the dialogue partner as far as possible on a subject without violating one's own integrity; where one can go no further, there is where the authentic difference is, and what has been shared up until that point are commonalities. Experience informs us that very often our true differences lie elsewhere than we had believed before the dialogue.

One communal goal in looking to learn the commonalities and differences two religions hold is to bridge over antipathies and misunderstandings – to draw closer together in thought, feeling and action on the basis of commonalities held. This goal, however, can be reached only if another principle is also observed: Inter-religious, inter-ideological dialogue must be a two-sided dialogue – across the communal divide, and within it. We need to be in regular dialogue with our fellow religionists, sharing with them the results of our inter-religious, inter-ideological dialogue so they too can enhance their understanding of what is held in common and where the differences truly are, for only thus can the whole communities grow in knowledge and inner and outer transformation, and thereby bridge over antipathies and draw closer. Further, if this two-sided dialogue is not maintained, the individual dialogue partners alone will grow in knowledge, and experience the resultant transformation, thus slowly moving away from their unchanging community, thereby becoming a third reality, a *tertium quid* – hardly the intended integrative goal of dialogue.

It is clear that it is important to learn as fully as possible the things we share in common with our dialogue partners, which most often will be much more extensive than we could have anticipated beforehand; we will thus be drawn together in greater harmony. Likewise, however, it is important that we learn more comprehensively what our differences are. Such differences may be (1) complementary, as for example, a stress on the prophetic rather than the mystical, (2) analogous, as for example, the notion of God in the Semitic religions and of *sunyata* in Mahayana Buddhism, or (3) contradictory, where the acceptance of one entails the rejection of the other, as for example, the Judeo-Christian notion of the inviolable dignity of each individual person and the now largely disappeared Hindu custom of *suttee*, widow burning. The issue of the third category of differences will be discussed below, but here we can note that the differences in the first two categories are not simply to be perceived and acknowledged; they should in fact be cherished and celebrated both for their own sakes and because by discerning them we have extended our own understanding of reality, and how to live accordingly – the main goal of dialogue.

VI. The Means of Dialogue

A great variety of means and techniques of dialogue have been successfully used, and doubtless some are yet to be developed. The overall guiding principle in this issue, however, should be, (1) to use our creative imaginations and our sensitivity for persons. Techniques that have already been utilized range from joint lectures and dialogues by experts from different traditions that are listened to by large audiences on one extreme, to personal conversations between "rank and file" individuals from different traditions on the other. One important rule to keep in mind, however, whenever something more formal than the personal conversation is planned is that, (2) all the traditions to be engaged in a dialogue be involved in its initial planning. This is particularly true when different communities first begin to encounter each other. Then dialogue on the potential dialogue itself becomes an essential part of the dialogic encounter.

It is clear that in the first encounters between communities, (3) the most difficult points of differences should not be tackled. Rather, those subjects which show promise of highlighting commonalities should be treated so that mutual trust between the partners can be established and developed. For without mutual trust, there will be no dialogue.

Vital to the development of this needed mutual trust is that, (4) each partner come to the dialogue with total sincerity and honesty. My partners in dialogue wish to learn to know me and my tradition as we truly are; this is impossible, however, if I am not totally sincere and honest. Of course, the same is true for my partners; I cannot learn to know them and their traditions truly if they are not completely sincere and honest. Likewise note: we must simultaneously presume total sincerity and honesty in our partners as well as practice them ourselves, otherwise there will be no trust – and without trust there will be no dialogue.

Care must also be taken in dialogue, (5) to compare our ideals with our partner's ideals and our practices with our partner's practices. By comparing our ideals with our partner's practices we will always "win," but of course we will learn nothing – a total defeat of the purpose of dialogue.

There has already been earlier mention of several other "means" of dialogue: (6) each partner in the dialogue must define her or himself; only a Muslim, for example, can know from the inside what it means to be a Muslim, and this self-understanding will change, grow, expand, deepen as the dialogue develops, and hence perforce can be accurately described only by the one experiencing the living, growing religious reality. (7) Each partner needs to come to the dialogue with no fixed assumptions as to where the authentic differences between the traditions are, but only after following the partner with sympathy and agreement as far as one can without violating one's own integrity will the true point of difference be determined. (8) Of course, only equals can engage in full authentic dialogue; the degree of inequality will determine the degree of two-way communication, that is, the degree of dialogue experienced.

An indispensable major means of dialogue is (9) a self-critical attitude toward ourself and our tradition. If we are not willing to look self-critically at our own, and *our tradition's*, position on a subject, the implication clearly is that we have nothing to learn from our partner – but if that is the case we are not interested in dialogue, whose primary purpose is to learn from our partner. To be certain, we come to the dialogue as a Buddhist, as a Christian, as a Marxist, etc., with sincerity, honesty and integrity. Self-criticism, however, does not mean a lack of sincerity, honesty, integrity. Indeed, a lack of self-criticism will mean there is no valid sincerity, no true honesty, no authentic integrity.

Finally, the most fundamental means to dialogue is, (10) having a correct understanding of dialogue, which is *a two-way communication so that both partners can learn from each other, and change accordingly*. If this basic goal is kept fixed in view and acted on with imagination, then creative, fruitful dialogue, and a growing transformation of each participant's life and that of their communities will follow.

VII. The Subject of Dialogue

We already spoke about choosing at first those subjects which promise to yield a high degree of common ground so as to establish and develop mutual trust, and the three main areas of dialogue: the cognitive, active and spiritual.

In some ways the latter, the spiritual area, would seem to be the most attractive, at least to those with a more interior, mystical, psychological bent. Moreover, it promises a very great degree of commonality: the mystics appear to all meet together on a high level of unity with the Ultimate Reality no matter how it is described, including even the more philosophical systems, e.g., Neoplatonism. For instance, the greatest of the Muslim Sufis, Jewish Kabbalists, Hindu Bhaktas, Christian Mystics, Buddhist Bodhisattvas and Platonist Philosophers all seem to be at one in their striving for and experience of unity with the One, which in the West is called God, *Theos*. At times the image is projected of God being the peak of the mountain that all humans are climbing by way of different paths. Each one has a different way (*hodos* in Christian Greek; *halachah* in Jewish Hebrew; *shar'ia* in Muslim

Arabic; *marga* in Hindu Sanskrit; *magga* in Buddhist Pali; *tao* in Chinese Taoism) to reach *Theos*, but all are centered on the one goal. Consequently, such an interpretation of religion or ideology is called theocentric.

Attractive as is theocentrism, one must be cautious not to waive the varying understandings of God aside as if they were totally without importance; they can make a significant difference in human self-understanding, and hence how we behave toward our selves, each other, the world around us, and the Ultimate Source. Moreover, a theocentric approach has the disadvantage of not including non-theists in the dialogue. This would exclude not only atheistic Humanists and Marxists, but likewise nontheistic Theravada Buddhists, who do not deny the existence of God but rather understand ultimate reality in a non-theistic, non-personal manner (theism posits a "personal" God, *Theos*). One alternative way to include these partners in the dialogue even in this area of "spirituality" is to speak of the search for ultimate meaning in life, for "salvation" (*salus* in Latin, meaning a salutary, whole, [w]holy life; similarly, *soteria* in Greek), as what all humans have in common in the "spiritual" area, theists and nontheists. As a result, we can speak of a soteriocentrism.

In the active area dialogue has to take place in a fundamental way on the underlying principles for action which motivate each tradition. Once again, many similarities will be found, but also differences which will prove significant in determining the communities' differing stands on various issues of personal and social ethics. It is only by carefully and sensitively locating those underlying ethical principles for ethical decision-making that later misunderstandings and unwarranted frustrations in specific ethical issues can be avoided. Then specific ethical matters, such as sexual ethics, social ethics, ecological ethics, medical ethics, can become the focus of inter-religious, inter-ideological dialogue – and ultimately joint action where it has been found congruent with each tradition's principles and warranted in the concrete circumstances.

It is, however, in the cognitive area where the range of possible subjects is greatest. It is almost unlimited – remembering the caution that the less difficult topics be chosen first and the more difficult later. That having been said, however, every dialogue group should nevertheless be encouraged to follow creatively its own inner instinct and interests. Some groups, of course, will start with more particular, concrete matters and then be gradually drawn to discuss the underlying issues and principles. Others on the other hand will begin with more fundamental matters and eventually be drawn to reflect on more and more concrete implications of the basic principles already discovered. In any case, if proper preparation and sensitivity are provided, no subject should *a priori* be declared off-limits.

Encouragement can be drawn here from a for some perhaps unexpected source, the Vatican Curia. The Secretariat for Dialogue with Unbelievers wrote that even "doctrinal dialogue should be initiated with courage and sincerity, with the greatest freedom and with reverence." It then went further to make a statement that is mind-jarring in its liberality: "Doctrinal discussion requires perceptiveness, both in honestly setting out one's own opinion and in recognizing the truth everywhere, *even if the truth demolishes one so that one is forced to reconsider one's own position, in theory and in practice, at least in part*." The Secretariat then stressed that "in discussion the truth will prevail by no other means than by the truth itself. Therefore, the liberty of the participants must be ensured by law and reverenced in practice" (Secretariatus pro Non-credenti, *Humanae personae dignitatem*, August 28, 1968). These are emphatic words – which again should be applicable not only to the Catholics of the world, but in general.

VIII. When to Dialogue – and When Not

In principle, of course, we ought to be open to dialogue with all possible partners on all possible subjects. Normally this principle should be followed today and doubtless for many years to come because the world's religions and ideologies have stored up so much misinformation about and hostility toward each other that it is almost impossible for us to know ahead of time what our potential partner is truly like on any given subject. Consequently, we normally need first of all to enter into sincere dialogue with every potential partner, at least until we learn where our true differences lie.

In this matter of differences, however, we have to be very careful in the distinctions we need to make. As pointed out above, in the process of the dialogue we will often learn that what we thought were real differences in fact turn out to be only apparent differences; different words or misunderstandings merely hid commonly shared positions. When we enter dialogue, however, we have to allow for the possibility that we will ultimately learn that on some matters we will find not a commonality but an authentic difference. As mentioned, these authentic differences can be of three kinds: complementary, analogous or contradictory. Complementary authentic differences will of course be true differences, but not such that only one could be valid. Furthermore, we know from our experience that the complementary differences will usually far outnumber the contradictory. Similarly, learning of these authentic but complementary differences will not only enhance our knowledge but also may very well lead to the desire to adapt one or more of our partner's complementary differences for ourself. As the very term indicates, the differences somehow complete each other, as the Chinese Taoist saying puts it: "Xiang fan xiang cheng" (Contraries complete each other).

Just as we must constantly be extremely cautious about "placing" our differences *a priori*, lest in acting precipitously we mis-place them, so too, we must not too easily and quickly place our true differences in the contradictory category. Perhaps, for example, Hindu *moksha*, Zen Buddhist *satori*, Christian "freedom of the children of God," and Marxist "communist state" could be understood as different, but nevertheless analogous, descriptions of true human liberation. In speaking of true but analogous differences in beliefs or values here, we are no longer talking about discerning teachings or practices in our partner's tradition which we might then wish to appropriate for our own tradition. That of course does, and should happen, but then we are speaking either of something which the two traditions ultimately held in common and was perhaps atrophied or suppressed in one, or of something which is an authentic but complementary difference. If this difference, however, is perceived as analogous rather than complementary or contradictory, it will be seen to operate within the total organic structure of the other religion-ideology and to fulfill its function properly only within it. It would not be able to have the same function, i.e., relationship to the other parts, in our total organic structure, and hence would not be understood to be in direct opposition, in contradiction to the "differing" element within our structure. At the same time, however, it needs to be remembered that these real but analogous differences in beliefs or values should be seen not as in conflict with one another, but as parallel in function, and in that sense analogous.

Yet, at times we can find contradictory truth claims, value claims, presented by different religious-ideological traditions. That happens, of course, only when they cannot be seen as somehow ultimately different expressions of the same thing (a commonality) or as complementary or analogous. When it happens, however, even though it be relatively rare, a profound and unavoidable problem faces the two communities: What should be their attitude and behavior toward each other? Should they remain in dialogue, tolerate each other, ignore each other, or oppose each other? This problem is especially pressing in matters of value judgments. What, for example, should the Christian (or Jew, Muslim, Marxist) have done in face of the now largely, but unfortunately not entirely, suppressed Hindu tradition of widow burning (*suttee*)? Should s/he try to learn its value, tolerate it, ignore it, oppose it (in what manner)? Or the Nazi tenet of killing all Jews? These, however, are relatively clear issues, but what of a religion-ideology that approves slavery, as Christianity, Judaism and Islam did until a century ago? Maybe that is clear enough today, but what of sexism – or only a little sexism? Or the claim that only through capitalism – or socialism – human liberation can be gained? Making a decision on the proper stance becomes less and less clear-cut. Eventually it was clear to most non-Hindus in the nineteenth century that the proper attitude was not dialogue with Hinduism on *suttee*, but opposition; but apparently it was not so clear to all non-Nazis that opposition to Jewish genocide was the right stance to take. Furthermore, it took Christians almost two thousand years to come to that conclusion concerning slavery. Many religions and ideologies today stand in the midst of a battle over sexism, some even refusing to admit the existing of the issue. Lastly, no argument need be made to point out the controversial nature of the contemporary capitalism-socialism issue.

Obviously, important contradictory differences between religions-ideologies do exist and at times warrant not dialogue, but opposition.

Individually we also make critical judgments on the acceptability of positions within our own traditions and, rather frequently, within our personal lives. But certainly this exercise of our critical faculties is not to be limited to ourselves and our tradition; this perhaps most human of faculties should be made available to all – with all the proper constraints and concerns for dialogue already detailed at length. Of course, it must first be determined on what grounds we can judge whether a religious-ideological difference is in fact contradictory, and then, if it is, whether it is of sufficient importance and of a nature to warrant active opposition.

IX. Full Human Life

Because all religions and ideologies are attempts to explain the ultimate meaning of human life and how to live accordingly, it would seem that those doctrines and customs which are perceived as hostile to human life are not complementary or analogous but contradictory, and that opposition should be proportional to the extent they threaten life. What is to be included in an authentically full human life then must be the measure against which all elements of all religions-ideologies must be tested as we make judgments about whether they are in harmony, complementarity, analogy or contradiction, and then act accordingly.

Since human beings are by nature historical beings, what it means to be fully human is evolving. At bottom everything human flows from what would seem to be acceptable to all as a description of the minimally essential human structure, that is, being an animal who can think abstractly and make free decisions. It has been only gradually that humanity has come to the contemporary position where claims are made in favor of "human rights," that things are due to all humans specifically because they are human. This position, in fact, has not always and everywhere been held. Indeed, it was for the most part hardly conceived until recently.

Only a little over a hundred years ago, for example, slavery was still widely accepted and even vigorously defended and practiced by high Christian churchmen, not to speak of Jewish and Muslim slave traders. And yet this radical violation of "human rights" has today been largely eliminated both in practice and law. Today no thinker or public leader would contemplate justifying slavery, at least in its directly named form of the past (see the Universal Declaration of Human Rights by the United Nations in 1948; art. 4). Here we have an obvious example of the historical evolution of the understanding of what it means to be fully human, i.e., that human beings are by nature radically free.

What in this century has been fundamentally acknowledged as the foundation of being human is that human beings ought to be autonomous in their decisions – such decisions being directed by their own reason and limited only by the same rights of others: "All human beings are born free and equal in dignity and rights. They are endowed with reason and conscience and should act toward one another in a spirit of brotherhood" (Universal Declaration art. 1). In the ethical sphere, this autonomy, which Thomas Aquinas recognized already in the thirteenth century,[9] expanded into the social, political spheres in the eighteenth century – well capsulated in the slogan of the French Revolution: "Liberty, Equality, Fraternity" (contemporary consciousness of sexist language would lead to a substitute like "Solidarity" for "Fraternity"). With the term "Liberty" is understood all the personal and civil rights; with the term "Equality" is understood the political rights of participation in public decision-making; with the term "Solidarity" is understood (in an expanded twentieth-century sense) the social rights.

Though frequently resistant in the past, and too often still in the present, the great religious communities of the world have likewise often and in a variety of ways expressed a growing awareness of and commitment to many of the same notions of what it means to be fully human. Hence, through dialogue humanity is painfully slowly creeping toward a consensus on what is involved in an authentically full human life. The 1948 United Nations "Universal Declaration of Human Rights" was an important step in that direction. Of course, much more consensus needs to be attained if inter-religious, inter-ideological dialogue is to reach its full potential.

---

9.   Thomas Aquinas, *Summa Theologiae*, I-II, Q. 91, a. 2: "Among other things, however, the rational creature submits to divine providence in a more excellent manner in so far as it participates itself in providence by acting as providence both for itself and for others." "Inter cetera autem rationalis creature excellentiori quondam modo divinae providentiae subiacet, inquantum et ipsa fit providentiae particeps, sibi ipsi et aliis providens."

X. Conclusion

The conclusion from these reflections, I believe, is clear: Inter-religious, inter-ideological dialogue is absolutely necessary in our contemporary world. Again, every religion and ideology can make its own several official statements from the Catholic Church about the necessity of dialogue, starting with Pope Paul VI in his first encyclical:

> Dialogue is demanded nowadays...It is demanded by the dynamic course of action which is changing the face of modern society. It is demanded by the pluralism of society, and by the maturity man has reached in this day and age. Be he religious or not, his secular education has enabled him to think and speak and to conduct a dialogue with dignity (*Ecclesiam suam*, no. 78).

To this the Vatican Curia later added:

> All Christians should do their best to promote dialogue between men of every class as a duty of fraternal charity suited to our progressive and adult age.... The willingness to engage in dialogue is the measure and the strength of that general renewal which must be carried out in the Church [read: in every religion and ideology] (*Humanae personae dignitatem*, August 28, 1968, no. 1).

ATTITUDES OF JUDAISM TOWARD NON-JEWS

by

Rabbi Daniel Polish

So many of us are veterans of gatherings such as this – indeed many of us in this room have studied together in formal settings or informally over the years-that we take for granted what a *novum* this moment is in the religious history of humankind. As we talk about the attitude of our respective traditions toward others, we must begin by recognizing that the thrust of so much of tradition is in the direction of rejection. The faith of other people is perceived as a "folly" or a "stumbling block" in the words of I Corinthians (1:23). Biblical Judaism – and the Rabbis after it – is clear in its repudiation of the polytheistic practices of its neighbors. The prophets railed against the inefficacy of idol worship in a way which, if failing to represent the reality of the self-understanding of those who made use of idols in worship, was unequivocal and pungent in the expression of their rejection of the practice. Isaiah 44:9-20 says:

> They that fashion a graven image are all of them vanity,
> And their delectable things shall not profit;
> And their own witnesses see not, nor know;
> That they may be ashamed.
> Who hath fashioned a god, or molten an image
> That is profitable for nothing?

Behold, all the fellows thereof shall be ashamed;
And the craftsmen skilled above men;
Let them all be gathered together, let them stand up;
They shall fear, they shall be ashamed together.

This attitude carried on into Rabbinic literature which accords *avodah zarah* the highest rank among sins (*cf.* Sanhedrin 74a which equates idolatry, sexual immorality, and murder), and generally reflects the attitude expressed in the Mechilta to Ex. 23.4: "idolators are everywhere designated the enemy of Israel." This despite the fact that removed as we might find such practice and belief from our own, "idol worship" has a legitimate place among the religious options of humankind. The Jewish tradition has, moreover, never adequately understood, or at least depicted, such practices. No religious tradition actually worships elements of the natural world. No one prays to sticks or stones or to objects manufactured from them. What such traditions do practice is a worship of those forces inherent in the physical object or manifest through it. The physical object is not regarded as the recipient of prayer, but the focal point for prayer. It is not the deity, but the valence through which the deity is manifest.

The sacred texts of Christianity have long been understood as having as their starting point a repudiation of Judaism and the arrogation of religious truth to its own, new dispensation. Similarly, Muhammad begins his career of preaching with the assertion that the Jewish and Christian communities which preceded him misunderstood and corrupted their religious text. His teaching alone, he asserts, is a correct representation of the will of the one God. Such attitudes, explicit in the formative teachings of the various traditions, can hardly be called accepting of other traditions. Their intent was to indicate that they alone were in possession of absolute truth. The teaching of others was to be understood as consisting of error, or worse, perverse mischief.

In part such attitudes were sustained by the nature of the pre-modern world. Members of different religious communities were able to maintain isolation from one another. Even if physically proximate, their interaction was limited only to such contacts as were absolutely necessary. Members of different communities were able to regard one another as different types of beings, and where political inequality permitted, were able to treat one another accordingly. Familiarity with the inner realities of other traditions was limited to religious virtuosi, and was certainly not made accessible to the ordinary members of the community. As it was, members of any community were exposed to perhaps one or two other traditions. Physical distance separated all the members of most communities from the multitude of other faith communities, all of which could be understood to make the same claim of absolute truth.

Our world is very different. The average member of any community lives in the midst of representatives of countless other traditions. The communication of our global village exposes us to still others farther away from us. The result is that while once various traditions could be assumed to be confined to one geographical site, today all traditions have established encampments throughout the world. The missionary journeys of devout Christians to the hinterlands of Asia have been reciprocated by the establishment of Hindu Ashrams in Texas, and of course elsewhere. We live in physical proximity to one another, and if we were not physically proximate, various forms of communication give us at least some exposure to one another's existence. Even more significant, it is not simply members of the various communities that are accessible, but the contents of those traditions as well. The "knowledge explosion" that characterizes this age has caught the teachings of the various traditions in its vortex. Even the most firmly rooted member of any community, at least in the West, has easy access to the teachings – and often teachers – of a whole gamut of other traditions. Printed material about the most arcane or remote religious tradition is easily accessible. Spokespersons for a whole range of faith stances are seen and heard on radio and television, thus literally entering the homes of those who, in earlier times, might never have known of their existence.

Against this background, the issue of how to understand the existence of other religious traditions presents itself not merely as the object of abstract speculation, but as a pressing existential concern. We live in a world of polyform religiosity. If we are to be religiously serious or authentic people, we must struggle to make sense of that fact. How do we understand the existence of religious traditions other than our own?

The existence of divergent traditions need not be regarded as altogether a new moment in religious history. A clear reading of the histories of any of the traditions reveals the extent to which its existence is dependent upon some other tradition, and the intensity of interaction with one or more other traditions over the centuries or millennia. Traditions have grown out of one another. Christianity stands upon Judaism, as Islam stands upon both of them–and the B'hai tradition upon it. The origins of the Buddhist tradition make sense only against the background of the religious teaching of India. Nor does the interaction end at the moment of birth.

The traditions have, over time, encountered one another with regularity, sometimes with animosity, surprisingly often in fruitful and constructive ways. Intent aside, the fact is that the various traditions have influenced and informed one another, knowingly or not. The exchange of ideas and patterns of religious expression has existed as long as the traditions themselves. Even before the advent of our "age of information," the religious traditions of humankind have taken turns sitting as master and then student at one another's feet. Religious polyformity should not confound us; it has been the stuff of our various careers.

When we look specially at the history of the Jewish people, and the unfolding of its religious tradition, we note that its primary interaction has been with first the polytheistic traditions of the ancient Near East, and then with Christianity and Islam. Its relations with the religious traditions of the East have been less substantial. However, even there, tantalizing questions of influence exist. One wonders about the relationship between the Manual of Discipline of the Qumran community with the *Vinaya*, the code of monastic law of Buddhism. Suggestive parallels exist between the account of Manu and the Flood in India, and the flood motif of the Bible. We also note that Jewish communities did exist in India and China, and it is interesting to observe the extent to which those Jewish communities appropriate some of the forms and patterns of the religious lives of their neighbors. Still as we look at the attitude of Judaism to non-Jews, it has been primarily the monotheistic traditions of Christianity and Islam that have dominated Jewish thought, and it is those traditions which shall take precedence in our discussion of Jewish attitudes.

Jewish attitudes toward non-Jews did not, of course, constitute a separate category of Jewish thought. Rather, those attitudes were reflected in various strands of what Max Kadushin refers to as the "organic thought" of Jewish life. Those attitudes reflect themselves most acutely in those strands to which we have given the label of revelation and the issue of chosen-ness. Our discussion of attitudes towards non-Jews, then, shall focus on these areas.

Revelation, as commonly understood, connotes the self-disclosure of God to human beings. As such it is an integral part of all religious tradition. Indeed, it has been argued, it is this element which differentiates the teachings of religion from those of philosophy. Further, it has been maintained, revelation is the centerpiece of the distinction between philosophy and theology; philosophy being the free pursuit of truth; theology being the presentation in philosophical/rational form – or the philosophical/rational defense – of ideas which have their origins in revelation.

Significant as revelation may be in other traditions, it is, in Judaism, the keystone, supporting the entire system of ideas and practices which constitutes Jewish religiousness. There can be no underestimating the centrality of revelation to the Jewish religious tradition. Every attempt, in the Middle Ages, to create a formulation of Jewish beliefs – an attempt, perhaps to create a Jewish equivalent of a *credo* – asserted the primacy of revelation. In our own time Franz Rosenzweig maintained that any complete or authentic expression of Jewish religiousness must reflect the concepts of creation, redemption and revelation. Emil Fachenheim states:

> if revelation must go, with it must go any possible *religious* justification for the existence of the Jewish people. In the absence of a binding commandment supernaturally revealed to a particular people, it makes as little sense to have a Mosaic religion for the Jewish people today, as, say, a Platonic religion for the modern Greek nation (*Quest for Past and Future*, p. 71).

Any conventional Jewish theology will include the category of revelation. Using the schema of organic thought articulated by Max Kadushin, revelation is interpenetrated with the ideas of covenant, of Torah, and of *Mitzvot* (commandments – religious practices). It is understood as an expression of God's love for God's creatures, and an emblem of God's assurances of ultimate redemption. It is, as Fackenheim persuasively argues, inextricably intertwined with the notion of Jewish peoplehood. It alone provides a rationale for the existence of the Jews as a separate and distinct group; and it alone provides warrant for the notion of chosenness – distinguishing that idea from simple ethnocentrism or chauvinism.

Of all the accounts of revelation in the *Tanach* ("Hebrew Bible") the revelatory experience *par excellence* is that at Sinai. Sinai becomes the most crucial event in the history of the Jewish people. Schemata of Jewish history regularly depict everything antecedent as leading up to it, and everything posterior as flowing from it. Sinai is celebrated in festivals. Its outline can be discerned in the liturgy surrounding the regular reading of the Torah. It is qualitatively unlike any other revelation described in the Torah. Unlike them, it is an event rather than an experience. It did not occur suddenly, unexpectedly, or in a vacuum; but was announced, anticipated and prepared for. It occurred not to a single individual, but to the people as a whole, the entire generation of the Exodus. It is understood as constituting not merely a self-disclosure but a covenant pertaining to – and binding – all subsequent generations of that people. The public quality of this revelatory experience is seized upon by Yehudah ha Levi as proof of its authenticity, and justification of the Jewish assertions of its superiority over any other purported claims to disclosure of the divine will.

After Sinai, the *Tanach* depicts God as continuing making self-disclosures to and through significant individuals in various ways. But Jewish teaching is clear that such revelation stopped completely with the destruction of the Temple, save to "children and idiots." Indeed, in one startling Rabbinic account, one contender in a legal argument among scholars invokes various forms of revelation to prove his case – including a public auditory assertion of his correctness, only to have the majority decide, "we do not pay heed to revelatory voices." This event is accompanied by the admonition that Torah is no longer in God's hands, but has been turned over to God's human children. Thus, the period of self-disclosure *per se* is understood to be brought to a close.

The issue of revelation raises several important questions which we shall here treat. It is my belief that in response to each of these questions there is no one authoritative position. Rather, in Judaism, as indeed in all religious traditions, there exists a spectrum of possible attitudes, including a more "normative" or generally held position ("generally held" is a difficult phrase to interpret. One never knows if by it an author means the one that was most common for the longest period of time, or the one held by most informed "believers" today, or more simply "my own").

The issue of revelation, more pointedly the revelation at Sinai, touches on the very difficult question of particularism and universalism. The particularist understanding of revelation asserts that God "chose us from among all peoples to give us His Torah." This orientation maintains, and rejoices in the fact, that Jews alone are recipients of God's word. Though one could well anticipate such a particularist reading of the phenomenon of revelation, there exists, significantly, a more universalistic treatment of this theme. There are in Rabbinic discussions of Sinai those who emphasize that revelation occurred simultaneously in all the seventy languages of humankind. It is also noted that that event took place not in the land of the Jews, which would thus make it pertinent to them alone, but in the wilderness – no man's land, or more properly, every man's land. This image is amplified in the explanation that as the sand, wind, and sky of the wilderness belong to no one and every one, so too is the Torah the possession of all human beings. One startling *Midrash* depicts God as giving the Torah to the Jews only after it had been rejected by all the other peoples of the earth. This story has both a particularist and a universalist thrust to it. Generally it is understood in its universalist sense.

There are those who argue, particularistically, that the Torah is the property of the Jews: received by them, in their language, for their own use. The opposite pole of this question understands Jews as being merely representative of all humanity when they stood at Sinai. Thus the Torah is given to human beings who only incidentally happened to be Jews. A common middle position is that Sinai did not confer chosen-ness upon the Jews, but rather a mission. That mission was not to keep the Torah for themselves, but to be its bearers to the world. The Jews, according to this understanding, received the Torah as Jews, but for the purpose of disseminating its teaching to all humankind.

Various understandings exist about the content of revelation. At its most fundamental level revelation can be understood to include the Ten Commandments spoken at Sinai. More inclusively, tradition understands the Sinaitic revelation to include the whole of the Torah, indeed all of the *Tanach*. In what Ellis Rivkin characterizes as a "revolution," the Pharisaic understanding of revelation, to which all Judaism is heir, extended the contents of the revelation at Sinai to include not only the *Tanach*, which it redefined as the "written Torah," but also what it identified as the "oral Torah" – that is, all authoritative teaching of the Rabbis. Thus, the teaching of later millennia came to be understood as revealed at Sinai.

The precise understanding of the foregoing is that all Torah is to be understood as having been given by God at Sinai, and thus is to be understood literally. Upon this literal understanding of the Torah (in the expanded sense of the term) rests the entire enterprise of commentary which constituted the major form of the tradition's self-expression. The premise of Rabbinic hermeneutics was the belief that the will of God was implicit in the words of Torah, and that if one probed those words correctly one could explicate that will more precisely. A similar assumption underlay the Kabbalistic strand of Jewish religiousness. The Kabbalists believed that the mind of God was made manifest not in the words of Torah alone, but in the very letters of the text themselves, in the arrangement of words on a page, even in the spaces between the letters. Nothing could attest more clearly to the belief that Torah constitutes literal revelation.

Other strands of Jewish belief hold less firmly to the concept of literal revelation. This spectrum can be characterized in a survey of various understanding of the giving of the Ten Commandments at Sinai. The literal understanding is troubled by the fact that variant versions of the decalogue are given in Exodus and Deuteronomy. The classical resolution of this apparent disparity is that God spoke both forms "in a single saying"/simultaneously, one version being recorded in each place. The purpose of this dual exposition was to enunciate specific shadings of instruction. Another teaching maintains that of the various commandments

God actually enunciated only the first one, which was a self-disclosure. The rest of the decalogue, it is here suggested, is the response of the people itself to this self-disclosure. Amplifying upon this theme, Herman Cohen, taught that God spoke not even the entire first commandment, but only the first word: *Anochi*/I; the people, Cohen states, responded by the formulation of the decalogue to that sense of divine presence. More radical still is the teaching of the Chassidic Rebbe Zev Wolf of Zhitomer (d. 1800). Zev Wolf taught that God did not speak even the whole of that first word, but only the first letter of the first word: the *aleph* – a silent letter. To that silent speaking of the presence of God, the people responded with the decalogue.

Early in its career, the Reform movement discarded a literal belief in revelation. The implications of this reformulation of Jewish theology, though beyond the scope of the present paper, are of incalculable significance to the ideology of Reform. Though it is frequently asserted that Reform differs from Orthodoxy only in practice and not in belief, its treatment of revelation represents a fundamental revision of the belief system and is essential to its reformation of religious practice. One cannot reform practices which one believes were literally commanded by God. In place of revelation, Reform postulated the concept of divine inspiration. People can be inspired by God and as a result of that inspiration have formulated the great classics of religious expression.

Closely akin to this concept is another Reform idea, that of "continuing revelation." Such inspiration by God, according to Reform, did not cease with the destruction of the Temple. Rather it is available to "the seers of all generations," including, it is to be assumed, the fathers of Reform themselves. Such divine inspiration, continuing through time as it does, is equally accessible to Jews and non-Jews, including the great teachers of all religious faiths. This reformulated view of revelation then, has the affect of dissolving barriers of time and group identity. It becomes available at all places and times, and to members of all peoples.

In the contemporary world, Jews are in contact with other communities of faith which make their own claims to being recipients of revelation. We turn, now to a brief discussion of how Jews understand the fact that Islam and Christianity have challenged Jewish claims to exclusivity in receiving revelation, and claim to be recipients as well. Here, as in other matters, there exists a spectrum of belief.

On one end of that spectrum is the school of thought which believes, that Muslims and Christians simply are in error. This error may be the result of mischievousness, perversity or malice or may be the product of simple human confusion. In any event, neither Jesus nor the Church, in that community, nor Mohammed in the other, can be believed to be the recipient of revelation. To the extent to which their teachings correspond to truths which were revealed to Israel, they may be of some value. To the extent to which their teachings diverge from those revealed to Israel, they are in error, and may even be dangerous.

On the other end of the spectrum are those who contend that no one has actually received revelation, that all such claims are the attempt of human beings to invest their own teachings with supernatural authority. To those who hold this position, all so-called revelations are equally true, and, more precisely, equally false. Somewhat less radical, but toward the same end of the spectrum are those who assert, in various ways, that the revelations of all communities of faith are, at bottom, identical; "all say the same thing." Some holding this position would assert the value of Jewish teaching by maintaining that of the various revelations, that one simply happens to be the one that is their own. More normatively there exists a recognition that both Christianity and Islam are authentically monotheistic faiths. As such they each have some claim to truth. To some extent this claim may be understood as involving the fact that both were influenced by Judaism. But ultimately the valuation of them as possessing truth extends beyond that. Indeed it rests on an implicit recognition that they both have, in some way, access to God's presence. As such each can claim that it possesses insight into God's will. Normatively Jews recognize this process as essentially identical with what in our own case is referred to as revelation.

Jews may, indeed, believe that the aspects of Christianity and Islam that cause those two communities of faith to diverge from Jewish belief and practice detract from their correctness. Nonetheless, there is a recognition that those two communities possess and impart revealed truth. As such

Judaism, normatively regards Islam and Christianity in the fullest sense of the term as sister religions, and, in some way, as vessels of divine truth.

If such an affirmation of the worth of other religious traditions, or the intimation that they might be recipients of revelation is posited, it would appear to run contrary to the idea of Jewish "chosen-ness." The idea of the "election" of Israel constitutes a scandal in the eyes of Christianity. It is a complex notion, and one not easily understood by Judaism itself, nor consistently interpreted. At first glance, election might seem to indicate a privileged place among the family of nations for the Jewish people – a status of manifest inequality. The major stream of the Jewish tradition itself has not understood election in that light. Election has not been confused with superiority. According to normative Jewish understanding, God charged the Jews with performance of a special task, but did not ascribe to them special merit. According to this understanding, each nation had its own special gift, its own innate talents, its own peculiar skills, the contribution that it alone could make to the human family. It was the "gift" of the Jews to carry Torah into the world.

In this light can Israel understand God to bless Israel along side of its historic adversaries: "In that day, Israel shall be a third partner with Egypt and Assyria as a blessing on the earth; for the Lord of Hosts will bless them, saying 'blessed be My people Egypt, My handiwork Assyria, and My very own Israel'" (Isaiah 19:24-5). More pointedly, Amos addresses the question of election itself and here has God as proclaiming the more universal vision of equality for all humanity: "Are you not as the children of the Ethiopians to Me, O children of Israel, says the Lord. Have I not brought Israel up out of Egypt? And the Philistines from Caphtor, and the Syrians from Kir?" (Amos 9:7). The Rabbis tell a poignant story about the moment when the Jews had safely crossed the Red Sea and the Egyptian pursuers had drowned in it. The Hebrews, safely on the dry shore, began to sing their song of exultation. So powerful was their singing that the angels in heaven joined in. According to the Rabbinic commentary, God then turned to the angels and demanded "How can you sing when my children are drowning?" This story rests on an idea that transcends any concept of election – that of the equality of all human beings.

In discussing the form of the Genesis account of humanity's origins, the Rabbis teach that the notion of God's creating a single human person serves to undergird the belief that all people are equal. None of us can claim superiority over another. All of us are B'nai Adam/children of Adam–human, and each equal to the first human. Furthermore, all of us are, in the light of this account, related to one another, all of us equally descended from the same first ancestor. No one can say, "my lineage is superior to yours," all of us trace ourselves back to the same roots. In such light, subscription to the Genesis narrative connotes belief in the ultimate importance of every individual, and the fundamental equality of all individuals.

The Jewish tradition has been consistent in advocating the equality of all the children of God. Another *Midrash* (Rabbinic elaboration of the biblical text) maintains that to form the first human, God took dirt from all four corners of the world, humus of all shades from which to shape that common ancestor of all people and races. The motif of human equality is sounded again in the story of Noah. With the destruction of all other people, Noah becomes the new Adam, the common ancestor of all who would people the earth. In this account, the commonality underlining racial differentiation is made manifest. The sons of Noah are explicitly identified as the ancestors of the various racial groups. The story indicates an awareness of political distinction among the various groups of humanity. But there is no escaping the lesson of their ontological equality. For they are clearly sons of one parent. They share the same flesh and blood, the same underlying humanity.

This fundamental equality is rendered in legal terms in the set of mandates given to Noah at the conclusion of the deluge. These rules, which came to be called the Noahide Laws, antedate Sinai and are directed equally to all the descendants of Noah–all humanity. All who live are regarded as equally defined by this set of "natural" laws. As the laws are equally binding on all people, so they have the effect of identifying all people as equal. Rabbinic teaching underscores the importance of the Noahide Laws as the common law of all humanity. They become, in effect, the judicial embodiment of the common descent of all humans.

All humans are biologically kin, by virtue of their common descent from first Adam, and then Noah, just as they are cosmically children of the creator God. It is as if the descendants of Noah were cosmicized by Malachi: "Have we not all one Father, has not one God created us...." The sense of the absolute equality of all people is reflected in a Talmudic account:

> Someone came to Rabba and told him: "the general of my town has ordered me to go and kill such and such a person, and if not, the general will kill me." Rabbi said to him: "Let the general kill you rather than him so that you do not commit murder. Who knows that your blood is redder. Maybe his blood is redder" (Babylonian Talmud Sanhedrin 74A).

The commitment to the equality of all people is embodied in the judicial system and process created by the Jewish people. The system of law represented in the Torah and elaborated by Rabbinic legal literature is one that guaranteed a fair trial to all people, home-born and stranger alike (Leviticus 24:22). Every person was entitled to a fair hearing before an impartial court. Judges were forbidden to accept bribes (Deuteronomy 16:19) and prohibited from showing favoritism in any way – to the needy no less than to the powerful (Leviticus 19:15). Throughout the period of their self-determination, the Jewish people prided themselves in this scrupulous fairness of their courts. Equality under law was more than an abstract ideal. It was the concrete embodiment of the basic tenets of the theology of the Jewish community.

The notion of "chosen-ness" is commonly related to a secondary idea of mission. That idea, so evolved in the thinking of the Christian community and so evident in a variety of forms in the activities of that community has, today, no correlative in Jewish life. Indeed, it is instructive that the term itself, when it was briefly employed in Jewish thought, had a meaning diametrically at odds with that conventionally understood to be its purport in Christianity. Reform Judaism, child of the emancipation, and conversant with Christian theological categories, appropriated the term mission for the Jewish people. Yet, as used by Reform Jewish thinkers early in this century, the idea of the "mission of Israel" did not carry any implication of the conversion of humanity, nor even of individual non-Jews to Reform in particular or to Judaism in general. Quite to the contrary, that notion designated a special role for the Jewish faithful. Jews were called to embody in their belief system an absolute, uncompromising and pure fidelity to the monotheistic vision, and in their actions a scrupulous devotion to the highest ethical standards – and ethical system corollary to that faith. The heart of the "mission of Israel" was the challenge that Jews be living embodiments of ethical monotheism.

This exemplification was not for the purpose of winning others to Judaism, but, rather, for calling others – and here it must be recognized that the main "others" early Reform had in mind were principally the Christians among whom they lived – to the highest aspirations of their own respective religious traditions. When advocates of the mission of Israel admonished Jews to be a "light to the nations," that light was not understood as a harbor light calling ships to one particular pier, but a flood light illuminating the proper channels to the various ports.

If there is any sense of movement implied in the concept of mission as articulated by early Reform, it is clearly not from outside of Judaism into it, but rather from all particular embodiments of monotheistic faith to the broadest, most universalistic expression of that faith. When early Reform asserted "My house shall be a house of prayer for all peoples," it did not intend that the nations would find their way to the doors of the Synagogue, but that when all humanity came to the recognition of God's unity, the walls of all particular "houses" would fall and all people, standing together, would inhabit the greater mansion. In this spirit did the liturgists of this persuasion amend the Sh'ma – the credal affirmation of Jewish faith in God's oneness – to declare "Hear O Israel, Hear all mankind, the Lord our God, the Lord is One."

Paradoxically, the concept of mission as employed in Reform Jewish theology of that period denoted not the particular enterprise of gathering others to one's faith, but the most universalistic impulses inherent in that term. There is some indication that this transvaluation of the meaning of mission was not altogether unself-conscious on the part of its proponents. Kaufman Kohler, the pre-eminent spokesman of early Reform theology wrote:

Noble as the heroic task accomplished by many a Christian missionary indisputably was, the task of the Jew during the dark medieval centuries of withstanding all trials, the threats, the taunts, the *auto da fes* and the alluring baits of the Church was by all means far nobler and more heroic, and it was performed not by individuals but by the entire people. It was a passive, not an active mission. Had they then gone forth among the nations to win the world for their teachings, they might have long ago been swallowed up by the surrounding multitude. Instead of this, the Jew proved to be the "Servant of the Lord" who "gave his back to the smiters," "the man of sorrows, despised and forsaken of men..." ("The Mission of Israel and its Application in Modern Times" in *Studies, Addresses and Personal Papers*, p. 189).

The fact is that Jews today live in a world religiously far different from the one in which their faith was born. Judaism, which emerged in a world sunk in the ignorance of the One God, and in thrall to idolatry, today finds its world to be one in which the vision of monotheism is shared by countless peoples. Doctrinal differences persist. Religious forms diverge. Communities of faith are divided. And yet, to Jewish eyes, the core truth is apperceived alike. The emergence of this situation thrust upon the Jewish community a profound question: should we seek to teach other monotheists the specific contours of Jewish faith, or are their own traditions and forms sufficient vehicles to convey the elemental teaching? There is a history of discussion within Judaism of this question: the application of the categories of Noahide Law to all human beings, even non-monotheists; the philosophical exchanges about whether Christianity and Islam were to be considered monotheistic or idolatrous: more recent writing about relations with Christians. Paramount among these is the notion articulated by Franz Rosenzweig of a dual covenant theory. Rosenzweig maintains that Judaism and Christianity are at bottom two distinct approaches to the same God, bearers, in two radically different forms, of the same truth. Rosenzweig would, no doubt, today extend that metaphor to include Islam. The challenge of this moment is how to conceive of the inclusion of traditions that are not formally monotheistic.

What is clear is that Judaism has not assumed the notion of chosenness to connote superiority, nor mission to demand the conversion of other peoples of Jewish faith. Rather, Judaism has taken a quite consistent attitude of the equality of human beings, and a progessively fraternal attitude toward other communities of faith, particularly those with whom it has the most in common, historically and theologically, those of a monotheistic orientation. The future may find us expanding our parameters to include a greater understanding of, and relationship to, traditions whose understanding of God is couched in non-singular terms.

For myself, there is a part of me that is very drawn to the teachings of the Qur'an where it is articulated that the One God has been perceived in a variety of ways, that there was not one messenger but many: "We sent forth to every nation a Messenger" (16.38). The forms of all these revelations are not identical. Rather, each is suited to the particular language and the particular needs of the people to whom it has been given:

> Every nation has been summoned to its book (45.27).
> To everyone of you we have appointed a right way and an open road (5.33).
> We have appointed for every nation a holy rite that they shall perform (23.65).

Our traditions have separated us. At their deepest level, however, they can unite us. This does not mean that we are called on to abandon the unique and characteristic aspects of our various traditions, to merge ourselves into some new configuration which encompasses all and submerges all individuality.

The greatest articulator of the Jewish collective unconscious in this age has, I think, been Franz Kafka. In one parable Kafka envisions a gate which a man might have entered but failed to. The guard standing at the gate throughout the man's long vigil says that this gate has been prepared especially for you. For each of our traditions has been fashioned especially for us as our own summons to the Ultimate. Each is our gate to the absolute and the only gate appropriate for us, indeed the only gate for which we have the key. We are called to examine the course our traditions have decreed for us. It might be that the various traditions find themselves to be wholly different roads. It may be that they prove to be different by-paths of the same trail, or perhaps they are, in truth, the same path, called by Jews Torah, and by others Tarigah, Dharma or Tao and that the end of that path is the same Ultimate One.

THE ATTITUDE OF ORTHODOX CHRISTIANS TOWARD NON-ORTHODOX AND NON-CHRISTIANS

by

Demetrios J. Constantelos

The attitude of Orthodox Christians toward the non-Orthodox is determined by their understanding of the origins and development of Christianity and the perception of themselves as its guardians and interpreters. Furthermore their attitude toward non-Christians is based on their comprehension of natural revelation and historical experiences.

There are two dimensions to my topic, the theoretical and the pragmatic. The theoretical dimension, which determines the theological attitude of modern Orthodoxy, rests on the attitude of early Christianity toward the lapsed and non-Christians. And yet in every age and time theory and practice are often inconsistent, so that realistically we should speak of Orthodox Christian attitudes rather than an attitude toward non-Orthodox. There are "official" positions, but also subjective opinion.

I

The Orthodox believe their faith, their Christian ethos, and even some forms of their worship, although never static, have an unbroken continuity with the experience of early and medieval Christianity which must be maintained. Thus they possess a strong historical consciousness. Continuity and change, unity and diversity have been major characteristics and fundamental traits of Orthodox Christianity.

This sense of continuity is explained in terms of both history and theology. They believe that the founder of Christianity is never the Jesus of Nazareth but always Jesus the Christ. Jesus was born in Bethlehem of Judaea, but the principal theater of his life and teaching was the region of Galilee. Eleven of his twelve apostles were also natives of the same province. But at the time of Jesus Galilee was heavily Hellenized: its inhabitants were viewed with disdain and their district was called "the land of the gentiles" (John 1:46; Mat. 4:15). For more than three hundred years Galilee was subject to influences of Greek ideas, customs and culture. This mixed and heavily Hellenized population of Galilee received Jesus as the Anointed one, the Christ. As Jesus the Christ, the founder of Christianity was accepted as the fulfillment of Hebrew messianism and Hellenic expectation, and as the point of convergence between Hebraism and Hellenism, the Jewish Messiah and the Greek Logos.

The Gospel of Matthew is the clearest source of the Hebraic understanding of Jesus while the Gospel of John reveals Christ as the Logos, the pre-existent God who in time and space assumed flesh and walked among human beings as God-human, as *theanthropos*. The Gospel of John more than any other new Testament book is in the heart of Orthodoxy.

Thus for Orthodox Christians–whether Greek speaking, Slavic, Arabic, or English, Jesus, the Hebrew fulfillment of Messianic expectations becomes the Christ whom the Greeks sought to see in Jerusalem (John 12:20-23). The long search of the Greeks culminated in the discovery of Jesus the Christ.

Theologically the coming of the Greeks to see Jesus is most significant. The Greeks represented the world outside Judaism, and their conversion to Christ secured Christianity's universalism. When Jesus exclaimed that "the hour has come for the Son of God to be glorified" he understood the ecumenical implication of the first Gentiles' meeting with Him. But this was more than a meeting between Jesus of Nazareth and the Greeks–symbolically it was a meeting between Christianity and the Greek inquisitive mind, between ethical Judaism and philosophical Hellenism.

In the person of Jesus the Christ, the Orthodox see the fulfillment of God's promise to all humankind. Early Christianity is as much Hebrew as it is Hellenic. The Orthodox are conscious of the fact that Christianity was born and raised in the Greek speaking and Hellenized Eastern part of the Roman Empire. In his excellent volume *The Spirituality of the Christian East*, Tomas Spidlik, a member of the Society of Jesus and Professor at the Oriental Institute in Rome, has summarized what the Orthodox consider a principle of great significance. He writes: "We must stress one principle and stress it hard, that the Latin church originated from the Greek church as a branch grows from a tree trunk. The Church was implanted by the Greeks and expressed itself in the Greek language until the end of the fourth century."[1]

The Church continued to deliberate in Greek and every one of the ecumenical councils of united medieval Christendom was held in the Greek East, recorded in the Greek language and with the assistance of Greek thought. This emphasis is not nationalistic or political, but based on historical realities. If we are to understand the theological disagreements which arose between the Greek Christian East and the Latin Christian West we must bear in mind that the Greek East spoke from a position of intellectual and cultural superiority which rightly or wrongly had been imbedded in their psyche for many centuries. Rome, on the other hand, was conscious of its past political power and spoke from a tradition of political superiority.

In any case the Orthodox Church has always seen itself as the genuine Church, in unbroken continuity with the early Church. Thus any deviation from this mainstream Church was perceived as heresy or schism. As the citizen in Greek antiquity realized his potentialities within the *polis*, which provided no justification for an *idiotis* (an idiot), the individual Christian is saved in the divinized human and divine *polis* – the Church. Thus even today some Orthodox Christians, including serious theologians, believe that all

---

1.   Tomas Spidlik, *The Spirituality of the Christian East*, tr. by Anthony P. Gythiel (Kalamazoo, MI: Cistercian Publications, Inc., 1986), p. 351.

Christian Churches and denominations should seriously seek their return to what they consider authentic Orthodox Christianity.

The method by which the early Catholic-Orthodox Church received back former members served as a prototype for many centuries in the Christian East. Practice varied considerably from diocese to diocese and from one metropolitan see to another. The theological argument used to justify a given tradition also differed.

Historical evidence indicates that uniformity in attitude from place to place and century to century was absent. Differences between Rome and Carthage, Alexandria and Constantinople, Antioch and Jerusalem, Asia Minor and Gaul were evident especially after the third century. Every geographical or ecclesiastical area had its own practice and ritual in receiving former heretics, schismatics, lapsed and apostates.

Likewise in the Orthodox Church today the reception of and the attitude toward non-Orthodox varies from one independent Church to another, from jurisdiction to jurisdiction. The theological debates over the proper practice is justified according to the specific situation and the historical experience of each autocephalous Church. *Oikonomia* rather than *akribeia* is the dominant principle that regulates the attitude of most Orthodox toward non-Orthodox. *Oikonomia* means flexibility, a discernment and practice according to circumstances. For example, when Orthodox autocephalous churches are to receive into sacramental communion non-Orthodox Christians or non-Orthodox clergy they follow different ways. Non-Orthodox Christians baptized in the name of a Triune God are not rebaptized but as a rule they are received through a confirmation, a rite of anointment with chrism. *Akribeia* means strict observance of Church canons and there are few Orthodox who rebaptize and re-ordain non-Orthodox.

While there are various attitudes toward several sacraments (baptism, marriage, ordination) all Orthodox unanimously maintain one disposition toward communion. Non-Orthodox are not admitted to eucharistic communion. Admitting non-Orthodox to a common chalice would mean organic union, an event that belongs to deliberations and decisions of a Pan-Orthodox Council. Organic union remains a serious yearning but it cannot be achieved without serious preparation.

Those who oppose the participation of the Orthodox Church in inter-faith and inter-religious dialogues usually count three major reasons: first, they are afraid of the gradual weakening of the Orthodox conviction that the Orthodox Church is the one, holy, catholic, and apostolic church of Christ. Second, they consider the possibility that the Orthodox Church may come to be viewed equal to heretical, schismatic, or even sectarian groups. They adamantly refuse to engage in dialogue with creeds which have been condemned by ecumenical councils for serious theological disagreements or to accept a branch theory ecclesiology. Third, they are fearful lest ultimately inter-faith dialogues will result in the reduction of the essence of dogmas, whose validity is believed to be diachronic, into human-made teachings subject to evolution and change. However at no time have the Orthodox been monolithic and monochromatic in their attitude toward non-Orthodox.

The very presence of the Orthodox in the Ecumenical Movement, the World Council of Churches in particular, indicates that the Orthodox, notwithstanding their strong beliefs about the genuineness of their Christianity, maintain a flexible and conciliatory attitude toward non-Orthodox. Though they stress the factors and forces of continuity which bind the past inextricably with the present, the Orthodox recognize the presence of forces both human and divine which enable them to accept change and seek reinterpretation.

II

As we turn our attention to the attitude of the Orthodox toward non-Christians, I need to emphasize that Orthodox Christians have co-existed with Jews and Muslims for many centuries. Frequently historical realities belie theoretical positions.

One of the factors which allows the Orthodox to see the divine presence outside of Christianity is their notion about *apocalypsis* (revelation) as source of truth. Truth, whether in terms of doctrine, ethics, worship, or daily moral practice, derives from one source – the Being in whom everything has its being, the Creator who brought the creation into existence. The human being as part of creation is not self-sufficient and autonomous for it owes its origin and existence to that Being whom we commonly call God. The human quest for identity and understanding of its place in the cosmos, for creative self-realization in history is realized in truths extant in and revealed by the Creator. And the Creator is both an inner presence and a cosmic reality, endocosmic and exocosmic. Because of this, Orthodoxy possesses a sense of the sacredness of the whole creation which encompasses the totality of life.

Thus truth has one source, but it is conveyed through two channels, the physical, or natural, and the metaphysical, or supernatural; one can become partially known through a personal quest and effort and the other is given as a gift, gratis. God is the originator and the human being is the receiver. Divinity and humanity have been in constant interaction. The divinity is "present in all places and filling all things" (*pantahou paron kai ta panta pleron*) and humanity "lives, moves, and has its existence" in the Divinity (*en auto zomen kai kinoumentha kai esmen*), as the ancient Greek philosophers and poets Epimenides and Aratos put it and Paul of Tarsus reemphasized (Acts 17:28).

The two channels by which truth is conveyed represent the two aspects of God's involvement in history the visible and the invisible, the physical and the metaphysical. God as Spirit, Power, and Essence is invisible but God as creative energies active in creation is visible and physical. God as the ultimate cause of laws, decrees, principles of morality, the urge of the human person to seek communion with the divine, the desire of the human being to rise above nature, is revealed in the world through various ways and diverse manners. Furthermore, human capacity to reason, the inward sense of non-material origins, the faculties which distinguish humanity from the plant and animal creation are considered sparks or rays of the Divinity and manifestations of "natural" revelation. Because of the commonalty between Divinity and humanity, the human reaches out for God and when the reach becomes unattainable, God takes the initiative and reaches out for the human.

In addition to their understanding of natural *apocalypsis* as a possession of all humanity, the attitude of Orthodox Christians toward non-Christian religions and beliefs is determined by the pneumatology, their conception of the nature of the *Hagion Pneuma* (the Holy Spirit) and its function in the cosmos – its revelation. In Greek the Holy Spirit is neuter.

Whether the Spirit is the cosmic and universal power or substance as in ancient Greek thought or as a *hypostsis* (person) sharing in the essence of Triune God as in Christian theology, the Pneuma has been an experience of humanity both Christian and non-Christian, Spiritual experience is a universal phenomenon. Even so, there have been communities of people such as ancient Israel and the Christian community (the Church) whose experience singled them out for a special awareness and consciousness, claiming uniqueness for themselves and their descendants.

The Spirit is an ever-present reality such that revelation is never finished but always active, unveiling things and invisible realities, making intelligible incomprehensible mystery, building bridges over fortresses viewed in the past as islands in themselves, tearing down walls perceived as impregnable. It is the Spirit which moves where it wills, whose presence and operation is everywhere and all encompassing. The Spirit of God may not be where one would like to see it and it may be where one refuses to see it. Thus it is impossible to define the boundaries of God's people.[2]

The Orthodox acknowledge the continuity of God's revealing truth before as well as after the incarnation of the Logos. The living God "in past generations allowed all the nations to walk in their own ways; yet he did not leave himself *amartyron* – without witness" (Acts 14:16-17), and "what can be known about God was known to them, because God revealed it to them. Ever since the creation of the world his Invisible nature, namely, his external power and deity, has been clearly perceived in the things that have been made" (Rom. 1:18-19). On the other hand Pentecost is an ongoing event. The Holy Spirit continues to guide to new interpretations and to new revelations. It is the same Spirit who creates, who spoke through the prophets, who guided the apostles, and "in whom we live, move, and have our existence" (Acts 17:28).

---

2.   On the importance of the Spirit in Orthodox theology see P. N. Trembelas, *Dogmatike tes Orthodoxou Katholikes Ekklesias*, 3 vols. (Athens, 1959-61), 1:257-268; Nikos A. Nissiotis, "The Importance of the Doctrine of the Trinity for Church Life and Theology," in *The Orthodox Ethos*, ed. by A. J. Philippou (Oxford, 1964), pp. 32-69; John Meyendorff, "The Holy Spirit, as God," in *The Holy Spirit*, ed. by D. Kirkpatrick (Nashville, 1974), pp. 76-89; Georges Khodr, "Christianity in a Pluralistic World – The Economy of the Holy Spirit," in *The Orthodox Church in the Ecumenical Movement*, ed. by C. G. Patelos (Geneva, 1978), pp. 297-307.

Christianity's claim to be inherently exclusive of other religions was an inheritance from its Hebraic roots. But as early as the apostolic age, Christianity became rooted in the Hellenic tradition as well. The tensions between the Hebraic and the Hellenic elements were constant in early Christianity. There is little doubt, however, that the future of Christianity was shaped not by people like Tatian and Tertullian, who rejected what the Orthodox call natural revelation, the truth of God outside the Hebrew Bible, but by Justin, Clement, and Origen of Alexandria. Synesios of Cyrene, Basil the Great, Gregory of Nyssa, and others who achieved a synthesis between indirect, or natural revelation, and direct – the self-disclosure of God in Christ. As already indicated, for the early Church as well as for the Orthodox Church today Christ is the point of convergence between the Jewish Messiah and the Logos of the Greeks.

As Hellenistic-Jewish writers of the pre-Christian era made significant compromises with Hellenism in their theology, likewise early Christian writers adjusted their theology to Hellenic thought and philosophical categories which they perceived as another form of God's revelation.[3] A great degree of syncretism occurred in late antiquity in both Judaism and early Christianity. By the fifth century Christianity had defined its major theological principles but in no one century was Christianity monolithic. What in the fifth century was described as a heretical church today is called a sister church.

The Hebraic and Hellenic tensions in early Christianity gave rise to two different attitudes toward the religious truths of the outside world. In his Areopagos speech, St. Paul implied that the Athenians who worshiped the unknown God were actually crypoto-Christians. The opening words of John's Gospel that in the beginning was the beloved Logos of the Greeks, prepared the way for early Christianity to take a positive attitude toward non-biblical truth.

---

3.   Justin, *First Apology*, 5.4; Clement of Alexandria, *Paedagogos* III.98.1; Iden, *Stromateis* VII.7.7; Origen, *Contra Celsum* III.62.79; Idem, *De Principiis*. The literature on the subject is enormous. Excellent summaries are provided by W. Jaeger, *Early Christianity and Greek Paideia* (Cambridge, Mass., 1961); H. Chadwick, *Early Christian Thought and the Classical Tradition* (New York, 1966).

St. Paul's attitude toward non-biblical truth, as expressed in the seventeenth chapter of Acts as well as in his epistle to the Romans determined Orthodox Christianity's positive attitude toward non-Christian religions. Justin, mentioned earlier, proclaimed that all who had lived according to the Logos, the Reason of God, were Christians before the coming of Christ. Clement of Alexandria, after Justin, stressed that it was to the whole of humankind that "God spoke in former times in fragmentary and varied fashion." And Origen, one of the great theologians of all times, emphasized that there is no truth independent of the direct action of God, whether in Judaism or in Hellenism. Gregory of Nazianzus, Gregory of Nyssa, Basil the Great, and Augustine, notwithstanding their condemnation of paganism, saw in history the presence of God guiding all to the truth. As Irenaeus wrote: "There is only one God who, from beginning to end, through various economies comes to the help of humankind."[4] The Orthodox maintain that "the good is part and parcel of the truth wherever found," as fourth century churchmen taught.

The Orthodox attitude toward non-Christians can be summarized in the words of Bishop George Khodr of Lebanon. In a notable address before the Central Committee of the World Council of Churches in Addis Ababa, Bishop George said:

> It has been an [Western Christian] error to identify the range of the Incarnate Christ and one of the holy Spirit with the salvation history that derives from the Old Testament. There is a divine dialogue with humanity, outside the Abrahamic and the Mosaic, because of the covenant in nature with universal man. The liberty of the Spirit is not confined to the frontiers of the Church as "the new Israel." It is Christ alone, who is received as the light when grace visits a Brahman, or a Buddhist or a Muslim, reading their own Scriptures. These extra-Christian data must be taken up into our theology. Our task is to reveal to the world of the religions the God there hidden, just as Paul, coming to Athens, found "Christians who

---

4. Irenaeus, *Adversus omnes haereses*, III.12.13

were not aware of their Christianity: he gave their God a name"...is the right adjective for the Orthodox Christian faith.[5]

III

While the theology of the Orthodox about the nature of revelation, both physical and metaphysical, provides a solid basis for intra-faith and inter-religious dialogues, the Orthodox remain uncompromising in their attitude toward Trinitarian theology as it has been defined by the early ecumenical synods. They believe that in Christian theology certain constants and inviolable articles of belief cannot be reduced in their essence in order to accommodate ultra-liberal Christologies and Pneumatologies (doctrines of the Holy Spirit).

Chalcedonian Christology, for example, is upheld as the best result of a synergy between Divinity and humanity. But Christology and Pneumatology complement each other and constitute two aspects in the context of *Triadike* – a Triune theology. What follows is an explanation of the theological reasons why Christology and Pneumatology are so important to the Orthodox.

For the Orthodox, Christ and Spirit, co-exist as two *hypostaseis* for one essence with the Being in whom both have their being. Though two persons, they are complementary to each other and their relationship is characterized by *symphonia*. The interrelationship of *Logos* (the Christ) and the *Pneuman to Hagion* (the Holy Spirit) is axiomatic in the New Testament, the faith and worship of the mainstream early Christian community, ancient baptismal confessions, patristic exegesis, and ultimately in the pronouncements of the first and second ecumenical synods. Christ had been accepted as "the identical icon of the divinity, of the same essence, will, power, and glory" in the words of St. Athanasios.[6] The Holy Spirit had been proclaimed as the Spirit of God, the Spirit of truth, Sovereign, "Sharing in or incorporated into,

---

5.   Cited by A. K. Cragg, *The Christian and Other Religion* (London and Oxford: A. R. Mowbray and Co., 1977), p. 78. Georges Khodr, "Christianity in a Pluralistic World – The Economy of the Holy Spirit," in Patelos, ed., *the Orthodox Church*, pp. 297-307.

6.   Athanasios of Alexandria, "Pros Serapiona Epistole A" 20., ed. by Niketas Tsiomesides, *Athanasiou Alexandrias Apanta ta Erga*, vol. 3 (Thessaloniki, 1979), p. 142.

the divinity" in the words of St. Basil.[7] Soteriology and ecclesiology make the communion and *alleloperichoresis* between Christ and Spirit indispensable. Being of the same essence, they both have their origins from the same entity - the Creator, the source of generation.

The question, however, of an organic and full synthesis between Christology and Pneumatology for soteriology and especially ecclesiology remains a serious problem. Admittedly Christology without Pneumatology is lame and Pneumatology without Christology remains blind – empirically an abstraction. The redeeming work of Christ and the sanctifying and recreative function of the Holy Spirit belong together. Without Christology there is no soteriology and without Pneumatology there is no ecclesiology – no Community which perpetuates Christ unto the ages. Without Christology, Christian anthropology becomes zoology.

God-in-Trinity is an incomprehensible mystery. In the classic words of John of Damascus; "God is infinite and incomprehensible; and all that is comprehensible about God is His infinity and incomprehensibility."[8] But the mystery of God as one-essence-in-three-persons is partially revealed, for God is a "living God..." and revelation is an ongoing process.[9]

Orthodoxy's understanding of God as one-in-essence-in-three-hypostaseis is reflected in the creed and the theology of the Synods of Nicea and Constantinople. But the basis of the Nicene-Constantinopolitan creed is the revealed testimony in the written word of the Scripture and the empirical witness of the Apostolic and post-Apostolic community. The biblical account which declares the oneness of the Father, Son, and the Holy Spirit, who proceeds from the Father through the Son, was proclaimed in the belief and prayer life of the early Christian community as well as read in the accounts of

---

7.   Basil of Caesarea, "Peri Hagiou Pneumatos," Ch. 24.55. 20, ed. by Theodore Zesis, *Baileiou Kaisareias tou Megalou Apanta ta Erga*, vol. 10 (Thessaloniki, 1974), p. 432.

8.   Ioannis Damascenos, "Ekdosis Akrives tes Orthodoxou Pisteos, A.4," ed. by Konstantinos G. Frantzolas, *Ioannou tou Damaskenou Apanta ta Erga*, vol. 1 (Thessaloniki, 1976), p. 68.

9.   Gregory of Nazianzus, "Oratio 45.4," ed. by N. E. Apostolakis, *Gregoriou tou Theologou Apanta ta Erga*, vol. 5 (Thessaloniki, 1977), p. 160.

Didache, Justin the Martyr, the baptismal creed of *Hippolytos*, *Clement of Rome* and others.[10] It needs to be emphasized, however, that neither scripture nor life and experience of the Apostolic and pre-Nicene Church justifies any unilateral emphasis, either Patromonism, Christomonism, or Pneumatomonism.[11]

Orthodox theology reiterates that Christ "reflects the glory of God and bears the very stamp of his nature" (Heb. 1:13) and that through the God-man Christ human beings can become "partakers of the divine nature" (2 Pet. 1:4). Christology has always been of extraordinary importance to Eastern Orthodox Christianity because without the Logos-made-man event the transcendent and the immanent, the separation of faith from knowledge, the chasm between divinity and humanity could not have been bridged and reconciled. Without the Incarnation of God's Logos God would be an incomprehensible abstraction in the realm of the empirically inaccessible.[12]

It is through the Christ event that the reality of communion with God's self becomes comprehensible. The Incarnation of the Logos has provided this possibility. The transcendent God "so loved the world that he gave his only begotten Son" (John 3:16) to assume human nature, to change, to walk among human beings that they may become participants in God's life. "The eternal Logos becoming like us bestows upon us the possibility of taking upon us the life proper to him as God."[13]

The life, ministry, and example of Jesus the Christ provide the foundations for a full justification of the Church's involvement in whatever pertains to the social welfare of the people. Jesus went "about all the cities

---

10.   Conveniently discussed by J. N. D. Kelly, *Early Christian Doctrines*, revised edition (New York, 1978), pp. 90-108.

11.   See my *Issues and Dialogues* (Brookline, MA, 1986), pp. 7-19 and Nikos A. Nissiotis, "The Importance of the Doctrine of the Trinity for Church Life and Theology" in *The Orthodox Ethos*, ed. by A. J. Philippou (Oxford, 1964), pp. 32-69, esp. 34-37.

12.   *Cf.* Christos Yannaras, "The Distinction between Essence and Energies and its Importance for Theology", *St. Vladimir's Theological Quarterly*, 19 (1975), p. 244.

13.   John Meyendorff, "The Holy Trinity in Palamite Theology" in *Trinitarian Theology East and West*, ed. by Michael A. Fahey and John Meyendorff (Brookline, Ma, 1979), p. 34.

and villages, teaching...preaching...and healing every disease and every infirmity" (Mat. 9:35; Mat. 4:24). Whatever Jesus did the Church is called upon to do, whether to defend social justice, human rights, world order and peace, or to improve the conditions of the poor and destitute.[14]

But social relationships and inter-religious dialogues are not meant to reduce Christian theology to sociology, nor to compromise the Christian Church as only an agent of social issues and political reforms. Thus the Orthodox emphasize a return to the biblical mind and the sources and experience of the ancient and medieval Church through what is known as Tradition. This re-emphasis should be expressed in modern categories but always in terms of the historical content of theological thought and religious experience. A balance must be maintained between the Jesus of Nazareth and Jesus the Christ – the eternal Logos.

Orthodox Christology has deep roots in scripture but also in early patristic thought which is an elaboration and a reaffirmation of biblical Christology. St. Irenaios (c.130-200) pronounced the now famous words: "Our Lord Jesus Christ, the Logos of God, of his boundless love, became what we are that he might make us what he himself is."[15] His Christology finds an echo in the theology of St. Athanasios (c.296-373). Early patristic thought insists that there is no possibility for the restoration of the human being to the original state of being except through the Incarnation. The Logos's union with the human being restored to fallen humanity the image of God in which it had been created. By his death and resurrection the Logos of God met and destroyed death, the consequence of the human being's rebellion against the Creator. "Christ, being God, became human, in order

---

14. Orthodox theology's view of Church and society has been discussed by several scholars but for our purpose here two need to be mentioned: Nikos A. Nissiotis, "Church and Society in Greek Orthodox Theology," in *Christian Social Ethos in a Changing World*, ed. by John C. Bennett (New York and London, 1966), pp. 78-104; Demetrios J. Constantelos, "Theological Considerations for the Social Ethos of the Orthodox Church," *Journal of Ecumenical Studies*, vol. 11.1 (1974), pp. 25-44.

15. Irenaeus, *Against Heresies*, 5, praef.

to deify us."[16] *Theosis*, eternal life of the human being in God, is the ultimate gift of the Incarnate Logos to humanity.

This theology of the Logos's Incarnation remains of absolute significance for Orthodoxy's anthropology which is concerned with the becoming and ultimate destiny of the human being. The human being is an evolutionary being and it achieves its ultimate purpose when it conforms to the image of the Divine-human, the *theanthropos Christos*. The human being is a historical and endocosmic being destined for an exocosmic existence. Like Christ, the human being is a physical and metaphysical being.

Orthodoxy's theological anthropology examines humanity from within and from without the Christian scriptures. Humanity and God are not placed at opposite poles, but on the two ends of the same pole. Each one moves toward a meeting with the other. The human person seeks and God responds. The two unite in the person of the Logos, the eternal God who appears among humans as the Emmanuel. Thus Christ brings to an end the old dispensation and inaugurates a new one. He recapitulates and moves forward to introduce the new redeemed epoch.[17]

The unredeemed, alienated somatic being of the pre-Christian era become the "pneumatic," the spirit-filled being without rejecting somatic qualities. The physical qualities are guided and ruled by the enlightened, the strengthened, the illuminated spiritual person. Ultimately it is the total person, a somatic-pneumatic integrated being, who is saved in the words of Irenaeus.[18]

The defeat of death and the recovery of eternal life, real freedom and growth toward what the human being was meant to be was made possible through the incarnate Logos who enabled the human to rediscover its divine nature. Christ is not only God manifest, but also the prototype of the total *anthropos*, the human being as it was ordained to become from the moment

---

16. Athanasios, *Against the Arians*, 1.39.

17. See Georges Florovsky, *Creation and Redemption* (Belmont, MA, 1976), pp. 95-159.

18. Irenaeus, *op. cit.*, IV 20.4. For an analysis of Irenaeus's anthropology see Gustaf Wingren, *Man and the Incarnation*, trans. by Ross Mackenzie (Philadelphia, 1947), esp. pp. 79-143.

of creation. As complete *theanthropos*, Christ is the link that united Divinity and humanity.

Christ's divinity should not lead to a Christomonism as an emphasis on God the Father should not be misunderstood as Patromonism. While the Father consents, the Logos descends, and the Holy Spirit overshadows and unites.

The Spirit appears as a person with personal qualifications and energies. In biblical thought the function of the Spirit is *koinonia*, the communion that operates between divinity and humanity: "The grace of our Lord Jesus Christ, and the love of God the Father, and the Communion of the Holy Spirit" (2 Cor. 13:14). It is this *koinonia* of the Spirit with the human being which effects the latter's regeneration, its spiritual growth into a new creation. The Spirit speaks personally to Moses, the Prophets, Apostle Philip (Acts 2:28) to Peter (Acts 10:19; 11:12), to the Christian community of Antioch (Acts 13:12) to the synod of Jerusalem (Acts 15:25), to the community of believers today and to the individual within the community.

It is this ever-present theological background which makes Orthodox theology today perhaps more optimistic than other theologies or any humanistic anthropology. The Orthodox believe that an alienation of Christian theology from its sources ultimately leads to distortions, misunderstandings, and pessimism. Teachings which tend to emphasize only the importance of God the Father, or Christ, contribute to the denial of the possibility of historical progress under the guidance of the ever present Spirit through whom the realization of God's likeness in the human being can be achieved, leading ultimately to *theosis*.

The Gospel is the good news that shows how humanity can be brought back to God's presence, but it is not a guide for all earthly issues or a blueprint of God's working in history. The Holy Spirit acts on specific occasions - the New Testament speaks of its "outpouring" (Acts 2:1-4, Rom. 5:5, Titus 3:6) – yet it has never stopped hovering over the earth (Gen. 1:2). The Spirit of God is a spirit of action over all humankind (*cf.* Joel 2:28) and meets people everywhere. The Spirit lifts up, inspires, and unites all in whom it dwells and bonds all humankind into the People of God. The "People of God" cannot be one branch of humanity as one part of the body cannot be separated from the other. Orthodox theology sees the particularism of ancient Israel and the "New Israel" Christendom not as God's work, but the result of self-reflective history, of a deductive self-serving system. It is on the basis of pneumatology that Christianity can improve its relations with other faiths.

IV

How do the Orthodox face the future and what do they foresee in their daily relationships with non-Orthodox and non-Christians alike? For many centuries millions of Orthodox Christians have lived amidst Muslims. And many more now live among atheists, agnostics, skeptics, and people of other creeds. Orthodox Christians have also been persecuted. Hundreds of neomartyrs have died rather than convert to Islam.[19] Historical events have exposed Orthodox Christians to religious pluralism.

Either because of historical circumstances or because of philosophical and psychological disposition, the Orthodox have viewed religion as the right *doxa*, (glory or glorification) right *praxis* (Orthodoxia and Othopraxia). Thus Orthodoxy is not so much right creed as right doxology-worship.[20] Prayer is not *religion*, a tie, a legalistic bond, but an unceasing quest and awareness of the human being's uniqueness and urge to seek communion with the divine. Since *praxis* means deeds, conduct, ethics, what counts is faith and conduct, humane personal and societal morality more than religious zeal or aggressive proselytizing. For this reason the Orthodox cannot sympathize with religious sentiment which leads to emotional movements such as the crusades, religious wars, coercive or subversive and divisive missions.

The theological objective of the Orthodox continues to be the divinization of humanity and of life itself, the elevation of the human being into God as the ultimate source of existence. The Orthodox call God a *Philanthropos Theos*, a God in love with creation, a concept which is not

---

[19]. See Demetrios J. Constantelos, "The 'Neomartyrs' as Evidence of Methods and Motives Leading to Conversion and Martyrdom in the Ottoman Empire," *The Greek Orthodox Theological Review*, 23 (1978), pp. 216-234; *cf.* James J. Stamoolis, *Eastern Orthodox Mission Theology Today* (Maryknoll, NY: Orbis Books, 1986), pp. 126-127.

[20]. *Cf.* Georges Florovsky, "The Elements of Liturgy," in Patelos, ed., *The Orthodox Church*, p. 172.

antithetical to the notion of *theosis*. *Theosis*, ultimate life in God, is the fruit of God's love for the human being[21] through Jesus the Christ who is never merely human or divine but always the *theanthropos* (divine-human), seeking to elevate God's supreme creation to *theosis*. As long as other religions have the same goal, the elevation of humanity to divine life, they are perceived by the Orthodox as instruments of God in God's world.

Searching for unity among fellow Christians for a better understanding with non-Christians, the Orthodox emphasize their belief that this is God's world and that God's revelations cannot be limited by human beings, for "The Spirit moves where it wills" (John 3:8). As the churches intensify their efforts in ecumenical dialogue and are exposed to each other's point of view, a new ecclesiastical syncretism will emerge. The Holy Spirit expects the synergy of human beings. It was a syncretic approach that won Christianity followers in the first five centuries. There was diversity of opinion among Christians of different countries and of different cities in the same geographical area; there were different rules and different customs, but the Church assumed "that those who agreed on the essentials of worship ought not to separate from one another on account of customs," as the fourth-century historian Sozomenos writes.[22] Worship in the early Church meant, as it does in modern Orthodoxy, the centrality of Christ in the Eucharist, in faith, life, and action. In the Eucharist the faithful express their unity in faith and spirituality, in theological and religious discourse, in love and care for each other, in a manner that encompasses the totality of humanity's needs of soul, mind, and body.

While in theory the Orthodox do not exclude the presence of the Divinity outside of Christianity, as already indicated, and their notion of revelation has ecumenical implications, in practice they are more exclusive and contradictory. They rely on canon laws which were issued by ecumenical and local councils of the first Christian millenium. In the application of

---

21.   See Demetrios J. Constantelos, "The Lover of Mankind," *The Way*, 9.2 (1969), pp. 98-106.

22.   Sozomenos, *Ecclesiastial History*, VII. 19.

canons the Orthodox are not consistent and their attitude depends on political circumstances and social and cultural realities.

But more and more the Orthodox recognize that there cannot be one attitude but attitudes, no model but models of Christian discipleship. Yet all models of Christian discipleship should allow the Spirit to inspire and to lead not to antagonisms, but to a closer approach to the ideal.

The present study synthesizes much of what I have written in three inter-related papers in three different intra-faith dialogues and published in the following volumes: "Models for Christian Discipleship: An Orthodox Perspective" in *Christ's Lordship and Religious Pluralism*, ed. by Gerald H. Anderson and Thomas F. Stransky (Maryknoll, NY: Orbis Books, 1981), pp. 181-191; "Varying Encounters with God in the Christian Life" in *Orthodox Synthesis: The Unity of Theological Thought*, ed. by Joseph I. Allen (Crestwood, NY: St. Vladimir's Seminary Press, 1981), pp. 117-126; "Christ and Spirit: From the Christocentric to the Trinitarian Dimension – A Coherent Theology," *World Council of Churches: Commission of Faith and Order*, FO/88.2.

MUSLIMS AND NON-MUSLIMS

by

Khalid Duran

The relations of Muslims with people of other faiths are determined by a variety of cultural, economic, historical and socio-political factors that constitute, at times, an intricate web of interrelated strands. In the present case priority is given to the religious dimension. This makes it necessary to distinguish between what is purely religious, in the sense of theological, and what is cultural or sociopolitical in the sense of historical accretions to – or elaborations of – the original core of tenets.

Theology is the self-understanding of Muslims as a *chosen community*. The term is not usually used by Muslims, who regard it as a Mosaic expression and take it to be indicative of Jewish exclusivism. And yet, in the final analysis, the concept of chosenness is fairly much the same in both religions. Al-Qur'an (the Koran) calls Muslims "the best community ever brought forth by God for the benefit of humanity," (*khaira ummatin ukhrijat li-n-nas*).[1] Muslims are also called the "people of the middle" or "a people in the center."[2] There is a whole literature on the exact or possible meaning of this term, with most commentators taking it to signify "model community," the community of the golden mean and, therefore, the community of

---

1.   Al-Qur'an II, p. 84.
2.   *Ibid.*, p. 143.

salvation, a community to be emulated by the remainder of humankind.[3] Muhammad Iqbal (d. 1938), who is acclaimed as one of the leading thinkers of Islam in this century, spoke of the Muslim community as a "model for the final unification of mankind."[4] This leads to the conviction that there can be no lasting peace in this world until Islam is spread to all the corners of the globe and made to prevail against other beliefs.

Such a missionary view need not cause conflicts, however, because there also are the clear-cut injunctions in Al-Qur'an that there should be no compulsion in religion[5] and emphatic statements such as "to you your religion and to me my religion."[6] And yet, it is self-evident that such a concept of chosenness is bound to collide with the assertion of other identities.

Quasi-theological is the belief that Islam is identical with political supremacy. There is little in Al-Qur'an to warrant such a belief, but the historical development of the community made Muslims see things that way. The Prophet's companions saw their new religion triumph during the lifetime of the founder. Unlike the Christians, they did not have to wait for three hundred years to attain worldly power. Early Islam was not a religion of the catacombs. Muhammad's followers had it the other way round; they experienced three hundred years of political triumph before suffering the first serious setbacks.

This engendered a belief that Islam and political power go together. Almighty God came to be seen as rewarding the believers with supremacy over others. The correctness of the faith came to be equated with a monopoly on government. After the "heathen" Mongols destroyed Baghdad in 1258 – the seat of the Caliphate and the greatest city of the world in those days – Muslims sought to counter such challenges by coining the motto "Islam is religion and state" (*al-islam din wa daula*). History had accustomed them

---

3. Khalid Duran, "In Quest of Muslim Identity," in Charles Fu & Gerhard Spiegler, eds., *Religious Issues and Inter-religious Dialogues* (New York/London: Greenwood Press, 1989).

4. Muhammad Iqbal, *The Reconstruction of Religious Thought in Islam* (Lahore/London: Muhammad Ashraf, 1930).

5. Al-Qur'an X, pp. 99-100.

6. Al-Qur'an CIX, p. 6.

to seeing religious commitment and worldly might go hand in hand. It would hardly be an overstatement to say Muslims had been pampered by the mundane success of their early history. Later on they often behaved like the spoiled children of history, and quite a few continue to do so even today, despite two centuries of European colonialism and its protracted aftermath.

It is an ingrained conviction with many Muslims that the loss of political supremacy is the result of a slackening of the faith. Things can be remedied only if the believers return to the pristine purity of the faith, if they become practicing and committed Muslims again.[7] Whatever lands have been lost can be regained once the believers are motivated by Islam, as in the olden days, instead of allowing themselves to be lured away by "foreign" ideologies. This idea became strong in twelfth-century Spain, prevailed in nineteenth-century India, when Hindus, Sikhs and Britishers took over from the Muslim rulers, and surged up again in the Near East after the disastrous 1967 defeat at the hands of the Israelis, when Jerusalem was lost to Islam once again as it had been lost to the Crusaders in the eleventh century.[8] Iqbal, the aforementioned poet-philosopher, expressed the conviction that Muslims could regain lost glory by a return to the right faith and correct practice in his little volumes of Urdu poetry entitled *Complaint* and *Answer to the Complaint* (*Jawab-e Shikwa*). Many others have done the same, and hardly less eloquently. We might even speak of a genre of literature devoted to such soul-searching: "What caused our downfall? How can we regain for Islam the glory it enjoyed during the days of our ancestors?"

This belief in the relationship between the correctness of the faith and the right to rule is symbolized by the institution of the Caliphate. This institution is not mentioned in Al-Qur'an and is, therefore, strictly speaking not part of Islamic theology (the tenet of the human being as God's Caliph, "vicegerent," on earth is a different matter altogether). However, the Caliphate played such an important role in history that it entered the Muslim

---

7.   Khalid Duran, "The 'Golden Age' Syndrome. Islamist Medina and Other Historical Models of Contemporary Muslim Thought," in *Revue suisse de sociologie*, No. 3, 1983. Republished in *Islam and the Modern Age*, Vol. 15, No. 2, (New Delhi: Islam and the Modern Age Society, May 1984).

8.   Fouad 'Ajami, *The Arab Predicament*.

psyche as an inalienable component of the belief system and came to be regarded as an element of "normative" Islam. No doubt, there have been attempts by Muslim theologians at divesting Islamic principles of this Caliphal legacy by explaining the Caliphate as an historical accident.[9] While such reasoning stands on firm ground as an academic exercise, it has failed to have much impact on the Muslim self-image as a community that regards the loss of political power as a kind of aberration. Outside Shi'ism few would go so far as Khomeini, who regarded the "Islamic state" as superior to all other categories, with the interest of the "Islamic state" having precedence over the norms of Islamic law and ethics. When he said that there could be "no Islam without tears," he actually meant "no Islam without bloodshed."[10] While this was an excess and obvious deviation from the hallowed norms, it nonetheless strode, albeit in a grossly exaggerated manner, in a direction along which some Muslims in their thought tend to move as a result of the historical development undergone by their community.

Political subjugation of others mostly did not imply forced conversion. The original rationale for the insistence on supremacy was that Muslims had to be protected, understandable enough in view of the persecution suffered during the Prophet's days in Mecca, the wars of the heathens from Mecca against the Muslims in Medina, as well as the threat of Persian and Roman invasions of Arabia. Soon enough, however, the right to rule was taken for granted, with no rationale required, because it was now regarded as a divine compensation and a distinction for God's chosen community.

The link with theology proper is provided by God's warning that another people might be chosen as God's favorites if the Muslims did not observe God's commands,[11] a warning reminiscent of that given to the Jews, whose chosenness depends on their being up to the mark–this, at least, is how some orthodox Rabbis interpret it. The distinction of being God's

---

9.   Leonard Binder, *Islamic Liberalism* (Chicago/London: The University of Chicago Press, 1988), Chapter 4.

10.   See the Khomeinist journal *Crescent International*, Toronto, Nov. 1, 1983. Reproduced in Khalid Duran: *Islam und politischer Extremismus*. Hamburg: DOI, 1985, p. 105.

11.   Al -Qur'an IX, p. 39; XXXXVII, p. 38.

favorites might manifest itself in many ways, political supremacy being certainly one of them, and for many Muslims the most plausible manifestation: "Seek ye first the political kingdom and all other things shall be done unto you."[12]

The association of Islam with rule is, therefore, more than quasi-theological. It is semi-theological. Outstanding theologians have come up with reinterpretations allowing for an Islam shorn of political power and yet secure and sovereign, a complete code of life, perhaps more cogently than the Islamists with their disfiguring of Islam as a political ideology. Nonetheless, such intellectualist reinterpretations rarely catch on with the masses. As a community, Muslims are burdened with the triumphalist legacy of an imperial past, making it difficult for them to integrate into a pluralist society where all are equal partners and no single community rules supreme.

1. An Insidious Numbers Game

A result of this near obsession with political power is the conflictive numbers game witnessed in most states with sizable Muslim populations. In many Third World countries correct statistics are hard to come by. Do Muslims in Nigeria and Tanzania constitute a majority or minority? With regard to both these states Christians claim to be in majority, giving the Muslims no more than 25-35%, with a few conceding to Islam some 45%. Muslims generally insist on being not less than 65% in both states, some Muslims going up to 75% in their estimates. More neutral academics with less religious commitment estimate the Muslim population in both Nigeria and Tanzania to be between 55% and 60%.[13]

Does Kenya have a Muslim population of 25-30%, or merely 15%? The same question is asked about Cameroon, Ghana, Liberia, Mozambique and several other states. Are the Muslims of Sierra Leone more than half of the population or less? What about Bourkina Fasso? Do Muslims constitute

---

12.   This is how the Lord's Prayer was 'misappropriated' by Kwame Nkrumah during Ghana's struggle for independence. That this is but vicarious for a larger phenomenon, especially in the world of Islam, was aptly recognized by Kenneth Cragg, *Counsels in Contemporary Islam* (Edinburgh: Edinburgh University Press, 1965), p. 31.

13.   Emilio Galindo Aguilar, *Encuentro Islamo-Cristiano*, Madrid, Aug. 1988

two thirds of Sudan's population or more? How about Chad? Everywhere there are claims and counter-claims.

Fundamentalist Copts claim that 30% of Egypt's population is Christian, while official estimates speak of only 12%, a figure corroborated by non-Egyptian Catholic academics in Cairo. The government does not want to disclose the correct statistics because if our real numbers become known, hotheads among the Copts argue, Egypt might turn into another Lebanon.[14]

It could be argued that correct statistics might put an end to the deadly numbers game. Just as likely, however, is that a census result would be disputed by everybody, with each party accusing the government of favoring the other side. Even if the census were conducted by an international agency, such as UNESCO, conflicts might fully erupt that have, so far, been only simmering. Muslims of Guinea Bissao, on learning that they stand no chance of forming a majority, might opt to secede. Muslims of Egypt might says: "Now that it has been established without any doubt that the Copts are only 15% and not more, they have to shut up once and for all."

In countries such as Sudan, however, devastated by decades of civil war, such clarity might prove wholesome, if in no other way then by finally bringing about the secession of the non-Muslim South, rather than have all the peoples involved bleed to death. To carry out a census in such a way as to obtain reliable results is, however, a Herculean task in war ravaged countries that never had the necessary infrastructure nor the trained personnel for such an endeavor.

Census information produced by many Muslim states is to be treated with much caution. Afghan government officers in charge of population counts under the *ancien régime* have readily admitted to the manipulations they were asked to carry out by their ministry because it was thought advisable to inflate the numbers in order to obtain larger funds from UN agencies. While the number of Afghans was officially given as being above 16 million, such officers hold the view that in reality the figure was closer to 13 million, possibly as low as 11. At the same time they admit the difficulty

---

14.   Personal communication during interviews in Egypt in November-December 1981.

of obtaining the correct number of females. While 11 million Afghans were counted, 2 million were added as the approximate number of females they had not been able to count because of culturally motivated resistances. To this were added another three million for UN purposes. This is but one instance to illustrate the problem.[15]

2. The Bane of Muslim Separatism

Senegal, with a Muslim majority of almost 90%, was ruled for two decades by a Christian president, Leopold Sedar Senghor. Christian president Julius Nyerere ruled for 24 years over Tanzania with its Muslim majority. Chad was likewise ruled for more than a decade by Christian presidents, although Muslims are probably in the majority. Islamists were unhappy about this state of affairs, and many non-Islamist Muslims too. The rule of Christians over Muslim majorities was often regarded as the effect of colonialism. On the other hand, no objection was raised to the Muslim Amadou Ahidjo ruling over Cameroon despite the fact that Muslims constitute hardly more than one third of the country's population. When Ahidjo ceded the presidency to Paul Biya, a representative of the Christian majority, this was deplored and Muslims rose in revolt, which in turn provoked a backlash by the Christians. Uganda has barely a 10% Muslim population but there were no Muslim objections when dictatorial Idi Amin brought his country into the ICO (Islamic Conference Organization).

In the meantime Leopold Senghor ceded peacefully to his chosen successor, Abdou Diouf, a Muslim. Julius Nyerere did the same with Hasan Mwinyi. Tanzania, thus, has a Muslim president. But Sudan has been ruled by Muslims since independence (1956) and they show no preparedness to hand power over to a non-Muslim, despite the fact that Dr. John Garang, leader of the SPLM ("Sudanese People's Liberation Movement") is admittedly the ablest politician and most qualified administrator.[16]

---

15. Personal communication by the officers in charge of the census with whom I happened to be associated in resistance activities. Several of them have confirmed, independent of each other, that Afghanistan's population might not have been more than 13 million, possibly as low as 11-12 million.

16. See my short biography of "Colonel Dr. John Garang de Mabior," in *Orient*, Journal of the German Orient Institute (Opladen, W. Germany: Leske Verlag, Fall 1985).

This shows a basic unpreparedness of many Muslims to accept being ruled by non-Muslims or to enter into a genuine power sharing as the prerequisite to a democratic pluralism.

A further result of this concern with political supremacy is the tendency found in many Muslim communities to secede from those areas of their state that hold a non-Muslim majority. The secession of India's predominantly Muslim areas from the rest of the overwhelmingly Hindu country in 1947 led to the establishment of Pakistan as a separate state for Muslims. This is but the most conspicuous example of a world-wide trend.

To be sure, there is no such thing as a Muslim separatism on purely religious grounds. Invariably, there is more than one factor of a very worldly nature involved. The difference from other types of separatism, such ones not involving any Muslims, is that various economic and political grievances are aggravated by the common Muslim proclivity to hold religious biases as primarily responsible for any discrimination suffered. The widespread and profound Muslim sense of being victimized because of Islam adds a special dimension.[17]

A comparable case might be the conflict between Sinhalese and Tamils in Sri Lanka, which is both ethnic-linguistic and cultural-religious. Both even where such parallels exist, the Muslim case is still burdened with the extra weight of its imperial legacy and the semi-theological notion that government over Muslims ought to belong to Muslims. Neither Sinhalese Buddhists nor Tamil Hindus are propelled by such motivations. For them it is a clash between two different nationalities or ethnic groups speaking different languages and professing different religions. They are not conditioned by a sacred law, such as the Islamic *shari'a*, stipulating that their faith cannot be properly lived as long as the rulers follow another faith. Many Muslims believe that Islam is not fully implemented if the government is not in the hands of Muslims, because only they will enforce the *shari'a*. The fact that most Muslim governments do not enforce the *shari'a* either, is a

---

17.　　Khalid Duran, "Die Geschichte christlich-islamischer Beziehungen aus muslimischer Sicht," in Jochen Wiezke, ed., *Islam* (Hamburg: Missionswerk der Evang. Kirche, 1986).

different matter. The important thing is that the choice rests with Muslims.[18] Occasionally, though, opinions are voiced that a tolerant non-Muslim government might be preferable to a rule of such Muslims as are totally opposed to the *shari'a*. In the sixties and seventies many Turks left home for West Germany because they realized that there they could observe certain *shari'a* injunctions outlawed in Turkey (e.g., the wearing of traditional oriental costumes and headgear, the running of certain types of private religious schools).[19]

Furthermore it goes without saying that the notion of the unicity of religion and state in Islam might be allowed to fall into oblivion when material conditions are particularly favorable and might be jeopardized by an insistence on the *shari'a*. Thus the privileged and prosperous Muslim community of Sri Lanka never entertained any separatist ambitions. The fact that it is a small minority of less than 10% played a role too. Incited by Islamist missionaries from abroad, even Sri Lankan Muslims began to demand a partial introduction of the *shari'a* for their community, such as the raising of *zakat* (the traditional Islamic tax for charitable purposes). It is not to be ruled out that a swelling of the Sri Lankan Muslim community to 20% or more might have induced them to envision some kind of separatism too. The tendency is universal. While it is usually only a minority within Muslim minorities that nourishes separatist ambitions there is always the likelihood of an increase in times of crisis.

A few examples might serve to further illustrate this phenomenon. Muslim separatism in Burma and Thailand is essentially ethnic in nature. Burmese Muslims are mostly of Bengali stock, speak Bengali and are concentrated in the area adjacent to Bangladesh. They are a kind of spillover of overpopulated Muslim Bengal into what used to be lesser populated Burma, as in the Indian province of Assam to the north of Bangladesh. The Muslims of Thailand live mostly in the Pattani region bordering on Malaysia. They are Malay by origin, speak Malay and would

---

18.   Khalid Duran, *Re-Islamisierung und Entwicklungspolitik* (Cologne/London: Weltforum Verlag, 1983).

19.   Khalid Duran, "Der Islam in der Diaspora: Europa und Amerika," in W. Ende & U. Steinbach, eds., *Der Islam in der Gegenwart* (Munich: Verlag C. H. Beck, 1984).

not be citizens of Thailand had not Thai imperial rule expanded southward
into Malay areas.

In both cases there is a clash of interests between the ethnic majority,
the *Staatsvolk*, and the minority that is linguistically and culturally oppressed,
politically outcast, economically exploited and educationally disadvantaged.
On top of this, the governments of Burma and Thailand do at times display a
kind of Buddhist chauvinism in no way less oppressive then, let us say, the
Muslim chauvinism of some Indonesian authorities toward their non-Muslim
Chinese citizens.

It is, therefore, difficult to say what factor is more decisive in those
minorities' resistance. It seems primarily to be a fight for equal rights in a
state dominated by an intolerant ethnic majority. The religious dimension
provides a powerful symbolism, often causing the protagonists to believe that
it is all about Islam and its survival in a hostile environment. The struggle,
then, becomes a *jihad*, a "holy war."

If the Arakan region were to secede from Burma and join Bangladesh
or emerge as an independent state, Muslims in other parts of Burma would
suffer all the more. They would then be treated as the fifth column of an
enemy state. Since there are not many Muslims in other parts of Burma, the
problem would not be a huge one. It was, however, an enormous difficulty
for Indian Muslims after the establishment of Pakistan. Today, Pakistan has
a Muslim population of roughly 100 million. Almost the same number of
Muslims continues on the other side of the border as citizens of the Hindu-
dominated secular state of India. This is not only the largest Muslim
minority anywhere in the world, it is probably the largest of all religious
minorities in our age. More than a million Indian Muslims migrated to
Pakistan and almost another million died in the bloodshed at the eve of
India's partition and the subsequent pogroms.

This migration, one should hold, was an exercise in futility, causing
enormous suffering without any gain. Had the Indian Muslims stayed on, the
community in India would be stronger and in a better position to maintain its
own among the Hindu majority. In Pakistan, the refugees became a burden
not only economically, but they also proved to be linguistically and culturally
quite different from the "sons of the soil," notwithstanding the uniting bond of

the Islamic faith. The Islamic bond had been overestimated. It is, no doubt, strong, but it is not a miracle weapon. Forty years after the establishment of the separate Muslim homeland, those refugees from India, who remained a distinct ethnic group, created their own political party to defend their interests against the indigenous majority population.

The party is called *Muhajir Qaumi Mahaz* ("Refugee National Front"). However, the term *muhajir* has a much deeper meaning than the word refugee. There is a religious connotation to it that provides the clue to understanding the phenomenon of Muslim separatism. A *muhajir* performs a *hijra* (*hegira*), that is, he migrates from where he lives, and where he cannot practice his religion properly, to another place where he is in a position to live Islam fully. The pattern was provided by the Prophet when he left his beloved Mecca for Medina and set up the first Muslim polity over there. This "flight" or "migration" is called in Arabic *hijra*, and the Prophet and his Companions who migrated in this manner become *muhajirin* – refugees in the path of God, not migrants for worldly gains.

3. A Manichean Partition of the World

The event was taken to be so crucial that it became the Year One of the Islamic calendar, called the *hijri* calendar. Islamic history did not start with the birth of Muhammad, but with his migration for the sake of establishing Islam on sure grounds. Ever since, oppressed Muslims have sought to emulate the "good exemplar" and migrated to safer areas without restrictions on Islamic practice. This concept provided a stimulus for Muslim separatism, because it was taken for granted that Muslims left behind in "enemy" territory would come over, being religiously obliged to do so. Many socio-political developments in countries with Muslim populations cannot be properly understood unless these notions are taken cognizance of. They provide the key to the understanding of the Muslim psyche.

For instance, at the beginning of the Afghan war (March 1979 and, more intensely, January 1980) many refugees headed for Pakistan and Iran not just to escape the horrors of war, but because they believed – or were told by their religious leaders – that there was no other way left but to perform *hijra*. Soon resistance leaders realized that such a mass exodus only served the interests of the Russians and began to encourage their compatriots to stay on in Afghanistan as long as humanly possible. The millions that crossed over into the neighboring countries then did so merely for the sake of physical survival without even a chance to dream of spiritual bliss. However, the initial impulse to flee was provided by the age-old pattern of *hijra* and the Afghans in Pakistan are called *muhajirin*, whereas political refugees without a religious motivation are called *panahgir*.

A century earlier Muslims fled in the other direction – from what is now Pakistan (then British India) to Afghanistan, because some of their leaders held the view that India under infidel rule was no longer a place for Muslims to live. Tens of thousands migrated to Afghanistan, with most of them perishing on the way through what was then a desolate wilderness.

The concept of *hijra* cannot be fully understood without reference to the *Manichean* division of the world that developed fairly early in Muslim history and found its way into the *shari'a*, the ancient law of Islam that became sacrosanct to many Muslims. This Manichean partition of the world envisions an "abode of peace" (*salam, islam*) and an "abode of war" (*harb*). A *muhajir* performs the *hijra* from the *dar al-harb* to the *dar al-islam*.

Many a time Muslims were locked in dispute whether to declare a certain territory as *dar al-harb* and make *hijra* incumbent upon the believers or not. A typical example is the above-mentioned case of British India. Only a minority among Muslims decided for *hijra*; the majority came round to the comforting view that since the British did not prevent Muslims from practicing their religion, there was no justification for declaring India to be *dar al-harb* and to migrate to the nearest part of *dar al-islam* (Afghanistan). The same controversy erupted after the establishment of Pakistan when the majority of Indian Muslims was convinced by their leaders, such as the Minister of Education, Abu l-Kalam Azad, that they could live in India as in *dar al-islam*. It was a difficult proposition for those suffering frequent pogroms that made India look like a real *dar al-harb* to them. All the same, it was still the most reasonable option in a situation altogether desperate.

According to the *shari'a*, a major criterion for a territory being either *dar al-islam* or *dar al-harb* is the freedom to hold the weekly service (Friday) in the name of the Caliph as the supreme Muslim leader. The Caliphate was abolished by Kemal Ataturk in 1924 only, and ever since there have been several attempts at re-establishing it. Till 1924 most Sunni Muslims used to hold the Friday service in the name of the Ottoman Calpih, even in territories never under Ottoman suzerainty. An exception is Morocco, the king of which holds a position comparable to that of the Ottoman Caliph. In India, too, Muslims used to conduct the Friday service in the name of the Ottoman Caliph. The British aggression against the Ottoman Empire during World War I, therefore, caused a crisis. The "Khilafat Movement" in India was launched with the aim of protecting the Caliphate against the British. Later, Indian Muslims attempted to persuade Kemal Ataturk not to abolish the Caliphate. The abolition of the Caliphate meant that they could no longer conduct their Friday service in the name of the spiritual head of Islam, and therefore, India would no longer be *dar al-islam* and they would then have to perform *hijra*. Realism made them stay on in India even after the abolition of the Caliphate. Many of them, however, have never been fully reconciled to the new circumstances – and this contributed to the creation of Pakistan, even though in Pakistan, too, there is no Caliph in whose name to perform the weekly service.

This *shari'a* legacy engendered a curious phenomenon in some Muslim regions of China where every Friday the weekly service is celebrated, after which the believers perform an ordinary noon prayer as on every other day. They are not sure whether they live in *dar al-islam* or in *dar al-harb*. They do not want to miss the Friday service, which is obligatory. However, since there is no Caliph in whose name to conduct the service, they feel that it might not be valid. To be on the safe side they also perform the daily noon prayer, hoping that at least one of the two will be all right, if not both.

Modern day Muslim laborers in Europe mostly know little or nothing about those ancient concepts of *dar al-islam* and *dar al-harb*. Residual notions, however, persist. Many view their sojourn in a non-Muslim society as a temporary necessity and long to return to sources of purity that become more and more imaginary. Their low social status in the host country prevents them from getting better acquainted with the foreign culture in the midst of which they live. What they get to know are mostly superficialities; large segments of society remain inaccessible to them; their knowledge of the people among whom they live remains restricted; they perceive only a few aspects of life in the West. The host country remains largely foreign to them. It is repellent and threatening, because they witness the absorption of their children into this strange world.

The picture looks all too familiar, scarcely different from that of any Chinatown in New York or San Francisco. In the case of Muslims there is always a likelihood of traditionalists reverting to the divisive concepts of old. The community learns from them about *dar al-islam* and *dar al-harb*, age-old terms that acquire a new tangibility. European xenophobia and new racial tensions become all the more explosive once they are made to fit into a religious frame of reference. A laborer from Turkey or Tunisia, on learning that leading West German politicians hold Islam responsible for the resistance to cultural assimilation among those immigrant communities, is prone to discover the meaning of *dar al-harb* afresh, because he actually lives in a world that is not his own, that is hostile to him as a Muslim. He yearns for the *dar al-islam*, an "abode of peace," where he can feel at home. Misery, however, prevents him from returning to his country of origin, unless he is forced to.

Others, more confident of the dependence of affluent societies on immigrant labor, set up islands of *dar al-islam*, self-chosen ghetto communities attempting to be as self-sufficient as possible. They do so by making full use of the legal possibilities offered by Western democracies without subscribing to those democratic norms within the narrow confines of their own communities. This turns their ghettos into virtual bastions of *dar al-islam* within the *dar al-harb*. They now seek to obtain the semi-independence of the Ottoman *millet* system, this time not for non-Muslim communities in an Islamic state but for Muslim communities within a non-Muslim state. Since the host society is not used to Muslim minorities and not prepared for such an eventuality, there is aggressiveness on both sides.

Some such Muslim diaspora communities demand separate schools and the enforcement of their family laws, their law of inheritance etc. Controversies such as the one over the Rushdi affair help to galvanize their demands.[20]　　While the insistence on following their own (*hijri*) calendar – important because of the holidays – might seem justifiable in a democratic society, other demands are not. Authoritarian education and the infringement upon their youngsters' free choice of a professional line or marriage partner pose serious problems. Most critical are the restrictions on the freedom of Muslim women, especially the *shari'a* prohibition for girls to marry non-Muslims.

4. From Aggressive Proselytizing and Communal Chauvinism To a New Sense of Mission

There is no gainsaying the fact that Islam is a missionary religion, with a sense of mission comparable to that in Christianity. Some Muslims tend to dispute this, but this is evidently a modern reaction against a concept of missionary work that has come under fire in a secularized West. It would be futile to enter into a discussion of minute details such as the question whether certain missionary practices dear to some Church organizations are acceptable from an Islamic point of view or not. Over the centuries, Muslim missionary activities have developed differently in different parts of the world. Most present-day Muslims are not aware of those rich varieties of missionary practices within their own tradition. To give just one example, mention could be made of the Indo-Pakistani type of singing called *qawwali*. Nowadays it is solely associated with Islamic spiritual values. *Qawwali* are Sufi songs sung by three or more singers. Only specialists know that this is based on an old Hindu tradition. Early Muslim missionaries merely changed the terminology, so that the texts of those songs are now devotionally Islamic and no longer Hindu.

Qawwali were a potent means whereby large masses of Hindus were converted to Islam. The instruments to accompany these songs are the tabla and harmonium – a harmonium adapted to a singer squatting on the ground rather than standing. This type of harmonium seems indispensable to much of Indo-Pakistani music. Few people realize that it was introduced only

---

20.　　Daniel Pipes, *The Rushdie Affair: The Novel, the Ayatollah, and the West* (New York: Birch Lane, 1990). ·

around 1800 by Christian missionaries seeking to emulate Muslim missionary practices.

Such observations are stunning to many Muslims who see things only the other way round and believe that Islamic mission has always been blunt and direct, unlike the Christian mission which is considered to be devious and surreptitious. As a result of the colonial experience, many Muslims regard Christian missionary activities as some kind of a subversion, an enticement of people by hook and by crook, camouflage and stealth.

The Islamic sense of mission is expressed in the famous dictum *wa ma 'alaina illa l-balagh* ("our task is only to pass on the message"). In other words, there should be no attempt at brainwashing. The more subtle ways of influencing people in order to prepare them for the message are to be eschewed as unethical. While this is a widely shared belief, there have always been many Muslims who thought differently. To be an effective missionary has been the aim of many who devised all kinds of strategies and tactics indistinguishable from those of their Christian counterparts.

The present-day organizational disadvantage of Muslim missionary work is due primarily to the general backwardness of the societies concerned, but the situation is changing rapidly. Oil-rich states have put enormous sums at the disposal of newly created missionary organizations who are now in a position to recruit well-educated personnel. Seeking to surpass Christian missionaries, they concentrate – just like those – on providing educational and medical facilities.[21] In 1990 Islamic missionary endeavors are still a far cry from their well established Christian counterparts, but it is not to be ruled out that the two might be at par in the not-too-distant future.

The fact that Islamic mission as an organized effort at proselytization at all lags behind Christian missionary activities is due chiefly to the colonial interlude, but not solely so. Another factor is a certain haughtiness and self-conceit that developed during periods of Muslim political supremacy, an attitude to the effect that Muslims felt it below their dignity to win people over. "Truth speaks for itself," was the argument of a ruling community that

---

21.   See such publications as the Saudi daily newspaper *Al-Riyadh*, Nov. 14, 1989: "Al-mamlaka takaffalat bi-ta'lim ad-din al-islami...."

regarded it as a privilege to be Muslim. Traces of this attitude can still be found in various parts of the Muslim world, making converts feel ill at ease.[22]

Important in the present context is that both attitudes bear the potential of friction. While the missionary attitude is confrontational, the overbearing posture of the exclusivists is generally discriminatory, not very different from racism or communal antagonisms in places such as Los Angeles or New York. There is manifold divisiveness among Muslims themselves, preventing, e.g., Indian Muslims of East Africa from being one with their native fellows-in-faith, or Arab Muslims in the United States from harmonizing with African-American converts, etc. Given such superiority complexes inherited from an imperial past, it is small wonder that many French people loath Iranian Muslims as self-conceited, or that many Germans complain about the obnoxious self-righteousness of the Turks in their midst.

Hindus ridiculed Muslims for their self-righteousness by saying jestingly "let them set up their Pakistan ('land of the pure')." Muslims responded by actually naming their separate homeland Pakistan – a name necessarily provocative to Indians. Muslims accused Hindus of *Apartheid*, but ended up by responding in kind instead of ridding themselves of the attitudes they originally revolted against.

All the same, Islamic religion – or "normative" Islam – provides ample scope for a concept of mission adjustable to a pluralist society. Expanding the aforementioned dictum that "we have no other obligation but to pass on the message," Muslims would quote such verses from Al-Qur'an as "We sent you but as a conveyor of the glad tidings and as a warner," or "You are not to dictate them."[23]

From there it is not far to the other central theme of Al-Qur'an, namely, humanity's responsibility for this world, its mission as God's vicegerent – humanity as the administrator (Calpih) of the earth. This is a broader sense of mission and a more essential one than that of mere

---

22. This observation is based on some two dozen interviews with converts from various countries.

23. Al-Qur'an III, p. 144; VII, pp. 184, 188; XV, p. 89.

proselytizing. Muhammad Iqbal emphasized this central notion in his famous *Reconstruction of Religious Thought in Islam*,[24] and Ali Shari'ati, the intellectual pathfinder of Shi'ite resurgence in Iran, did likewise.[25]

As such, there is no inherent inability in Islam to conceive of mission as something above and beyond proselytizing. The difficulty lies with an onerous historical legacy that has come to be misunderstood as Islam per se. It would be patently wrong to gloss over this formidable obstacle to pluralism. Muslims need to be made aware of disparities between their faith and their practice. This will remain difficult as long as education remains the privilege of a few percent of the population, with the standards of religious education, moreover, on the decline.

5. Secularism Needs a Second Start

Relations between Muslims and non-Muslims might be vastly improved if secularism were to be given a second try. Indonesia, Iraq, Syria and Turkey are the only countries in the world of Islam that are avowedly secularist, apart from the large minority of Muslims in India and the near-majority in Nigeria. In all of these states, secularism has been discredited by a variety of factors.

Indonesia is perhaps the least critical, but also the least typical case. Many Indonesian Muslims are only superficially Islamized. They subscribe to the basic tenets of Islam, but rarely in an exclusivist manner, while their lifestyle is scarcely affected by the Middle Eastern patterns of behavior that accompany the *shari'a*. Indonesian Muslims may be more devout than their coreligionists in various other countries, yet they are generally less cut off from their roots in indigenous traditions. Significantly, a fundamentalist insurrection called itself *dar al-islam*, because Islamists feel that Indonesia has yet to be properly Islamized. Although it is the state with the largest Muslim population in the world, Indonesia has remained, in many ways, a rimland of the realm of Islam – different from India (Pakistan) which

---

24. Muhammad Iqbal, *The Reconstruction of Religious Thought in Islam* (Lahore/London: Muhammad Ashraf, 1930), Chapter I.

25. Ali Shari'ati, *On the Sociology of Islam*, translated from Persian by Hamid Algar (Berkeley: Mizan Press, 1979).

changed from a rimland into a heartland, replacing, in more than one way, the Arab world and Turkey as the core of Muslimhood.

Indonesian secularism, enshrined in the "Five Principles" (*pancha sila*) of the state's constitution, is special in that it postulates belief in God. It does not postulate adherence to a given religion, but rejects atheism. In principle, this should be acceptable to Muslims, and indeed, it has been hailed by many, because Al-Qur'an calls upon other believers to join Muslims on a common platform, namely, the worship of God. Al-Qur'an appeals to all believers with the words "let us get together on a word between us (dialogue)."[26]

Indonesian secularism, thus, is different from secularism elsewhere, as for instance in India and Turkey, which adopted the Western concept of the state's neutrality with regard to religion. And yet, Indonesian Islamists object to it because they hold that since the overwhelming majority of Indonesians are Muslims, the country should be turned into an "Islamic State," a concept of which there exist at least two dozen different definitions.[27] Many Muslim traditionalists demand that Indonesia should, at least, declare Islam to be the religion of state, as is the case in most Muslim majority countries that are not "Islamic States" in the Islamist sense. This controversy, which has sometimes deteriorated into insurrections on some of the islands, is almost exclusively religiously motivated, though envy against the wealthy Chinese minority plays a role just as much as fear of the disproportionate influence in public affairs of a Christian minority which is ahead in education.

Indonesian Muslim traditionalists and Islamists might gladly have subscribed to the state ideology of *pancha sila* had Muslims been a minority in Indonesia. In any event, the majority of Indonesian Muslims seems to stick to *pancha sila*, and the concept has been generally beneficial to all communities, liberal Muslims just as much as Christians and other minorities.

Turkey is a kind of counterpole in the sense that *laiklik* (laicism) as enshrined in the Turkish constitution goes beyond the secularism of most Western states, because it imposes certain restrictions upon the religious

---

26. Al-Qur'an III, p. 64.

27. Khalid Duran, *Islam und politischer Extremismus* (Hamburg: DOI, 1985).

practice of government servants, who are not allowed to attend religious functions while in office or to perform prayers in their office precincts, a common practice in other Muslim countries. Restrictions on religious education have been abandoned, but there are strong resentments among many Turks against *laiklik* because of the severity with which it was originally enforced and maintained by more or less dictatorial military regimes.[28]

The "Socialist Party of Arab Rebirth" (*Baath*) ruling in Iraq and Syria is secularist, aiming at uniting all Arabs regardless of their adherence to Islam or Christianity or other sects and heterodoxies as well as atheist ideologies. Both regimes, however, rose to power through military coups, lack a sufficiently large popular base and have been at times severely repressive. This has discredited secularism and allowed Islamists to become the strongest force of opposition.[29]

Opposition to secularism is widespread and not limited to the Islamists. Even liberals and reform theologians tend to reject it as something pertaining exclusively to the intellectual development of Western Christianity. Not even Sudan's radical humanist, Mahmoud Muhammad Taha (d. 1985), was prepared to profess secularism, although from the viewpoint of a political scientist his ideas would have to be classified as secularist.[30] Iqbal branded secularism Machiavellism, because he too understood it as the separation of politics from ethics.[31]

This understanding of secularism as unethical politics might have been generated by a school of radical secularists in England, headed by George Holyoake, who were uncompromisingly anti-religious. The crux of the matter, however, seems to be the problematic translation of the term, as well as the fact that it was introduced into the Arab world by Christians with socialist tendencies, such as Salama Musa in Egypt in the 1930s.

---

28.   Khalid Duran, "Atatürk's Laicism in the Light of Muslim History", in Sencer Tonguc, ed., *The Reforms of Atatürk* (Istanbul: RCD Cultural Institute, 1975).

29.   Khalid Duran, *Islam und politischer Extremismus* (Hamburg: DOI, 1985), documentation pp. 33-38.

30.   Mahmoud Mohamed Taha, *The Second Message of Islam*, translated from Arabic by Abdullahi A. An-Na'im, (Syracuse University Press, 1987).

31.   Muhammad Iqbal, *Jawab-e Shikwa* (Lahore: Muhammad Ashraf, 1944).

In Arabic, "secularist" is sometimes rendered as *'alamani*, making it look like "worldly" (from *'alam*), or "this worldly" as opposed to "other worldly" – which does indeed come close to the original Latin *saeculum* (century = age = world). Sometimes "secularist" is translated as *'ilmani*, which denotes something like "scientific" or "scientistic," smacking of "materialistic." It has also been translated as *la dini* ("irreligious"). This is how it appeared in Urdu, a language spoken by some 150 million people. No wonder, then, that secularism was not well received. Secularists such as Abu l-Kalam Azad in India, one of Islam's towering religious thinkers in this century, translated secularism as "neutrality in religious affairs" (*madhabi ghair-janibdari*). However, while Azad is hailed for his superb translation of Al-Qur'an, Pakistanis declared him a political outcast because he remained faithful to his ideal of an undivided India. New Delhi's espousal of secularism has always been derided by Islamabad as fake.

Pakistan understands itself as an ideological state analogous to Israel because both countries lay claim to a religious scripture as the basis for their statehood. Under the military dictatorship of General Zia ul-Haq (1977-88), the propagation of secularism became a punishable offense. The founding father of the state, Muhammad 'Ali Jinnah (d. 1948), was quite explicit in his profession of secularism. The Islamist dictatorship, therefore, issued a decree prohibiting Pakistanis from "misconstruing" Jinnah's statements as expressions of secularist intent. In Islamist propaganda, "Secularism, Zionism, Communism" became a trinity of evil. There are numerous volumes by Islamist writers solely with the purpose of combating secularism. Few Muslims have dared to refute that kind of propaganda with religious arguments. Nationalist parties ruling in Egypt and Tunisia do in actual fact adhere to a secularist conception of state, and yet the issue is rarely discussed in a direct manner.

The separation of East Pakistan from West Pakistan and the creation of the independent state of Bangladesh in 1971 made matters worse because the Bengalis fought their Pakistani brethren-in-faith under the banner of secularism, translated into Bangla as *dharma niropekkhota* ("non-interference in religious affairs"). This was to assure the Hindu minority that in an independent Bangladesh the Muslim majority would no longer discriminate against non-Muslim citizens, with the hope that Muslims in the neighboring Indian state of West Bengal would likewise no longer face discrimination by the Hindu majority there.

Secularism was enshrined as a principle of state in the first constitution of independent Bangladesh. The new nation, however, survived only thanks to generous financial aid from Saudi Arabia and Kuwait. The Arab coreligionists saw to it that secularism was soon dropped. It no longer figures as a principle in the revised constitution of Bangladesh, but surfaces whenever the songs of the 1971 *mukti bahini* ("freedom fighters") are played – battle songs which glorify secularism.

Under the constraints of the colonial situation some Muslim leaders did understand the benefits of secularism as a means of achieving the best possible *modus vivendi* with non-Muslims. The leader of the Moroccan nationalist movement, 'Allal Al-Fasi, who also was a scholar of religion and a reformist thinker, analyzed secularism as being in the interest of Muslims, especially in French-ruled Algeria.[32] All the same, he failed to realize the need for secularism as a means of protecting Muslims against themselves, or, more precisely, of protecting some Muslims against some others – not to speak of secularism as a protection of non-Muslims from Muslims. After independence the plight of several non-Muslim minorities became less and less enviable. To be sure, this was due mostly to nationalistic motivations and less to religious bigotry. However, for the people concerned what counts are the practical effects on their lives, not the rationale behind one or the other government decree.

With a Muslim diaspora in Western Europe soon numbering seven million, Islam has become an important factor in Western life. Everywhere Muslim communities are clamoring for equal rights and want to see their religion recognized at a par with the Christian denominations and Judaism. In order to achieve those rights, they make full use of secularist constitutions. The host communities rarely refuse them those constitutional rights. At the same time, however, the demand for reciprocity is raised more and more vociferously. The increasing inter-penetration of different national societies

---

32.   'Allal Al-Fasi, *An-naqd adh-dhati* (Tetuan, 1951).

and religious communities has created new conditions that make such reciprocity incumbent upon communities less and less homogenous. The Muslim argument that secularism is not a homespun device, that the very term as such is foreign to Islamic vocabulary, makes little sense. The term secularism is new to the West too. It is a highly technical term of recent coinage, a concept not understandable unless explained and commented upon. A few Muslim scholars have indeed understood this and endeavored to make it accessible by interpreting it within an Islamic frame of reference.[33] Much depends on a resumption of those seminal efforts, against the heavy odds of bigotry and chauvinism.

---

[33]   Sayyid Qudrat-Allah Fatimi, *Pakistan Movement and Kemalist Revolution* (Lahore: Institute of Islamic Culture, 1977). Hichem Djait, *La personnalite et le devenir arabo-islamique* (Paris: Editions du Seuil, 1972). Mohammed 'Aziz Lahbabi, *Le personnalisme musulman* (Paris: Presses Universitaires de France, 1967).

OUTSIDERS-INSIDERS:
HINDU ATTITUDES TOWARD NON-HINDUS

by

Kana Mitra

Sri Krishna Prema, a Westerner who embraced Hindu monastic life under the discipleship of a woman mystic, wanted to worship in the Jagannath temple in Puri. His white skin made him an outsider and the priests did not allow him to enter the temple. However, in Vrindavana, where the worship of Krsna is as central as in Puri, white skin is not a deterrent to *darsana* (viewing) of the deity. In the diversity within the different groups of the Hindus there is also a diversity of attitudes regarding who is an insider and who is an outsider. Some groups of Hindus consider the followers of their guru or the founding saint as the most intimate inside group and those of other gurus or other saints as less intimate and belonging to the outer circle of a believing community. Similarly, there are rare individual spiritual leaders and even fewer Hindu communities who consider non-Hindus or non-India born people as insiders. The early scriptures of the Hindus – the Vedas (approximately 1500 B.C.E.-1200 B.C.E.) and the Upanisadas (approximately 800 B.C.E.-600 B.C.E.) do not have any clear statement regarding who is inside and who is outside of the believing community. The concern of these texts, commonly referred to as *Srutis*, are the human goals of life and how can they be achieved. The Dharma Sastras (approximately 700 B.C.E.) deal with the question of what are correct or incorrect forms of actions or who are within or outside of noble society, but not who are true or untrue believers.

Thus in the early history of Hinduism we can note the attitude towards *anarya* or barbarians. Some Indian born and all non-India born were considered as barbarians. The basis of classification was not religious beliefs, but rather, whether the behavior was *sanskrita*, or cultured, i.e., according to the standards of that time. It is common knowledge today that Hinduism is not one religion with a common creed, common ritual, or common scripture. It is the common name for a multitude of religions of the Indian sub-continent. Until the twentieth century all Hindus were of Indian ancestry. Yet, anyone who studies the divergent scriptures of the Hindus and the worldview by which the people of India live will see at least family resemblances, if not exact similarity. Thus, any categorical statement about Hinduism is incorrect – but generalization is not totally unjustified. In dealing with the question of the Hindu attitude toward non-Hindu religions it is thus possible to make some general remarks which are justified.

The issue of the plurality of religions and singleness of ultimate truth is usually treated by the present day Hindu ideologues in terms of the Rg-Vedic statement, "There is one Truth, people call it by different names." Currently a statement by the nineteenth century Ramakrishna, "there are as many ways as there are faiths," is commonly referred to. Thus it seems that the commonly held view of many Hindus, primarily the literate and devout ones, towards other religions, is that the different religions of the world are different views or different ways of expressing the one truth. The Hindus face difficulty when a particular religion claims that not only is there one truth but there is also only one way of expressing that truth. In other words, the denial of pluralism is unacceptable to the Hindus. Following the rule of consistency, the Hindus need to accept the exclusive claims of others, which they cannot, and thus they have developed the idea of peaceful co-existence – each religion upholds its own view but also lets others retain their own.

Until the nineteenth century there was not much consciousness among the Indians of any thing like Hinduism. There were different religious groups having different leaders. Before the time of Samkara (8th century C.E.)

there was not any organized monastic order, although there were wandering monks. There are wandering monks even today, although now there are many monastic orders as well. Often these monks are the sources of guidance in the spiritual quests of the Hindus. Religious guidance is also provided by family gurus or charismatic religious individuals like Meher Baba or Satya Sai Baba or Anandamai Ma–twentieth century spiritual leaders, men and women. Most of them are not scripture specialists and some of them may not even have any direct acquaintance with the scriptures of the Hindus. The *acaryas* or theologians of Hinduism are the specialists of the scriptures and some of them are religious leaders also, but not necessarily so. Who can be considered an *acarya* is usually dependent on public opinion, although until the present they needed to demonstrate their proficiency in the scriptures by way of public encounter with each other. For example, Vinova Bhave (Gandhi's associate), although he is not much of a scripture specialist, is called *Acarya Vinova Bhave*, because his grassroot reform attempts were based on the Bhagavad Gita Chaitanya, the most important person related with Krsna consciousness, in order to prove his skill in scriptures needed to argue with Sarvabhauma, a famous scholar of the sixteenth century. Some of these *acaryas* discussed the issue of who is a true believer and who is not. For example, in the Sammkara there are polemics against dualists, and the worshipping of deity with a form; further, the ritual worship of deity is considered a lower form of worship, although not a false worship. Similarly, Chaitanya considered the Samkarites deluded. Thus, we note that within the Indian traditions, which we now identify as Hinduism, there have been controversies of such a nature that they are comparable to the controversies between Hindus and Buddhists, Hindus and Muslims, etc.

From the early part of this century the West came to know about Hinduism on a mass scale after the Parliament of World Religions (1893) held in Chicago. Since then Hindu teachers came to the West and the "evangelical" activities of the Hindus outside of India have become apparent. In India Dayananda Saraswati (1824-1883) introduced the idea of the conversion of non-Hindus to Hinduism. Before that the religious leader of one group often tried to influence other groups of Hindus to follow his or her way, but not those who were not born as Hindus. Even Dayananda converted only Indian non-Hindus to Hinduism and did not go outside of India. Prior to the twentieth century there was a sense that all Hindus are Hindus by birth and not by affiliation with any ideology. This was expressed in Hindu society in the caste system. Those who were born as Hindus are Hindus and from birth were born into a specific caste. Those who were not born into the Hindu castes are outside of the caste system, are outsiders.

In the Dharma Sastra by Manu these people are often treated in the same way as those Indian born who are outcastes or untouchables. The Dharma Sastra of Manu is not considered a revealed text. It is thought to have been written by a law giver to guide Hindus in moral behavior. Manu indicates that caste members, Brahmanas, Kshatriyas, Vaisyas, are twice born, and Sudras are only once born. There are only four castes, there is no fifth (Manu X:4).

Children born from parents belonging to different castes were considered to belong to the lower caste parent. All children of confused caste are base born. Some are more so than others. For example, the Chandalas are described as the lowest of the mortals. We need to take note of the point that caste as it is described in Manu or in other religious texts of the Hindus is not the same as it is in Indian society. The different field studies that are done on the Hindu caste system make it evident. Manu describes in detail how one is placed outside of one's caste. For example, if children born from parents of same caste do not keep up their sacred duties they must be considered *vratyas*, outcastes (Manu X:20). Not only non-observance of duties but commitment of offences like adultery places one outside of one's caste. Manu also indicates that all those tribes which are neither Brahmana, Kshatriya, Vaisya or Sudra are *Dasyus* (enemies), whether they speak the language of the *Mlechhas* (barbarians), i.e., non-Sanskrit or of the *Aryans* (nobles), i.e., Sanskrit (Manu X:45).

It is obvious that Manu was not interested in spreading Hindu wisdom to the outsiders. For him all non-Indians are outside of *arya* society and some of those who are born in India also are outside of *arya*, or noble, society due to various reasons. In Manu there are considerations about who are within and who are outside of the cultured society but no reference to what is true or what is untrue religion. In Manu there seems to be inclinations toward treating different people differently, but not on the basis of differences of religions. In other words, from Manu we find reflections regarding attitudes towards the outsiders of *arya* or noble society but not any reflections about attitudes toward non-Hindu religions. In fact, in Manu's time (the current consensus of scholars regarding Manu's date is 200 B.C.E.- 100 B.C.E. although many indigenous scholars think it must have been prior to Buddhism as they find mention of Manu in the Buddhist texts) there does not seem to have been any consciousness among those who were addressed by Manu or Manu himself regarding distinctions between Hindu and non-Hindu religions. *Dharma*, which is often considered as equivalent to the notion of religion, has different connotations than the word religion. *Dharma* suggests the constituents of beings – their nature. Thus every one has *dharma*. As water has its inherent nature so also the Brahmana, the Kshatriya, the Vaisya, the Sudra – each has his or her *dharma*. Those who are outside of the caste have *dharma*, but, according to Manu, are unlikely to attain spiritual perfection, although the possibility is not totally denied because besides the birth characteristics there is an eternal or perennial nature inherent in all beings, not to mention in human beings. According to Manu neither Sudra nor women are likely to attain spiritual perfection. Manu suggests that from birth, due to ancestry, humans have such natures that it is almost impossible to overcome them totally. Manu suggests that all humans are not born equal, in the sense that one is born with different personality traits and one's birth characteristics are so powerful that it is almost impossible to change them. Only the spirit of renunciation can lead to the transformation of one's birth characteristics. A person born in any caste can be a renouncer (*sanyasi*). In Manu there are suggestions that birth in a particular family is not a guarantee of belonging to a particular caste. People may fall from a caste. But it is not possible to change one's caste in the sense of raising oneself to a higher caste. By becoming a *sanyasi* one goes outside of caste. The difference between *sanyasi* and *chandala*, outcastes, is that the former, the monk, because of renunciation transcends the *dharma* that s/he was born with (*sva-dharma*) and realizes the universal *dharma* which is the true and ultimate *dharma* (*sanatana dharma*), the ultimate nature-reality of all. Any one with a strong spiritual longing has the potential for the realization of ultimate nature as it is inherent in all beings. However, often birth characteristics are detrimental to such spiritual longing. In any case, it can be easily noted that Manu's concern is not about non-believers or wrong believers but for those who do or do not act according to the rules of noble society. According to Manu, a person who belongs to the noble society acts according to his or her inherent gifts and not according to some outside incentive. The statement of the Bhagavad Gita which asserts that it is better to perish following one's inherent nature than to live following that of others is analogous to Manu's perspective. However, from Manu we cannot gain any idea of the attitude of Hinduism toward non-Hindu religions.

The quest of Hinduism is a quest which started after Hinduism's encounter with the West. The encounter with the West had a tremendous impact on Hinduism. We may even say that what we now call Hinduism is a result of India's encounter with the West. Non-missionary Hinduism acquired the characteristic of a missionary religion. Hinduism is no longer a religion just for people of Indian ancestry but it is now a world religion. There are now white-skinned Hindus as there are brown-skinned ones and black-skinned ones. However, it needs to be noted that although the different gurus of Hinduism who try to spread the wisdom of Hinduism to non-Indians may consider their converts to be Hindus, the Indian born Hindus, even today, hardly recognize the non-Indians as Hindus. This can be seen in the attitude of the majority of Indian born towards the Hare Krishna movement. Many Indians do not have any less suspicion towards them than do many people in United States. White-skinned people to not gain entry in Temple of Puri, even today. Via encounter with the British, India became exposed to the ideologies of democracy, nationalism, etc. That led to a tremendous change in the Hindu's self-understanding and understanding of others. Thus British colonialism, which was responsible for the slave mentality among many Indians, also enabled many other Indians to look at their ideologies in some different ways.

Hindus came in contact with the non-Hindus early in history. Buddhism and Jainism originated in opposition to Hinduism – or rather, at that period it is more appropriate to speak of Brahmanism or ritualistic Hinduism, as it can be noted in the literatures known as the Brahmanas (800-

500 B.C.E.). Brahmanical Hindus opposed the Buddhists and Jains. Zoroastrianism originated outside of India but hardly encountered any opposition from the Hindus when it came to India after the Islamization of Persia. Jews also hardly ever faced any opposition from the Hindus, when they came to India after the destruction of the Temple by Romans in 70 C.E. The relationship between Hinduism and Christianity and Islam is more checkered. The absolute monotheism of Islam with its Arabic cultural expression was too alien to Hinduism. The circumstances of encounter between Hinduism and Islam also are responsible for the relationship of alienation between the two.

When Christianity came to the Indian subcontinent early in the Christian era there was not too much opposition to it. Later, however, missionary activities, as it was dictated by Western leadership and colonial oppression, led to opposition to Christianity, although it did not take the violent form it did with Islam. Until coming in contact with the British, Hindus tried to maintain their identity by putting up barriers to others and considering themselves noble in comparison with the others who were inferior. Western education however shook the confidence of the educated Hindus. Many educated Hindus were drawn towards British culture – its system of government, its industrial affluence, its empirical philosophy. At the same time, via exposure to the ideologies of individualism, democracy etc., there developed a spirit of nationalism which led to nationalist movements and opposition to British rule. Christianity and colonialism also became associated in the minds of the Hindus and thus both attraction and repulsion in regard to Christianity can be noted.

In the nineteenth and twentieth centuries many reform movements began. Hindus started to be self-reflective. The reformers started to emphasize the Upanishads and the Bhagavad Gita, which offer a perspective of religious truth within a broad horizon, and that Hinduism does not need to be understood only as the religion of people of Indian origin. Some Hindu thinkers and religious leaders started to defend Hinduism against the criticism of the outsiders, especially the Christians. Some also started missionary activities, spreading the messages of Hinduism to non-Hindus. Thus it become possible for people of non-Indian origin to be Hindus.

Hence, the issue of the Hindu attitude toward non-Hindu religions is a modern issue addressed by modern Hindus.

Dayananda Saraswati, the previously mentioned Hindu who started the conversion of non-Hindus to Hinduism, established the Arya Samaj or the Society of the Nobles. He criticized Islam, Christianity and post-Buddhist Hinduism in his book *Satyartha Prakash*. To him, Vedic Hinduism was the only true religion. However, his is an exceptional view. The majority of modern thinkers express the view that the universal true religion transcends all religions and the plural religions are ways of realizing transcendence or transformation.

Ramakrishna Paramahamsa (1836-1886) and his disciple Vivekananda (1863-1902) were the most influential advocates of the singleness of truth and plurality of religions. Rammohan Roy (1772-1833) attempted to harmonize the plurality of religions on an intellectual basis and established Brahmo Samaj. Yet his impact was primarily on the intellectuals and not on masses. Ramakrishna's impact however was equally on the intellectuals as well as on the masses. This rustic illiterate mystic wanted to learn everything from experience. In his different spiritual phases he lived the different forms of Hinduism – sakta, vaisnava, ramait – the different devotional forms of Hinduism, as well as vedantic Hinduism. He pursued Christian and Muslim ways, and always came back to devotion of "Mother." He insisted on the unity of all religious experiences. All biographers agree about his "God realization." According to him, all religions can be considered true because each can lead to "God realization." He stated that every religion has imperfections. Everyone thinks that his/her watch is giving correct time, but each watch goes wrong occasionally. So once in a while it is necessary to check with the sun. Ramakrishna suggested that if anyone seeks God earnestly s/he can experience God no matter by what name God is named. If a young child cannot say "father" properly but only says "pa" the father still answers the child. He pointed out that one usually thinks that only my religion is true: I understand God and others are wrong. But such dogmatism is unjustified because God answers every sincere call.[1]

Vivekananda, being Western educated, was going through a phase of agnosticism when he came to know Ramakrishna. The affirmative answer of Ramakrishna to his question whether he saw God pricked Vivekananda's interest and he also eventually attained illumination. Although he died at the age of thirty-nine, within his short span of life he was successful in making the Hindus aware of the need of purifying their religious and social life, and in carrying the messages of Hinduism abroad to the United States and England. At the 1893 Parliament of Religions in Chicago he said: "Sectarianism, bigotry and its horrible descendant, fanaticism, have long possessed this beautiful earth. They have filled the earth with violence, drenched it time and again with human blood, destroyed civilization and sent whole nations to despair."[2] There is need for unity. But that cannot be by uniformity. He said:

> If anyone here hopes that this unity will come by triumph of any one of these religions and the destruction of the others, to him I say, Brother, yours is an impossible hope. Do I wish that the Christian would become Hindu? God forbid. Do I wish that the Hindu or Buddhist would become Christian? God forbid. The seed is put in the ground, and earth and air and water are placed around it. Does the seed become the earth or the air or the water? No, it becomes a plant, it assimilates the air, the earth and the water, converts them into plant substance and grows a plant. Similar is the case with religion. The Christian is not to become a Hindu or a Buddhist nor a Hindu or a Buddhist to become a Christian. But each must assimilate the spirit of the others and yet preserve its own individuality and grow according to its own law of growth.[3]

Thus Vivekananda advocated plurality but mutual influence and enrichment. But he was also a proud Hindu. In his Chicago address he said: "I am proud to belong to a religion which has taught the world both tolerance

1.   *The Gospel of Sri Ramakrishna* (New York: Ramakrishna Vivekananda Center, 1977).

2.   Address at the Parliament of Religions: Sept. 11, 1893. Nikhilananda Swami, ed., *Vivekananda. The Yoga and Other Works* (New York: Ramakrishna-Vivekananda Center, 1953), p. 183.

3.   Address at the final session, Sept. 27, 1893, *ibid.*, p. 197.

and universal acceptance. We believe not only in universal toleration, but we accept all religions as true. I am proud to tell you that I belong to a religion into whose sacred language, Sanskrit, the word 'exclusion' is untranslatable."[4] However, Hindus also consider some to be insiders and some to be outsiders. Some outsiders are shunned; for example, caste Hindus shun outcastes, and among non-Hindus, Muslims in particular. Some Hindus treat non-Hindus with politeness as one does guests, but only a few Hindus can and do treat all people as real neighbors. From Ramakrishna and Vivekananda's perspective this is due to the differences of levels of spiritual maturity of the various Hindus and they suggest that this is true among people of all religions. Ramakrishna and later Vivekananda used to tell the story of the frog in the well to indicate the reasons of denying other ways. A frog living in the well knows only its own ways and thinks it is the only way. But when it experiences rivers and oceans, its horizon increases. In Upanisadic Hinduism it is usually taught that one starts one's spiritual journey with body consciousness. At this stage as one identifies oneself with one's body and identifies God with another body and other humans with their bodies. Self-identity at this stage is in terms of opposition with others. God at this stage seems to be more a disciplinarian than a loving one. Other humans also are looked at with suspicion. At this point other humans seem to have the characteristics described by Freud, or they seem to be "hell," as Sartre says. With spiritual maturity one identifies one's self with mind and God is understood more in terms of mental characteristics than simply another being and other individuals more in terms of mental relationship than physical. God at this stage appears as a loving parent-protector and preserver and other humans as siblings. There is still a relationship of opposition, but it is toned down by love, which is not yet totally pure. Thus, although God is a loving protector, God is also a judge. In the same way, although other humans are loved the way one loves one's siblings, yet there is sibling rivalry.

When one identifies oneself with soul, God appears as Universal Soul and others as different souls. At this point, the relationship is no longer in

---

4. *Ibid.*, p. 183.

terms of opposition but more in terms of a part and the whole. This is the stage of peaceful co-existence which is not simply indifference. The last stage of spiritual experience is advaitic where the unity or interrelatedness of all reality is realized and pure love or love without hatred is actualized. Ramakrishna often referred to the story of Hanumana and Rama to illustrate the point. Hanumana said to Rama that when Hanumana feels himself to be a body he then feels Rama to be his king and he as Rama's servant; when he feels himself to be a soul then Hanumana feels Rama to be the whole and Hanumana to be Rama's part; but when Hanumana feels himself to be the Atman then he feels non-duality with Rama. According to Ramakrishna all religions in concrete divergent ways tend to lead their adherents to this similar spiritual journey. Thus all religions in their concrete details are unique and there consequently are many ways, but they are also one because each leads to spiritual maturity. Tagore, Gandhi, Radhakrishnan and many other modern Hindus basically agree with the view of unity in diversity position advocated by Ramakrishna-Vivekananda. Thus this view can be considered the ideal of the modern Hindu attitude towards non-Hindu religions. The prescription of each of these thinkers for the resolution of conflicts between different religions and the ways of cultivating spirituality are somewhat different. However, all agree that the cultivation of spiritual maturity is the way to world peace.

THE ATTITUDE OF BUDDHISTS TOWARDS NON-BUDDHISTS

by

Chatsumarn Kabilsingh

It is indeed an honor to be addressing a gathering of scholars with such a multi-religious background. I am honored because such a gathering fulfills the basic requirement of the openness needed to be able to listen and to try to understand the points of view offered by members of other religions often very different from their own. That is the beauty of this auspicious conference.

I have been given the assignment of speaking on "The Attitude of Buddhists Towards Non-Buddhists." Buddhism is not a simple single trend of thought but a religion with many characteristics – so much so that when I try to focus my thought on the given topic, I realize that it is not as simple as it may appear at the beginning. In order to come to some understanding of this topic, I would rather share with you some points, hoping that they will serve as a basis for further discussion and open up dialogue.

Buddhism is Non-Theistic

I purposely use the term "Non-Theistic" rather than atheistic. Buddhists do not deny God as such, but whether God exists or not is not our immediate concern when human beings are suffering. The classic example is that of a man wounded by an arrow. He should not waste time asking about the source of the arrow, who shot him, etc. but should exert every effort to concentrate on how to overcome the immediate suffering.

In this sense, A Buddhist will not indulge him/herself by arguing about the existence of God for he/she finds it ethically unprofitable. For members of other religions who believe in God, that is well and good, as long as it leads them out of the present suffering. In this respect a Buddhist can remain at peace among atheists as well as theists.

Philosophically if one wants to pursue a dialogue along the line of "God or no-God" a Buddhist scholar may introduce the concept of "Nirvana," which is the ultimate spiritual goal of Buddhists, and may try to compare this concept to the "God" of the theists, realizing of course, that "God" is the personalized form of that ultimate reality. The philosophical concept of Brahman in Indian philosophy is also indescribable and characterless. Therefore, Buddhist scholars should have no problems with either the concept of God or no-God. That is, they should not feel alienated from people believing in God or not believing in God.

No Supreme Religious Authority

The office of a "Pope" as supreme religious authority as in Catholicism finds no place in Buddhism. Instead, the Buddha introduced and established a democratic structure of administration to be followed within Buddhist communities. In each Buddhist country, the "Sangha" or community of Buddhist clergy follows the collective decision arrived at through democratic consensus and passed down to its members to put into practice.

Meditation, a very common mental practice among the Buddhists, may be prescribed according to each one's temperament. Here one sees clearly the respect for individual differences. In fact there are forty types of *samatha* (concentration) and six different types of *vipassan* (insight meditation).[1] Therefore, even at the personal level, Buddhism recognizes individual differences and encourages variety. Yet within its framework there is unity among the differences which all finally lead to the same goal.

---

[1]   *Thai Tripitaka*, vol. XIII, *Mah vaccha gotta Sutta* (Bangkok: Department of Religious Affairs, B.E. 2525 [1982]).

This open-mindedness was seen even in the teaching of the Buddha himself when he preached to the Kalamas in the *Kalama Sutta*[2] that one should not believe simply because it is the word of a teacher or even the Buddha. One should consider a statement acceptable only after having put it to the test in one's own experience. Such an attitude leaves much room for Buddhists to listen to the teaching of religions or teachers other than their own. In general, however, they will have difficulty understanding the situation where a religion or religious leaders appear authoritarian.

Self-reliance

Buddhism is a religion of this world, and therefore puts a strong emphasis on the responsibility of one's self, particularly in early Buddhism. One's own spiritual development depends totally on one's own effort here and now. One cannot control the actions of the past but one can control the future by laying a foundation of good actions in the present. With this emphasis, no one, not even the Buddha, can help another person towards his/her own enlightenment. Such an approach demands a very strong, mature personality. With a sense of inadequacy, Buddhists of a later period developed a belief in Bodhisattvas (Buddhist saints or saviors) who vow to help sentient beings achieve their spiritual goal.

This development, though later, cannot be rejected as non-Buddhist, for in Buddhist teaching itself there is much room for compassion, and the concept of Bodhisattva fits in well with the overall teaching of Buddhism. Though it is true that such a belief encourages a psychological leaning on "other power," in reality in the end one must depend on oneself in working towards her/his spiritual goal. Having faith in Bodhisattvas or Buddhas must be coupled with one's own effort.

The belief in "other power" at the practical level may in fact lead to the practice of polytheism, the belief in many gods. But Buddhism finds itself flexible enough to adjust to even such a belief within its structure and explains that even the gods are not free from the samsaric (the round of rebirth) world.

---

2.   *TP*, vol. XX, *Anguttara Nik yas*, Tikanip ta.

Non-missionary

Within the Buddhist context, there is no need for missionary work. Buddhists do not see the necessity of finding converts. Buddhism is a path of life and never claims to be the only way to Truth. Hence making converts becomes irrelevant to Buddhists. Buddhism as a religion grew out of diverse religious contexts with tolerance as a basic requirement. The Buddha sent his first group of disciples (60 in all) out in different directions to make known to society the *dharma* (teaching) with the idea of simply making the teaching available. If a person finds it fitting to follow, that is well and good. But if the teaching does not appeal to a person, that is also fine, for the disciples have done their job (of offering the teaching). There was no sense of forcing the belief or way of life upon anyone. Religion is a matter of a committed heart which cannot be brought about by force. Hence Buddhism spread in its own silent and humble way without any imposition upon others.

Once it takes hold of society, however, it can be of great force in that land. For example, throughout the more than a thousand years that Buddhism was a state religion in Japan it developed a strong and rich religious and cultural heritage. Through recent political and economical changes, Japan may have changed considerably, but many practices and beliefs in present-day Japanese society can still be traced back to Buddhist origins.

Possibility of Dialogue

Traditional Buddhist countries are primarily in Asia. One has to accept that one major cultural characteristic prevalent in Asian countries is that Asians avoid confrontation. Confrontation is considered improper. One has to learn, often painfully, to go round about in order to make some simple statements. Of course, to have a successful dialogue one has to be sincere about the issue at hand. However, there will be issues when one will find oneself at the opposite pole from members of other religions – then one will find oneself in confrontation. However, Asians in general are too polite to confront directly. Out of politeness they will try to save their opponent's face, and thus may choose to give more importance to courtesy rather than truth.

From my own experience, dialogues among members of different religions at certain levels is much more beneficial than dialogue among members of the same religion. In the latter case the barrier ironically is mainly the strong egoistic attitudes displayed by each party.

There are Buddhists who would agree that God is supreme in Christianity, Islam, etc., but the concept of Nirvana in Buddhism is after all for them much superior. We may compare it to the example of climbing the mountain. Are we climbing the same mountain or different ones? A Buddhist with the above reasoning would believe that we are climbing different mountains, and his/hers is the highest. But philosophically if each religion is aiming at ultimate reality (whatever it may be called, e.g., God, Allah, Nirvana) that ultimate reality must be only One Truth, otherwise how can it be ultimate?

Popular Buddhism

The teaching of the Buddha as found in the Buddhist texts of each tradition is known as textual or canonical Buddhism, which is agreed upon by scholars of each Buddhist tradition. The practices as found among the Buddhists are known as popular Buddhism, which is as a rule a mixture of local beliefs, Hinduism, Buddhism and traditional practices which have become part of that culture. Popular Buddhism differs in each country depending on geographical, historical and social contexts.

Buddhism has an encompassing attitude; that is, it has the tendency to incorporate many other practices and beliefs already prevalent in each country as long as they do not contradict the essential teaching of Buddhism. Before the arrival of Buddhism, Tibetans followed the Bon tradition which was full of beliefs in ghosts and menacing spirits. Buddhism, when it spread to Tibet, was accepted only after a Buddhist teacher who was believed to possess magical power successfully defeated the local spirits. Therefore Tibetan Buddhism is a set of beliefs with Buddhist values on the upper level of the triangle, whereas at the base the local beliefs of spirits, now transformed into "*dharma* protectors" of various different types, persist. In this way Tibetans could till retain their former beliefs and be totally

Buddhists. The example of Tibet is not an exception but rather the rule in all the countries where Buddhism has successfully spread.

On the one hand, textual Buddhism may emphasize self-reliance, but on the other hand popular Buddhism as practiced by the local people provides more comfort with Bodhisattvas, *dharma* protectors, etc. as spiritual guides to help them not only on the spiritual path but also in gaining a comfortable worldly life.

Textual Buddhism may not concern itself about God and often reminds us that gods are also subject to the wheel of life and birth, but popular Buddhism may pay sincere respect to gods. This may be seen as a reflection of psychological needs by which local people express themselves, and on this basis it should be as valid as textual Buddhism.

Buddhist Sense of Superiority

A good Buddhist who follows the teaching of the Buddha truly should not have any sense of superiority. But as we know, members of a religion do not necessarily all have the same level of understanding or commitment. Therefore a sense of superiority is the result. Buddhists, at least in Theravadin countries, often maintain a superiority complex, believing with conviction that their religion is the best. Surprisingly very few of them have studied any religion other than Theravada Buddhism.

Another point to be considered in this connection is that Buddhists seem to be content and satisfied with the answers provided by Buddhism, especially on questions regarding life and death. The law of *karma* seems to handle the question of inequality in society very well. A person who is rich but corrupt may be explained by saying that he is enjoying his riches as a result of his collected good karma of the past and that his corrupt actions will definitely bear fruits in the future. This explanation seems to satisfy the inquiring mind of an ordinary Buddhist.

In Thailand, Christian missionaries, who have been trying to propagate their faith for more than two centuries, have not been the least successful. This is the one country in the region that seems to be able to maintain its religious unity to a great extent. In general, however, Buddhists are very tolerant towards the propagation of other religions.

Among missionaries, Protestants seem to have been more successful in their work through providing education and medical services by establishing schools and hospitals. They made some Thai converts in the beginning but as soon as the foreign missionaries returned to their homelands, these so-called converts returned also to the services of Buddhist temples. From the Christian point of view, these Thais were seen as insincere. But the Thais who joined the church (hence were converts according to the Christian understanding) understood their action (of joining the church) as a means of expressing their appreciation and gratitude to the missionaries.

In Thailand Buddhism has so interwoven itself into the culture and tradition of the country that it is almost impossible to be Thai without being Buddhist. This point needs to be understood by people from other cultural and religious contexts.

Though some Theravadin Buddhists may maintain an attitude of superiority, they will always remain tolerant of and humble toward other religions or religious ideas. This attitude also makes it more difficult to start any meaningful dialogue with other religions.

Buddhists at large actually have a sympathetic attitude towards members of other religions, thinking that they do not have the path to the real truth of life. Often local venders in Asia refer sympathetically to Western tourists as "the poor uncultured Westerners," especially when they see them in shorts and sneakers. Mahayana Buddhists seem to be able to handle the problem better with their strong emphasis on compassion largely seen through the concept of Bodhisattvas. In Tibetan Buddhism, for example, the teaching is very strong about making oneself the lowest in order to be able to serve other sentient beings.

Being with Others

So how does a Buddhist stand with people from different religions? Academically, Buddhist teaching of all schools has much to offer to other religions. The Buddha had an opportunity to spread his teaching for 45 years as compared to Jesus Christ's short term of service to humankind or even to Muhammad who had to take on the responsibility of both religious and political leader. Buddhist teaching is rich in various aspects and Buddhists (at any level) feel that they have much to offer to the world. This attitude becomes even stronger in Mahayana Buddhism. In the Bodhisattva's precepts, it's not enough for a person to be good but s/he should also try to instill goodness in others and should try to prevent the ills of the world.

Violence finds no support from the teaching of Buddhism. However, there are stories of Buddhist rulers in the past who have tried to justify violent acts in the name of Buddhism. There is also the exception that a Bodhisattva might choose violence as a means to end further violence, but even then s/he has to sacrifice him/herself for the cause. Thus, for whatever purpose, true Buddhists do not approve of violence.

Peace and freedom in the ultimate sense are nothing but the manifestations of Nirvana, the Buddhist ultimate spiritual goal. Buddhists will have difficulty reconciling themselves with any other religions propagating otherwise. Peace and freedom in the world is very much related to peace and freedom within. One is meaningless without the other.

It is necessary, therefore, that members of different religions should come together to find ways they can work together to bring about peace and freedom at both levels for our society. This conference is ideal in its attempt to bring about a basic understanding among people of the world through the understanding of each others' religion, helping thereby to establish peace and freedom for humankind.

CHINA'S "THREE RELIGIONS"

by

Julia Ching

Is religion part of the Chinese heritage? This question draws different responses from people who have different degrees of acquaintance with China, and varying definitions of religion. In this article, I am taking as point of departure the Chinese claim to having had "three teachings," or "three religions": Confucianism, Taoism and Buddhism.

How do Chinese religions regard the outsider? This question might have seemed odd to a Chinese of the past who regarded him or herself to be living in the then-known world. But it is important to today's *Oecumene*. We shall also seek to give an answer.

As an expression, China's "Three Religions" (*san-chiao*) is a late coinage, representing a retrospective outlook on the results of historical developments. As noted, they refer to Confucianism, Taoism and Buddhism, especially in their later, developed forms. We can call them the "Three Religions," bearing in mind those features that have helped to identify them as *religions*. These include the important place given to rites in the Confucian tradition, the belief in a pantheon of gods in the popular Taoist tradition, and the devotional-mystical traditions in Buddhism.

Of these three religions, Buddhism was introduced into the country from the outside, that is, from India and Central Asia. Buddhism also became a universal religion, a world religion, whereas Confucianism is sometimes identified with the peoples of China, Japan and Korea in a special sense. Certainly, it was a tradition that developed in a land that considered itself *the Oecumene*. Taoism, on the other hand, is a "Chinese" religion, perhaps more associated with the people of China. Although it was also introduced into Korea and Japan, it lost its distinctiveness as a religion, especially in Japan, and did not witness its full development in Korea as it did in China.

In one sense, we may say the insider/outsider dichotomy does not hold in a country that considered itself the world. In the case of Buddhism, however, an outsider religion eventually became an insider religion. However, the insider/outsider dichotomy can be discerned in the interrelationships *between* China's three religions.

Confucianism: the Ritual Religion

The term *li-chiao* (ritual religion), which is often applied to Confucianism, emphasizes the doctrinal as well as ritual prescriptions for "proper behavior" in family and society. The Chinese word *li* signifies *both* ritual and propriety. Confucian teachings helped to keep alive the older cult of veneration for ancestors, and the worship of Heaven, a formal cult practised by China's imperial rulers who regarded themselves as the keepers of Heaven's Mandate of government, a kind of High Priest, a mediator figure between the human and the divine order. With the official establishment of Confucianism, its classical texts were inscribed in stone, and a corpus of commentaries and sub-commentaries were collected, establishing various traditions of textual exegesis. This took place during the period of time spanning the Han and the T'ang (618-906 C.E.) dynasties. Among these texts, the *Spring and Autumn Annals* in particular gave rise to allegorical interpretations that drew in *yin-yang* metaphysics, offering a new cosmological and historical vision, while the *Book of Rites*, with its elaborate instructions for correct deportment, especially regarding mourning and funerals, became the backbone of Chinese society.

The proper observance of rituals is meaningful when accompanied by certain interior dispositions. Otherwise, it tends to formalism and even hypocrisy – and these are problems which have plagued Confucian society through the ages, as they have also the Christian religion. Besides, as any official orthodoxy, Confucianism abhorred dissent, thus stifling creativity and spontaneity. It took the combined popularity of Taoism and Buddhism to arouse a movement of return to the roots of Confucian inspiration, a movement which has sometimes been called Neo-Confucianism.

The Neo-Confucian philosophers reformulated Confucian philosophy on the basis of a smaller corpus of texts, the Four Books: The *Analects* of Confucius, giving the conversations between Confucius and his disciples, the *Book of Mencius*, presenting the conversations between Mencius and his disciples, the *Great Learning* and the *Doctrine of the Mean*, which are chapters taken from the *Book of Rites*, the former making moral and spiritual cultivation the beginning of good rulership, and the latter concentrating on the inner life of psychic equilibrium and harmony. In so doing, Confucian scholarship oriented itself increasingly to metaphysical and spiritual questions, and even assimilated much from Buddhist and Taoist philosophies in its own discussions about the world and human psychology. The result is a new *Weltanschauung*, which builds on the old moralist answer, giving it a clearer metaphysical framework and spiritual profundity, oriented to the quest for self-transcendence in the achievement of sagehood. This took place especially during the Sung (960-1279) and Ming (1368-1644) dynasties.

Neo-Confucianism was the official philosophy for China during the last thousand years that preceded the establishment of a republic; the textual commentaries written or compiled by its representatives had been all that time the basis of the examination curriculum. The Jesuit missionaries, however, including especially Matteo Ricci, had tended to prefer classical Confucianism to the later development. They thought that the earlier philosophy lacked a belief in the deity, and that this "vacant place" could be taken over by the Christian God. They also opposed the metaphysical dimensions of Neo-Confucian philosophy, which bore a pantheistic imprint of Buddhist influence. More recently however, in our own times, leading Chinese scholars have complained of this missionary attitude as one that overlooked the rich spiritual dimension of the Neo-Confucian tradition. Indeed, it is not existentially possible to separate Confucianism and Neo-Confucianism. The Confucian tradition has lost ground in modern times, but it is not dead. Like Christianity, it has been confronting the challenges of science and technology in modern times. Like Christianity, it is also confronting the political and social challenges of a Marxist regime. Recent indications point to an increasing recognition on the part of the Marxist regime itself of the vitality of the Confucian tradition, and of its moral relevance. The encounter between Marxism and Confucianism began only a short while ago. The encounter between Christianity and Confucianism is not yet over.

Taoism: the Alchemical Religion

If Confucianism is called a ritual religion grounded in ethics which developed a great metaphysical system as well as a spirituality for the attainment of wisdom and sagehood, Taoism can be described as a nature-oriented philosophy giving rise to philosophical and political treatises and commentaries, which have been cited as their inspiration by a conglomeration of popular cults including especially that of the search for physical immortality through alchemy and yoga. This conglomeration has been called Taoist religion, in contradistinction to the classical philosophy from which it claimed derivation but with which it also differed in many respects. Indeed, the Taoist religion has been very selective in its inheritance of earlier Taoist teachings, making of personal survival the principal human quest, and basing it on the text *Lao-tzu* while making of the alleged author of this text a deified figure. To the extent that this indicated a serious self-transcending intentionality – giving expression to the very human desire to overcome the finitude of our situation – Taoism offers a deeper dimension, which is usually hidden underneath a surface of longevity cults as well as the worship of an apparent pantheon of deities inhabiting the microcosm of the human body and also the universe, its macrocosm.

Taoist interest in "survival" and the striving after immortality gave impetus to folk medicine as well as certain health cults, and the best known of these, formerly based in the Dragon-Tiger Mountain of Kiangsi, has had a hereditary "celestial master" and an ecclesiastical hierarchy with hereditary priests since the second century C.E. It witnessed various vicissitudes of fortune, and the recent death, without a son, of the last celestial master,

(1984) who had been living in exile in Taiwan, has also threatened the unity of the movement.

But Taoism should not be identified exclusively with the immortality cult, since the Taoist religion also encouraged practices of public prayer and penance, as well as of meditation and mysticism, aimed at the union between human beings and the divine. Although Taoist outer alchemy, or the search for an elixir of immortality through the transmutation of mineral and other substances, is better known to the outside world than Taoist inner alchemy, the latter practice of meditation with the help of the circulation of breath, has given the religion more depth. The goal of such meditation is the production within oneself of an ethereal and immortal body that would outlast the physical one. Its pantheon includes mythical figures, as well as many who were divinized human beings, under the supremacy of the highest, often called the Jade Emperor – or today, in Taiwan, *T'ien-kung* (colloquial for Lord of Heaven). Its explicit beliefs embrace that of a hereafter, whether Heaven(s) or Hell(s), and it spurns a complex ritual system, including a quasi-sacramental regard for rituals of initiation, of purification and renewal in the life-cycle and development of the human person. Its admonitions extend also to the moral life as the best preparation for health on earth and a blissful eternity. Indeed, "Taoist religion" is a pragmatic designation, since in actuality it is almost impossible to separate the Taoist religion from folk Confucianism (in its moral teaching) and folk Buddhism (in its religious beliefs and in some of its rituals).

Historically, there had been a serious encounter between Confucianism and Christianity, especially in the sixteenth and seventeenth centuries, during the time when Jesuit and other missionaries sought to evangelize China – although the consequences were ambiguous. But Western scholars and missionaries had not then taken the Taoist religion seriously, regarding it rather as superstition. More recently, the attitude has changed, especially among scholars, but also among missionaries. The rich history of the development of religious Taoism, its many sects as well as its very complex Taoist canon is now being studied with some care and earnestness. Missionaries working in Taiwan, Hong Kong, and Southeast Asia are increasingly recognizing the hold that the Taoist religion continues to maintain over many people, especially among those for whom the more rationalistic teachings of Confucianism are not adequately satisfying. How should Western scholars regard religious Taoism? With its diffused influence also felt in other parts of East Asia, including Korea and Japan, Taoism deserves more attention.

Buddhism: the Devotional-Mystical Religion

The introduction of Buddhism to China was an event with important consequences for the development of Chinese thought and culture as it was for the evolution of Buddhism itself. By that time (1st century C.E. or earlier), this religion of Indian origin had already undergone several centuries of development both in theory and practice. It acted as a harbinger of civilization in many areas, introducing a written script, as well as inspiring art, literature and philosophy. But China was already home to a vigorous civilization with an ancient canon – the Confucian classics – and time-hallowed traditions. The meeting of the Buddhist religion and Chinese culture became the occasion for conflicts and controversies, which were resolved only when Buddhism adjusted itself to the Chinese environment, taking account of Confucian moral values, such as filial piety, while making use of Taoist ideas and terminology for its own survival and advancement.

The Buddhism that went into China included both Theravada (Shravakayana) and Mahayana sects, although the latter prospered while the former declined. Eventually, many Buddhist texts were translated into Chinese; indeed, Chinese itself became an essential language of the Buddhist religious canon, since translations have survived where the originals are no longer extant. Buddhism turned its attention to problems of cosmological theories as well as of suffering in the universe of sentient beings. It introduced the presupposition of rebirth or transmigration, and the practice of monastic life, into a society where ancestors were venerated and descendants desired. But Chinese realism and pragmatism also influenced Buddhism, affirming this life and this world, including the values of family, longevity and posterity. For a long time, under state patronage, especially from the fourth to the ninth centuries, Buddhism flourished in China, establishing several major schools of thought, and inspiring an entire tradition of art and literature. In the meantime, Buddhist presuppositions also gained increasing acceptance, especially among Taoist circles, winning over many to the beliefs in transmigration and numerous heavens and hells. However, a series of persecutions, especially that of 845 C.E., broke the hold of Buddhism over China, including its landed wealth, and the Buddhism that emerged afterwards was mainly devotional (Pure Land Buddhism) or mystical (*Ch'an* Buddhism, called *Zen* in Japanese) in orientation. Its philosophy would continue to interest a few intellectuals, while its "savior figures," especially in their Chinese forms, including the female Kuan-yin (Sanskrit: Avalokitesvara) and the "Happy Buddha," Mi-lo (Sanskrit: Maitreya), kept their places in the hearts of the devout masses. The major historical question concerning Buddhism in China is: Has it been the "Buddhist conquest of China," or the "Chinese conquest of Buddhism"? The historical as well as missiological question that would interest Christians is: Would the course of Christianity have been different had it allowed more cultural adaptation, and to what extent could it have been possible, given *its* dogmatic presuppositions?

Syncretism and Harmony

And so, China has been the land of at least three religious traditions, of which two have been native and the third foreign in inspiration. It is perhaps to be expected that the ruling dynasties of native origins tended to favor Confucianism, whereas those of alien or mixed backgrounds offered more protection to Buddhism and Taoism – these latter two finding themselves more compatible with each other, and in a position of protest *vis-à-vis* Confucianism. It has also been observed that Taoism and Buddhism offered more escape and consolation during the times of disunity, such as between the third and sixth centuries, whereas Confucianism contributed more directly to social and political cohesion during the times of national unity. The three religions actually complemented one another, since they attended to different areas of human concern. Especially during and after the Ming dynasty, they tended to converge in a syncretistic movement until today; Confucius, Lao-tzu and the Buddha have sometimes even been joined in veneration and worship by its adherents.

Certainly, there had been rivalry, even acrimony, among these three traditions, and yet it appeared that they were eventually able to coexist and complement one another. We see here a spirit of harmony and reconciliation which is perhaps most characteristic of traditional Chinese culture – a harmony of parts within a whole, in which each religion serves a socially useful function. In Confucianism, such harmony has been directed to human social relationships; in Taoist philosophy, it has been turned to humanity's relationship with the rest of nature. Taoist religion presents a contradiction since the desire for physical immortality prompted proto-scientific experiments which were consciously undertaken *against* the spirit of harmony and in the name of *wresting* from nature itself, the secrets of life and longevity. On the other hand, Buddhism offered an entirely new outlook on life and the world, only to become itself conditioned by the pervading Chinese culture. It filled a certain spiritual vacuum, by addressing itself to questions largely ignored by both Confucianism and Taoism. Even outside of any particular syncretistic cult, many Chinese have found it possible to follow all three teachings at the same time. For example, a man could be a Confucian in his active life, responding to multiple social responsibilities, a *philosophical* Taoist in his leisure hours, reading poetry and enjoying nature and wine, while also practising some health regimen associated with *religious* Taoism, and both he and his wife – or at least, she – would frequent the Buddhist temple to offer prayers for special intentions. The coexistence of all three religious traditions, and the possibility for the same persons to be involved in all of them, testifies to a certain pluralism within the Chinese – and the East Asian – civilization, a pluralism that was not known by Europe and the Middle East.

But – is there one Chinese religion, or are there three? The question may seem strange after the above descriptions of the Three Religions, and yet, it is useful on account of the *shared* heritage called Chinese culture, which is inseparable from the religion(s). This inseparability has led formerly to a denial, on the part of some, that there is anything religious in Chinese culture. It also accounts for much that is common between the religions themselves. Here I am speaking especially of the religions of Chinese origin, Confucianism and Taoism. To the extent that both of these are derived from an ancient religious heritage, and continue to share beliefs, rituals and values, especially on the popular level, it is possible to speak of Chinese religion as singular, with manifestations in the plural. Such a description of Chinese religion, however, does not include Buddhism, even if Buddhist influences have penetrated "folk religion." For this reason, and for others, it is useful to continue to regard Buddhism as a religion of foreign origin.

Conclusion: the Modern Dilemma

The happy harmony of traditional Chinese society existed of course more as an ideal than as fact. Among other factors, the three major teachings were never the *only* religions in China. The country has also known Islam and Christianity, although the adherents of these *Western* religions have always been a minority in the population, and Muslims have usually come from specific ethnic groups, refraining from making converts from the majority. In any case, China faced the onslaught of Western intrusions, both political and cultural, especially from the late nineteenth century onward. This was the age of imperialism, when Asian and African nations were confronted by Western European – and also North American – ambitions of domination, supported by modern science and superior military technology. This has been a most severe test for Chinese culture and society, and the occasion for a long period of self-doubt and self-criticism, which has not yet ended. The dilemma has been how to modernize, without losing a cultural identity and a rich heritage. In the ensuing struggle, a particular Western ideology, that of Marxism, emerged victorious, and would combat both traditional religious values, considered as outmoded and a feudal force, which were keeping the country backward, as well as the more recently introduced Christian religion, considered as an ally of Western political and cultural imperialism. Under the Communist government of Mao Tse-tung, the Cultural Revolution (1967-1977) unleashed the primitive forces of cultural and religious iconoclasm, destroying temples and statues and persecuting all and any associated with religion. China appeared once more as it was in the early third century B.C., unified, but culturally devastated.

Marxism showed a certain Western doctrinal intransigence and even militant aggressiveness that had not been found to the same extent in China's traditional religions. In a sense, it is the tradition that distinguishes *most* between insiders (party members, especially those in high positions) and outsiders (the rest of the population). But the Cultural Revolution proved to be too extremist for most people, including most Communists. The death of Mao (1976) was followed by the fall of the "Gang of Four" and the implementation of a radically new policy with growing openness to the West as well as an increasing readiness to permit a critical inheritance of traditional heritage, and a tolerance for Western religions. Under these circumstances, the future remains an open question for religion, or religions, in China. This is at least an "outsider's" view of things. The military crackdown on the student demonstrators (June 4, 1989) has been too recent for us to reevaluate the religious landscape, and we can only hope that things will not change for the worse.

THE ATTITUDE OF YORUBA RELIGION TOWARD NON-YORUBA RELIGION

by

'Wande Abimbola

The purpose of this paper is to examine the attitudes of the Yoruba religion towards other faiths and other poles. But first, I propose to review the nature and scope of the Yoruba religious heritage and its socio-religious values in order to bring out what is relevant to our defined goals and objectives.

The Nature of Yoruba Religion: An Overview

The Yoruba profess some belief in a supreme deity. This deity is never a direct object of worship. Rather the supreme being is approached through a plethora of intermediaries or lesser deities who are objects of cult. There is the metaphor that the Yoruba pantheon is inhabited by four hundred and one divinities. They are the immediate surveyors of both good and evil. The moral values with which they regulate the relationship among human beings also apply to them.

One can say that the Yoruba traditional religion contains both monotheistic and polytheistic elements. This does not create any conflict whatsoever in the minds of the people. For example, the Yoruba can easily explain this system in terms of their socio-political structure. Just as the *Oba* (king), the divine-human ruler and head of the kingdom, cannot be approached directly by his subjects but through the council of Chiefs, so *Clodumare*, the Supreme God, is approached in prayer and sacrifice only through the *Orisa* deities.

The Supreme Being, the lesser deities, the ancestors, and a host of spirits present the Yoruba people with a sense of powerlessness in the face of the reality of these sacred beings. As a consequence, life and human power are seen as temporal and a constant proximity of death is always felt. Death of course, as far as African belief is concerned, is not the end of human life.

The Yoruba experience of the world is one in which the sacred and the secular are symmetrical. The ordinary human experience is mimetic of the supernatural world. In this primal culture, the whole of the human experience is grounded on cosmological myths which operate in sacred time and space. In most cases these myths describe how the world was created and how the patterns of human action became established. These narratives about divine beings, their actions and their intervention in the world of humans are experienced as real and not just fanciful tales.

Furthermore, in the cosmogonic myths there are stories about the making of primordial objects, about the first humans and the culture's heroes. The consequence of the cosmogonic myth is that the whole of reality is infused with a hallow of the sacred, one significant aspect of which is the reciprocal relationship which exists between the primal Africans and nature.

From these beliefs and ritual practices have arisen Yoruba religious attitude to non-Yoruba beliefs and peoples. Next, I shall attempt to provide a descriptive analysis of these attitudes and also discuss their implications for our theme on "Religious Education for Dialogue and Peace."

Yoruba Religious Worldview and
Culture and Other Peoples

I wish to begin with the metaphor that the Yoruba pantheon is inhabited by four-hundred-and-one divinities. The notion of the one odd divinity over the four hundred which inhabit the Yoruba pantheon represents the everpresent possibility of accretion by one in the population of the divinities.

This explains why, for example, the *Orisa* of a vanquished people may be acquired even where their institutions are either untouched or destroyed. This certainly cannot be considered unreasonable if divinities are in fact custodians of the values which order these institutions in the first place, particularly where the latter may be unwieldy in any way, even where they may not be physically threatening.

Another related aspect of the Yoruba pantheon to ponder is the local adaptability of the *Orisa*. For example, both *Ogun*, the divinity of iron, and therefore of all forms of manufacture, and *Obatala*, the archdivinity and the creator *de facto* of all beings, manifest themselves in as many forms and acquire as many attributes as there are communities which recognize them. And no contradiction in form or practice is ever encountered. The same applies to all other *Orisa* in the Yoruba pantheon.

Indeed, evidence exists in the Yoruba oral tradition which points to the fact that Islam and Christianity, although they came to this land at different times, when each came, its central figure was welcomed just as if it was another new arrival into the Yoruba pantheon. The exclusivity sometimes ascribed to either Islam or Christianity in certain quarters constituted very hard lessons for most of their Yoruba adherents to learn to this day. Nor is this unconnected with the ambivalence and consequent loss of orientation often observable among adherents of certain non-autochthonous religions in Nigeria. This contrasts sharply with the serenity observed among practitioners of the *Orisa* tradition even among the Yoruba of the diaspora. The lesson here is that only a belief system which predisposes us not just to accommodate other systems but to grow qualitatively by profiting from the experience of other systems is suitable for the modern world with a proliferation of religious traditions whose myriads of sects is emblematic of resistance to local adaptability.

Also, from the Yoruba creation myth emerges two central themes – interpersonal relationship and the unity of creation. It is believed that the creator deity (*Obatala*) is responsible for molding human beings: black, whites, albinos, hunchbacks and the Yoruba people themselves. The disabled and invalids created by this deity are regarded as *eni Orisa* (the rotaries of the deity), for they are accorded a place of honor in the *Obatala* household. This is partly the Yoruba explanation for evil and suffering in the world, and the reason why the less privileged ones in and outside the Yoruba communities, especially the invalids and those born with defects, are never laughed at, but rather accorded respect and dignity as they are believed to be sacred.

Ile-Ife, the place of creation and the city of the gods, is regarded as the center of the world. It is from here that the entire human race took its origin. Indeed, in contemporary time, over-enthusiastic oral narrators, in an attempt to prove this point of the unity of creation, have substituted biblical names for such significant landmarks in Ile-Ife such as *Edena* (which is now being corrupted with garden of Eden) – an attempt to show that the biblical creation myth took place here in Ile-Ife. The practical aspect of this is that the Yoruba regard all human beings as kin. Most prayers and invocations offered in Ile-Ife are deemed incomplete until prayers are offered to the people of the entire universe (*agbala aye gbogbo*), who are regarded as having had their origin in Ile-Ife.

Such kinship relationship is equally established with things in nature: animals, plants, water and all natural phenomena. They are all regarded as living beings created along with men and women. The feeling generated by this common bond results in a degree of solidarity and strong feelings of ethnic identities, loyalties and community. This is equally extended to people, places and objects through an ideology of common descent.

There are examples in Yoruba mythology where a stranger is honored and given valuable things even as soon as he enters the town. In one such occasion in *Odi Meji*, the fourth chapter of Ifa, a stranger who had just entered the town when the wealth of a dead king of Benin was being shared was given a part of the properties of the dead king. The verse is presented below:

> *Mo deere.*
> *Mo rin 're.*
> *Emi nikan ni mo morin arinkoo rin.*
> *A sese n kohun oroo 'le*
> *Ni mo wole de were*
> *Bi omo olohun.*
> *Emi e e somo olohun,*
> *Irin arinko ni mo moo rin.*

A difa fun ajogi godogbo
Ti o wole were
Nijo ti won a binro obaa 'Bini.
Ajogi godogbon sawoo rodee Bini,
Lo ba meeji keeta,
O looko alawo.
Won ni ajo o o dara fun un,
Sugbon ko rubo.
Igba to rubo tan,
Lo ba kori sona ibini.
Wiwo to wo 'Bini,
O sakoko iku obaa won.
O ni nje o ye ki oun agba awo.
O mo lo ki won bayii?
Bi won se n pinro Oba Ado
Ni ajogi wole de.
Bee ni bi won ba si pin in tan,
Apa kan re,
Ajogi ni won ko o o fun.
Ni awon ara ode ibini
Ba ko apa kan ohun oro naa fun ajogi godogbo.
Riro ti tajogi ro gbogbo nnkan oro naa nle,
Ilee re lo kori si.
O waa n yin awon awoo re,
Awon awoo reinyin 'Fa...
Won ni, "Ta hi o waa ba ni tunle yi se?
Ajogi godogboo,
N ni o waa ba ni tunle yi se."[1]

I return well,
I travel well,
Only I know how to travel with good luck.
Just as they were putting down valuable materials,
I entered unannounced
Like the son of the owner.
I am not the son of the owner,
O only know how to travel with good luck.
Ifa divination was performed for the Important Stranger
Who would enter unannounced
On the day they were sharing the wealth of the king of Benin.
When the Important Stranger was going to Benin to practise as
an Ifa priest,
He added two cowry shells to three,
And went to his diviners.
They predicted that his journey would be good,
But they warned him to perform sacrifice.
After he had performed sacrifice,
He went to the city of Benin.
As soon as he entered Benin,

---

1.   A poem from Odi Meji.

It happened that the king died.
He then wondered whether as an elderly Ifa priest,
It would not be necessary for him to go and console the king's
  relations.
It was at the moment when they were sharing the wealth of the
  king
That the Important Stranger came in.
And, according to tradition, as soon as they finished dividing
  the properties of the king,
One part of it
Should be given to a stranger.
So, the people of Benin
Gave one part of the properties to the Important Stranger.
As soon as the stranger gathered all the valuable properties,
He went straight to his own home.
He started to sing in praise of his diviners.
His diviners sang in praise of Ifa...
They said, "Who is going to help us to develop this land.
It is the Important Stranger,
Who will help us to develop this land."

Traditional Yoruba Pedagogy and the
Value of Peaceful Co-existence

In the traditional Yoruba educational system, myths, proverbs, stories and folktales play significant roles in the upbringing of the youth. In the olden days, it was customary for the head of an extended family to gather the household on the veranda under moonlight to tell stories, give proverbs and riddles dealing with various aspects of Yoruba social and cultural life. From these folktales, significant didactic lessons were derived, aimed at the proper socialization of the children and youth. A sizeable number of these deal with the value of good conduct, peaceful coexistence with one's neighbor, moral uprightness, the work ethic, and most significantly, good character. The Yoruba believe that a significant aspect of humanity's place in the world is that each individual has the responsibility to strive to have good character. This principle is known as *iwapele* in Yoruba thought. It is assumed that the person who has *iwapele* will not collide with any of the evil powers, either human or supernatural, which dominate the universe. This allows the individual to live in complete harmony with the forces which govern the universe. This is why the Yoruba people regard good character as the most important of all the principles of ethics, and the greatest attribute of any person. The essence of religious worship for the Yoruba consists therefore in striving to cultivate good character.

The rejection of brute force in communal living is also very important in the traditional Yoruba pedagogy. In one entertaining moral myth, contained in an Ifa divination text, is to be found the story of a forceful character known as *Kankan* (By-force) who employed all his neighbors in a collective manual labor known by the Yoruba as *owe*. He placed each person next to his enemy as follows: Grasshopper, Hen, Wolf, Dog, Hyena, Hunter, Baboon-Viper, Walking-Stick, Fire, Rain, Drought and Dew-Drops.

Since Mr. By-force did not give his friends anything to eat, at a certain stage during their manual activity, they became hungry and started to devour one another. When Dew-Drops, who was a common denominator to all of them, invoked the traditional rites of their forebears, they all revived and entered into a covenant to live in peace even in a situation in which one person was the arch-enemy of the other. They then started to sing:

> *Ogbedi kakaaka,*
> *Ogbedi kunkunkun.*
> *Ki ganmuganmu re*
> *Ko mo baa se han,*
> *Ko mo baa se ta jade.*
> *A difa fun Kankan,*
> *Yoo be Tata lowe.*
> *Yoo bagbebo adie lowe.*
> *Yoo be kolokolo.*
> *Yoo baja.*
> *Yoo bekooko.*
> *Yoo Bode.*
> *Yoo boka.*
> *Yoo bopa.*
> *Yoo bena.*
> *Yoo bojo.*
> *Yoo boda.*
> *Yoo beriwowo kanyiin won.*
> *Kankan lo waa baye je lonii o,*
> *Iriwowo waa tun se.*
> *Won n se, "Iriwowo*
> *Waa tun se o o.*
> *Iriwowo waa tun se.*
> *Kankan lo baye je lonii o...*
> *Irowowo waa tun se o."*[2]

---

2.   See 'Wande Abimbola, *Sixteen Great Poems of Ifa*.

Ogbedi the rugged person,
Ogbedi the strong man,
Tie it very well so that its edges
May not be visible,
So that it may not appear outside.
Ifa divination was performed for By-force
Who employed a Grasshopper in a collective work.
He employed a Hen.
He employed a Wolf.
He employed a Dog.
He employed a Hyena.
He employed a Hunter.
He employed a Baboon Viper.
He employed a Walking Stick.
He employed Fire.
He employed Rain.
He employed Drought.
And he employed Dew-drops last of them all.
Doing things by force has ruined the world of today.
Dew-drops, come and make repairs.
They were saying, "Dew-drops,
Come and make repairs.
Dew-drops come and make repairs.
Doing things by force
Has spoilt the world of today...
Dew-drops, come and make repairs."

Yoruba's Reaction to the Scriptural
Religions of Outsiders

The stories of Yoruba conversion to Islam and Christianity are numerous and scholars have carried out several studies of how and why many Yoruba people have given up their traditional religion. Several of these stores unfortunately present traditional religion as weak, crumbling in the face of a more powerful and superior religious world-view brought by Muslim Arabs and European Christians. This is far from the truth. As I remarked earlier in this paper, the Yoruba people often welcomed the newcomers, seeing them as additions to their already numerous pantheon of deities.

Yoruba attitudes toward Islam and Christianity also vary according to the initial attitudes and response of the two monotheistic traditions. It has been suggested that at this period, Islam was more tolerant of traditional religions than Christianity. Whereas Christianity insisted on a radical change from the old tradition to the new, the former did not insist on complete conversion to the tenets and practices of Islam, but rather viewed conversion as a gradual process from initial declaration of the *Shahada* (the profession of faith) to more detailed institutions in the Arabic language and moral law (*Shar'ia*). As a result of this, Yoruba religion began to cast aspersions on Christianity as evidenced in the following Ifa verses:

> *Aye la ba Ifa.*
> *Aye la ba Imole.*
> *Osan gangan ni Igbagbo wole de.*[3]

> We met Ifa on earth.
> We met Islam on earth.
> It was all of a sudden that Christianity emerged.

The insistence by Christianity that the Yoruba should destroy all the paraphernalia of traditional beliefs, should openly denounce their old faith and abrogate their ancient customs often led to a confrontation between the Christians and traditional believers. In reaction to this, Yoruba religionists argued that their beliefs constitute customs and traditions which can be practiced alongside the new religions.

Kingship Ideology and Religious-Civil Ceremonies

A central aspect of our inquiry is to investigate ways and means by which the Yoruba people and their religion have intellectually reacted to foreigners. As I observed in the last section of the paper, the two missionary religions, Islam and Christianity, constitute two major foreign influences which the Yoruba people and religion have faced and reacted to. The impression should not be given that Yoruba religion was intolerant of these religions. Rather, it reacted to them in a more accommodating fashion. As observed by a Yoruba scholar of religion, Jacob K. Olupona, at the level of cognition, Yoruba religion's reaction to the newcomers is evidenced in the kingship ideology rituals and ceremonies today. He observed that as the new religious traditions became rooted in Yorubaland and as they began to render implausible the plausibility structure of the old faith, the kingship ideology and rituals, which was pivotal to traditional religious beliefs and practices, became a new focus of pluralism and peaceful coexistence among

---

3.   A popular song of Ifa priests.

rival faiths. The *Oba* (sacred king), traditionally regarded as the custodian of his people's traditions and customs, also became the focus of attention demanding absolute support and obedience from the citizens and the foreign belief systems. In return the kingship system guarantees freedom of worship, peaceful coexistence among rival faiths. Through constant mediation and participation in their practices, the *Oba* became the source of tolerance and a new civil religion. The king's festivals and ceremonies are occasions when the new religious pluralism, tolerance and peaceful relations among the several religions in Yoruba communities are openly acknowledged and demonstrated.[4]

Yoruba Religion in the Americas

Yoruba peoples of the Americas grafted Christianity onto the fundamental elements of their traditional beliefs. Saints were assimilated *Orisa* on the basis of iconographic similarities, possession and other ecstatic manifestations with themes of Catholic mysticism, Protestant Pentecostalism and Yoruba traditional religion. In the New World situation, where the most extreme methods to eliminate African traditional religions were brought to bear, the tradition survived by assimilation. In their attitudes towards the religions of their oppressors the Yoruba found the sacred manifest, though turned to bitter service. This seems to indicate something of the genius of the Yoruba: the ability to see into the heart of various religions and find therein an authentic sacrality. An authentic experience of the sacred at the heart of other religions reduces questions of ritual and credal forms to the level of secondary importance by relativising them. The claims on the part of Christianity and Islam to exclusivity become questions of the second order, and therefore this should not, from the Yoruba perspective, obscure the truth of the first order: that the sacred has manifested itself to men and women of all cultures. The survival and continuous growth of Yoruba traditions, especially today, are a witness to the open-endedness and welcoming attitude of Yoruba traditional religion.

---

4.   Jacob K. Olupona, "Some Notes on the Religion of the Ondo-People in Nigeria: A Phenomenological Anthropological Study," *Bulletin of the International Committee on Urgent Anthropological and Ethnological Research*, No. 27 (1985): 47-58.

Conclusion

It remains for me to draw some general and wider implications from the foregoing on the Yoruba and African attitudes toward other faiths, peoples and traditions and indicate its relevance to the present attitude of intolerance prevalent in our contemporary society.

In the African primal traditions there is a continuing witness against violence, brute force and intolerance of each others' beliefs. The African point of view is one in which there is respect for all the religious traditions of humankind. While we hold steadfastly to our own beliefs, we respect the right of others to practice their own religions in their own ways, provided they do not infringe on the right of other people.

Furthermore, we believe that religious freedom is a condition precedent to world peace and individual freedom. We believe that we all can live together in peace if we are prepared to respect one another's point of view.

Our traditional belief system still remains the harbinger of the deepest truths that have become available to our society. A successful development in this particular area, i.e., a strong attention to these classical and spiritual resources contained in our primal traditions, will do much to redress the situation of paralysis and anomie in our societal life and guide us unto the right path. The famous historian, Arnold J. Toynbee, once observed that, "In the debate of religion in the next century, only the faith will endure which does not divide mankind on the basis of color, caste, dogma, creed, sex, status or nationality, but offers a quality of life which without distinction could be obtained and shared by anyone, equally, all over."[5] To my mind, African traditional religions present these solid spiritual and humane resources for an enduring faith which Toynbee was talking about.

---

5.   Cited from 'Wande Abimbola – An Address by the Vice-Chancellor of the University of Ife delivered at the Sixteenth Convocation Ceremony, 14 December, 1985, p. 16.

THE RELIGIONS OF OTHERS IN ISKCON'S EYES

by

William H. Deadwyler

(Ravindra Svarupa dasa)

Let me begin with a little recent history.

In the fall of 1965, a small and fragile-looking Bengali monk, the saffron robes of a *sannyasi* wound about him, disembarked from a nondescript Indian freighter out of Calcutta onto the wharves of Manhattan. He was quite alone; he had observed his seventieth birthday at sea; and his assets, beyond a parcel of personal items, consisted of the cash equivalent of seven dollars U.S. and a trunk packed with crudely printed volumes of the first canto of *Srimad-Bhagavatam*, the Sanskrit devotional classic he had begun translating into English and publishing at his own expense during the ten years preceding this improbable journey.

Abhay Charanaravinda Bhaktivedanta Swami, later known to his followers as Srila Prabhupada, found himself – providentially, they say – at the right place and the right time. Celebrated as the "downtown" Swami of the Lower East Side in the *annus mirabilis* of 1966, he swiftly attracted admirers and then followers largely from the counterculture's explorers of the outer limits. He accommodated as little as possible to the consuetudes of modern

America.[1] It is a measure of the cultural distance his disciples had to travel that they had to drop out not once but twice: from "straight" society into the counterculture, from the counterculture into the organization proleptic named the International Society for Krishna Consciousness (ISKCON).

But "reversal is the movement of the Tao." In going farther out, Prabhupada's followers found themselves coming back in: They shaved their heads close, rose daily before dawn to chant and pray, abstained from the flesh of animals, gave up the use of licit and illicit drugs, and even in wedlock avoided sex. Having gone farther out than the far-out, they became straighter than the straight.

In time Prabhupada's students began to grasp that they had joined a formidable religious establishment in its own right, that Prabhupada was grooming them painstakingly to become heirs to an ancient and venerable spiritual tradition, and scrupulous fidelity to its teachings and practices was of central importance to Prabhupada. He himself was simply a conduit; he claimed to act as nothing more than the servant of his guru, Bhaktisiddhanta Sarasvati Thakura, who had in turn been the servant of his guru, Gaura Kisora dasa Babaji, who similarly had served Bhaktivinoda Thakura, and so on. In the front matter to *Bhagavad-gita As It Is* Prabhupada listed a historical succession of spiritual teachers, going back to Krishna Himself.[2] This list was Prabhupada's credentials, the source of his teaching authority.

Thus, even though the International Society for Krishna Consciousness emerged as a radical novelty and still finds itself in the

---

1.   The "Uptown Swami" was Swami Niilananda, head of the New York Ramkrishna Mission, which could be regarded as the Hindu missionary establishment. Swami Nikilananda, whose followers were mostly "straight" middle or upper-middle class Americans, had counseled Prabhupada to follow his lead and adopt Western manners in dress and eating, advice Prabhupada rejected. For a history of beginnings of ISKCON see Satsvarupa dasa Goswami, *Planting the Seed: New York City 1965-66* and *Only He Could Lead Them: San Francisco/India 1967*, the second and third volumes of ISKCON's official six-volume biography of Srila Prabhupada, *Srila Prabhupada-lilamrta* (Los Angeles: The Bhaktivedanta Book Trust, 1980-1983).

2.   Complete edition (Los Angeles: The Bhaktivedanta Book Trust, 1985), p. 34. The list of succession from Krishna to Caitanya is taken from the seventeenth-century Gaudiya Vaisnava theologian Baladeva Vidyabhusana. See Surendranath Dasgupta, *A History of Indian Philosophy*, Vol. 4 (Delhi: Motilal Banarsidass, 1975), pp. 447-448.

situation of a "new religious movement," it is actually a contemporary extension of a branch of one of the four long-established Vaisnava traditions of India, a branch bearing the formal title of *Brahma-Madhva-Gaudiva sampradaya*. This tradition or community (*sampradaya*) traced itself back in historic times to the great Vaisnava theologian and religious leader Madhva (1238-1317), then more recently through Caitanya Mahaprabhu (1486-1533), who reformed and revitalized the tradition in Bengal (hence *Gaudiva*, from *Gaudi-desa*, an old name for Bengal).[3]

The historical tendency of Vaisnavism has been the increasing enfranchisement of spiritually disenfranchised people. The traditional teachings of "Hinduism" hold that only men born into priestly (*brahmana*) or occasionally royal (*ksatriya*) families can directly attain liberation. But the Vaisnava traditions teach that the Lord responds to sincere *bhakti*, devotional service, with a grace that destroys all the impediments produced by bad *karma*. Thus Krishna says in *Bhagavad-gita* that by taking shelter of him, women, merchants, and laborers – all traditionally considered ineligible for liberation – can attain the "supreme destination" (9.32).

Srimad-Bhagavatam goes even further, saying that devotional service will elevate even dog-eaters – that is, untouchables – to the highest position in Aryan culture and render them qualified to perform Vedic sacrifices (3.33.6-7). (These verses were spoken by Devahuti, who, like Queen Kunti, is one of the great women devotees in the *Bhagavatam* whose words are scripture.) Another *Bhagavatam* verse (2.4.18) names various untouchable communities-Europeans, Turks, Arabs, Chinese, and some assorted tribal peoples-and says that these and those even more sinful can be saved by "taking shelter of one who has taken shelter of the Lord."

Putting these texts into practice, Caitanya Mahaprabhu shocked the rigid and exclusive Hindu society of his time; he propagated devotional

---

[3]. For academic surveys of the history and thought of Gaudiya Vaisnavism see: S. K. De, *Early History of the Vaisnava Faith and Movement in Bengal*, 2nd ed. (Calcutta: K. L. Mukhopadhyay, 1961); A. K. Majumdar, *Caitanya His Life and Doctrine* (Chowpatty and Bombay: Bharatiya Vidya Bhavan, 1969); O. B. L. Kapoor, *The Philosophy and Religion of Sri Caitanya* (New Delhi: Munshiram Manoharlal, 1977); and Surendranatha Dasgupta, *A History of Indian Philosophy*, Vol. 4, chapters 32 and 33.

service everywhere, indiscriminately, and he offered both respect and high positions of leadership to followers like Thakura Haridasa, a Muslim by birth, and Rupa and Sanatana Goswami, *brahmanas* who had lost caste by serving in the Muslim government of Bengal. When Srila Prabhupada later came to America and put the sacred thread of a *brahamana* over the shoulders of foreigners, he simply implemented something already part of the tradition; he was on firm scriptural grounds, and he eventually succeeded in getting his actions accepted back home.[4]

In spite of the cultural boundaries he had to cross, Prabhupada endeavored greatly to maintain the integrity and continuity of the tradition. Thomas Hopkins, an authority on Vaisnavism who happened to encounter ISKCON in its very first days, found the eventual completeness of Prabhupada's transmission remarkable – although Hopkins understands Prabhupada's achievement in quite different categories from those who actually accepted what Prabhupada brought. Hopkins says:

> What became evident was that Bhaktivedanta Swami did, in fact, have a plan which he was gradually implementing – a plan that involved bringing more and more of the authentic tradition over from India and putting it in place in the American, or Western, movement. He made his students more and more familiar with the philosophy. This I was expecting. What I did not expect, and what really surprised and pleased me, was the degree to which the ritual tradition was also brought over and put into place. That's something that no other movement has succeeded in doing, nor even really tried to do: transplanting a traditional Hindu ritual structure into a Hindu religious movement in America.[5]

With all the exotic trappings of "a traditional Hindu ritual structure" thus in place, ISKCON appears to many to be heavily freighted with culturally conditioned forms and hence to exemplify sectarianism with a vengeance. It stands in contrast to *advaita-vedanta*, that earlier Indian export, whose philosophical abstractions and nondevotional orientation make

---

4. For an anthropological study of the way ISKCON devotees have come to be accepted in India as legitimate *brahmanas* and Vaisnavas, see Charles R. Brooks, *The Hare Krishna In India* (Princeton: Princeton University Press, 1989).

5. In Steven J. Gelberg, ed., *Hare Krishna, Hare Krishna: Five Distinguished Scholars on the Krishna Movement in the West* (New York: Grove Press, 1982), p. 107.

it appear universal, nonsectarian, and free from adventitious cultural and historical accretions.

Yet even after Prabhupada had everything in place, the Western youth who joined ISKCON never thought of themselves as "converting" to something called "Hinduism" or as participating in "a traditional Hindu ritual structure." The majority of them, I would say, had explored Eastern mysticism and had some familiarity with and even commitment to the ideas of *advaita-vedanta*, yet they did not think that in adopting ISKCON's practices they were plunging into the historically conditioned forms of a particular religious sect. Indeed, they usually did not think of themselves as practicing something called "a religion" at all.

Prabhupada managed quite compellingly to convey an altogether different vision. He did not function on a platform in which he saw himself as practicing some particular "religion" over against other "religions." His outlook was different, which was hard for some people – reporters, perhaps, most of all – to grasp.

I witnessed a revealing interchange in the early seventies. Prabhupada had finished an arrival press conference at Kennedy airport and, trailed by an entourage of disciples, was heading down a long concourse toward the exit, when a tardy television reporter came running up frantically, a huffing cameraman in tow. Thrusting a microphone in Prabhupada's face, the reporter gasped out: "How does your group differ from other Buddhists?" Looking the reporter in the eye, Prabhupada said, "We have nothing to do with this Hinduism or Buddhism. We are teaching the truth, and if you are truthful, you will accept it."

Flustered and bewildered, the reporter tried to get his question across to Prabhupada, but in vain. He did not know he had encountered the famous elusiveness of spiritual teachers. As Northrop Frye has pointed out, such teachers have their reasons for refusing to answer questions: "To answer a question...is to consolidate the mental level on which the question is asked."[6]

Prabhupada did not operate on the mental level in which the word "religion" refers to a collection of particular historical faiths – Hinduism,

---

6.   *The Great Code* (San Diego: Harcourt Brace Jovanovich, 1981, 1982), p. xv.

Buddhism, Christianity, Islam, etc. These denominations were of no relevance. To Prabhupada, "religion" was *dharma*, not some faith. He explained often that the root meaning of *dharma* is "that which sustains one's existence."[7] *Dharma* thus denotes the essential nature of something. The *dharma* of sugar is to be sweet, of fire to be hot. And, Prabhupada taught, it is the *dharma*, the essential nature, of each living entity, each soul, to render service to the Supreme Soul. It is our innate and natural activity. Thus, religion in the sense of *dharma* cannot denote a particular faith, which begins and ends in time, and which one can adopt or abandon at will.

Dharma has a further important implication: Religion cannot denote some specialized activity partitioned off from one's life; it cannot rightly mean, in fact, precisely what it has come to mean only in modern times, as Wilfred Cantwell Smith has so well shown: an addendum to human life, an extra appended to our ordinary activities.[8] *Dharma* allows no separation between our religion and our life.

This pre-modern concept of religion gives ISKCON that all-absorbing and self-contained character that disturbs so many. ISKCON has no place among the religions of modernity that orbit the huge planetary mass of Western secular culture like so many satellites. Rather, ISKCON is a complete alternative culture, a spiritual culture aimed at the total sacralization of human life, without remainder.

According to Gaudiya Vaisnava teachings, that complete realization of *dharma* is attained only in pure *bhakti*, pure devotional service to the Lord. A central text for our discussion here occurs early on in *Srimad-Bhagavatam*. A group of sages, gathered in the holy place of Naimisaranya to perform sacrifices, placed a number of questions before the great authority Suta Gosvami. Among them was this (1.1.11):

---

7.   *Srimad-Bhagavatam* (Los Angeles: The Bhaktivedanta Book Trust, 1972-1980), 1.1.6, purport. *Dharma* is derived from the Sanskrit verbal root *dhr*, which means to support or sustain.

8.   See *The Meaning and End of Religion: A New Approach to The Religions Traditions of Mankind* (New York: The Macmillan Company, 1962, 1963); and "The Modern West in the History of Religion," in the *Journal of the American Academy of Religion*, vol. 52, no. 1 (March, 1984), pp. 3-18.

There are many varieties of scriptures, and in all of them there are many prescribed duties, which can be learned only after many years of study in their various divisions. Therefore, O sage, please select the essence of all these scriptures and explain it for the good of all living beings, that by such instructions their hearts may be fully satisfied.[9]

Suta Gosvami answers (1.2.6):

The supreme occupation (*dharma*) for all humanity is that by which men can attain to loving devotional service unto the transcendent Lord. Such devotional service must be unmotivated and uninterrupted to completely satisfy the self.

The *para dharma*, the supreme religion or occupation, which is the essential instruction of all scripture, is defined as *bhakti*, loving devotional service to the Lord. It is intended for all humanity without restriction. Further, the specific standard of that *bhakti* is delineated: it must be unmotivated, that is, performed without any consideration of material or even spiritual return, and it must be uninterrupted, that is, every activity of life must be done so as to be service to God.

The criterion for accepting or rejecting any particular historical faith, then, is simply how much it inculcates pure *bhakti*. *Bhakti* is the original, natural, and innate activity of the soul, and to be engaged in uncovering that activity is not a matter of allegiance to this or that faith but of rediscovering one's true self.

God ceaselessly acts throughout the creation to help conditioned souls recover their real selves; out of that divine activity, historical religions are created and rectified over and over again. God descends repeatedly, *Bhagavad-gita* says (4.7-8), in age after age, whenever *dharma* goes into decline and ungodly people prevail. In each case his mission is to re-establish *dharma*, to protect the godly, and to disclose to the world something of himself. In commenting on 4.7, Prabhupada writes:

---

9.   All translations in my text from *Srimad-Bhagavatam* are Srila Prabhupada's (The Bhaktivedanta Book Trust edition). Known also as the *Bhagavata Purana*, *Srimad-Bhagavatam* is held in especial esteem by all Vaisnava *sampradayas*. The *Bhagavad-gita* is said to be propaedeutic to *Srimad-Bhagavatam*. The text gives prominence to Krishna; its famous tenth canto offers the most complete narration of his pastimes, and it declares in a verse Gaudiya Vaisnava regard of prime importance (1.3.28) that while all other *avataras* are expansions or expansions of expansions of the Lord, Krishna himself is *bhagavan svayam*, the original Supreme Personality of Godhead.

Each and every *avatara*, or incarnation of the Lord, has a particular mission, and they are all described in the revealed scriptures. No one should be accepted as an *avatara* unless he is referred to by scriptures. It is not a fact that the Lord appears only on Indian soil. He can manifest Himself anywhere and everywhere, and whenever He desires to appear. In each and every incarnation, He speaks as much about religion as can be understood by the particular people under their particular circumstances. But His mission is the same – to lead people to God consciousness and obedience to the principles of religion. Sometimes He descends personally, and sometimes He sends His bona fide representative in the form of His son, or servant, or Himself in some disguised form.[10]

A little further on (4.11), Krishna adds: "As all surrender unto Me, I reward [*bhajami*] them accordingly. Everyone follows My path in all respects."

This statement grants no particular tradition exclusive franchise on truth: "Everyone follows My path in all respects." But neither does it indiscriminately endorse any and all forms of religiosity; instead it offers a principle by which one can discriminate among (or without) them: "As all surrender unto Me, I reward them according."

The word *bhajami*, translated here as "I reward", has many implications. It is formed from the verbal root *bhaj*, meaning to distribute or share. *Bhakti* is formed from the same root, and *bhajami* also means to serve in love, or to worship. Here Krishna has stated a principle of equitable divine reciprocation. In proportion to the degree of our surrender to him, he "rewards" us – he gives or distributes himself, reveals himself – even so far as to enter into reciprocal relationships so intimate that "worship" is an accurate reading of *bhajami*.

The nature of pure *bhakti* has been further elucidated by the analysis of Rupa Gosvami, a direct disciple of Caitanya Mahaprabhu and one of the "Six Gosvamis of Vrindavan" whose writings established Gaudiya Vaisnava doctrine. Rupa Gosvami says that pure devotion (*bhaktir uttama*) means service rendered to Krishna in a favorable way that is free from all extraneous desires and from all taint of *karma*, acts done with a view toward

---

10.   *Bhagavad-gita As It Is*, p. 227.

enjoying the results, and *jnana*, philosophical speculation leading toward monistic self-deification.[11]

In the traditional Indian context, *karma* and *jnana* refer to specific forms of religious life. ("Religious," that is, to us today; to those so engaged, it was just life.) *Karma* indicates the discharge of the cycle of duties prescribed in the Vedas, especially the performance of Vedic ritualistic sacrifices (*yajna*); the result of the correct execution of these acts was future enjoyment of the goods of life, in this birth and those to come. *Karma* is this-worldly: Elevation through *karma* to the heavens of the demigods brings a vastly superior and prolonged enjoyment of the senses, although it finally ends. the culture of *karma* in India reached its apotheosis in the school of the *karma-mimamsa*, which held that the *yajna* in itself had the power to bring about the desired ends; it compels even the gods.

Jnana, by contrast, indicates the pursuit of liberation – release from all *karma* – through the renunciation of all desires, the cessation of all activities and the total absorption of the intellect in a radical theology of negation, thereby achieving dissolution of individual identity in a mystical union with an undifferentiated absolute spirit. *Jnana* is radically other-worldly: This world is rejected as false, unreal, or nonexistent, something with which the absolute spirit has no causal or ontological relation at all. At least this is the case in the *advaita-vedanta* propagated by the ninth-century thinker Sankara, in whom the culture of *jnana* finds its most complete "Hindu" exposition.

It is clear that the platform of *jnana* arises in a reaction against *karma; bhakti* in turn seeks to go beyond both. What becomes interesting is the way the relation of these three exhibits the progressive dialectical pattern of thesis, antithesis, and synthesis. The level of *karma* embodies worldly action and absorption in material name and form; *jnana* antithetically turns away from the world and action in it to seek liberation into a transcendence conceived as the negation of all name and form.

---

11. *Anyabhilasita-sumyam jnana-karmady-anavrtam/anukulyena krsnanu-silanam bhaktir uttama.* *Bhakti-rasamrta-sindhu* 1.1.11. Quoted, with translation and commentary by Srila Prabhupada, in *Sri Caitanya-caritamrta. Madhya-lila* 19.167 (Los Angeles: The Bhaktivedanta Book Trust, 1975).

Bhakti sublates and synthesizes features of both. On the platform of *bhakti*, there is "inaction in action" (*akarmani karma*, Bg. 4.18), that is to say, activities performed purely as an offering to God. Since the devotee acts wholly under the will of God, God is the doer, and the deed produces no karmic reaction, good or bad; from a material point of view, nothing has happened. In *bhakti* the world with its panoply of sense objects is neither to be enjoyed as in *karma*, nor rejected as in *jnana*, but used entirely in the service of God, who is its actual possessor and controller. And in *bhakti* the Absolute discloses, in addition to the undifferentiated impersonal aspect encountered in *jnana*, a further, personal feature which, although having no material name and form, possesses spiritual or transcendental names, forms, attributes, activities, and relations. According to Vaisnava teaching, the undifferentiated spiritual light apprehended by the *jnanis* is the effulgence emanating from the transcendental personality of the Godhead.

From the Vaisnava point of view, then, *jnana* represents the penultimate, not the ultimate, platform of spiritual realization. The incompleteness of *jnana* is shown by the way it remains bound to the previous platform of *karma*. Negations depend on that which they negate for their meaning; therefore negations alone cannot escape relativity and attain the Absolute. Nor can the transcendent unity be properly understood as the mere opposite of diversity: that absolute unity cannot exclude but must include variegatedness and diversity.

The paradigm of *karma*, *jnana*, and *bhakti* as representing three phases or moments in a dialectic of spiritual development has application beyond the particular forms of Indian religious life that exemplify them. All three of them are generically human, and can be seen instantiated in various ways in many cultures, embodied in numerous religions and ideologies.

Certainly, the major religious traditions have all these three strands of *karma*, *jnana*, and *bhakti* woven through them.[12] For example, every religion has an abundance of believers whose practice is directed primarily toward

---

12. I take the metaphor of "strands" from Ninian Smart, *Reasons and Faiths* (New York: The Humanities Press, 1958), where the cross-traditional analysis of religious discourse into "Mystical," "numinous," and "incarnational" doctrinal strands anticipates several features of the *karma-jnana-bhakti* typololgy and its application here.

satisfying their material desires, and who think of the divine much more as a means than as an end. People on this platform avoid dealing with the true God of *bhakti*, who makes unconditional and ultimate claims; often they explicitly traffic with a pantheon of specialized, lesser divinities, like spirits, saints, and *devatas*, who are not as formidable and are potentially more pliable and controllable.

Jnana is nearly as wide-spread as *karma*, a fact causing some of its advocates to name it "the perennial philosophy." As a generic phase of human spiritual development, we would expect to find it breaking out all over. It is not even surprising, then, to find strong expression of *jnana* in predominantly theistic traditions like Christianity and Islam. There we find often enough rigorous expositions of the theology of negation (apophatic theology or the *via negativa*), as well as the regular emergence of mystics like Meister Eckhart or al-Hallaj (who even indulge in expressions of self-deification).

The platform of *jnana* is most obvious to us in "religious" contexts, such as the Eleatic criticism of the Homeric gods or the Buddhist revolt against the cult of Vedic *vajna*. But the paradigm is also exemplified in "secular" ideological developments. For example, the historical movement we call the Enlightenment can be understood as a powerful instantiation of the culture of *karma*. The aim of *karma* is to attain material well-being by gaining control over natural processes. This was certainly at the heart of Enlightenment ideology: the central article of faith held that Newton's success in physics could and should be programmatically extended until all of nature – especially human nature in its psychological, social, and political manifestations – became subjected to rational ("scientific") manipulation and control. The reaction came quickly, and the stage of *jnana* became manifest in the form of the counter-Enlightenment (and then matured into the Romantic movement), with its exultation of intuition, holism, organicism, mysticism, etc.[13]

---

13. For a more detailed development of these applications of the *karma-jnana-bhakti* typology, see William Deadwyler, "The Contribution of *Bhagavata-dharma* towards a 'Scientific Religion' and a 'Religious Science,' in I. D. Singh, ed., *Synthesis of Science and Religion: Critical Essays and Dialogues.* (San Francisco: The Bhaktivedanta Institute, 1987).

The struggle between Enlightenment and counter-Enlightenment ideologies continues to shape the cultural dynamics of the West. The counterculture of the Sixties was simply a re-emergence of the original counter-Enlightenment, whose spirit had not been squashed by years of rational scientific and social progress. The emergence of the counterculture surprised and dismayed those who thought they had succeeded in establishing the method of empirical science as the only valid means of knowledge and in dismissing whatever was inaccessible to it as devoid of existence or significance. And the counterculture continues strongly today as the "New Age Movement" or the "Aquarian Conspiracy."

The *karma-jnana-bhakti* progression makes the emergence of ISKCON within the counterculture intelligible. As Prabhupada's "double-dropouts" abandoned "straight" society for the counterculture and then the counterculture for ISKCON, they lived that dialectic spiritual progression, each "dropping out" conveying them, so to speak, across a hyphen. Prabhupada's presentation of *bhakti* as the fulfillment of this progression and his critiques of *karma* and *jnana* were full of personal resonances for most who became his disciples. He was telling them the truth.

Thus, they did not "convert" to a "religion." The terms are alien, the categories inapplicable. And therefore they do not see people outside of ISKCON as practicing "another religion." "All people are following My path," as Krishna said, and that path progresses through various manifestations of *karma, jnana* and *bhakti*. People are distributed on different places along that path; some are hardly moving; others are going forward rapidly. In principle, any person, whether within or without ISKCON, confessing or not confessing a religion, is to be evaluated simply as an individual and by the same criterion that one evaluates oneself – by proximity to pure *bhakti*.

Yet it may be objected that ISKCON is, after all, a "proselytizing," "missionary" organization. Don't we in ISKCON actively seek converts, and doesn't that activity imply our own conviction of institutional superiority?

ISKCON hopes to teach people that pure devotional service is the highest aim of life and to provide them the means for practicing it. The positive influence it can exercise can be of two kinds: People may become

ISKCON members and practice devotional service, or people may realize the nature and importance of pure *bhakti* and seek to practice it within another historical tradition.

Bhakti is taught in many traditions, but so far I have not encountered in any but the Guadiya Vaisnava tradition the lucid, analytical reflection on spiritual experience which so precisely defines *bhakti* and isolates it from the elements of *karma* and *jnana*, as well as the explicit and consistent effort to inculcate such purified *bhakti*. My own conviction is that many Christians, for example, could benefit from this analysis, but they would not have to cease being Christians to do so. Rather, they could mine the resources of their own tradition to pursue pure *bhakti*, thereby becoming more devoted and spiritually advanced Christians.

For even in many devotional traditions the theology of negation has compromised and vitiated *bhakti*. The God one worships may be a person, but the God one thinks about becomes progressively evacuated of all personal features by a resort to abstraction and negation. The influence of *jnana* in theology checks and baffles the natural development of real *bhakti*. While *bhakti* impels us to praise God without ceasing, *jnana* tells us silence alone is valid and chokes the voice of praise and prayer.

Jnana presupposes that language originates here, in our traffic with the objects of this world, and it has no competence to deal with transcendence. When we extend it to speak of the divine, it snaps like an over-stretched rubber band. Such ideas are theological commonplaces, but from the point of view of *bhakti*, they are wrong. *Bhakti* understands that the language conveying the names, forms, attributes, activities, etc. of the transcendent person does not originate in this world. The origin of everything is God, and the original use of language is to praise, glorify, and offer prayer to God. Service to God is the proper and original use of everything. Forgetting God, we pervert that language to traffic with sense objects in this world. But when God reveals Himself and has that revelation conveyed in and through inspired language, language is restored to its original use. It is transcendental speech, and it must be taken with ultimate seriousness.

And is it therefore to be taken–as everyone always worries–"literally?" Rupa Goswami answers this question by saying that our materially contaminated mind and senses cannot apprehend the transcendental quality of the names, attributes, and so on of the Lord. Only when our senses–beginning with the tongue–have become purified by being engaged in devotional service, can they grasp the Lord's names, attributes, etc.[14] Thus, the language that describes God is to be understood literally, but in our conditioned state–with our mind and senses saturated with lust, greed, and anger–we are unable to understand the literal meaning. Yet even though our mundane meanings are perverted and distorted, the language remains real and valid. And even though we cannot grasp the language we use, we must use it unceasingly, for the use purifies our minds and senses so that we will come to understand fully what we speak.

Through "nonsectarian" arguments like this, ISKCON seeks to help encourage and foster the development of pure *bhakti* in any tradition. Yet many will fear that such fostering of *bhakti* is precisely the thing which will most injure the ecumenical spirit. For the negative theology of *jnana* has been widely promoted as the key to inter-religious harmony and even unity, while *bhakti*, with its conceptually specific object of devotion, is often held responsible for sectarian exclusivity and hostility. The claim on behalf of negative theology has perhaps been most strongly advanced by the proponents of *advaita-vedanta* (often still presented as normative "Hinduism"). But we should consider that *advaita-vedanta* "solves" the problem of religious pluralism and diversity by the expedient of wiping it out of the ontology. Only so long as the Absolute is an object of nescience, Sankara says, do the categories of devotee, object of devotion, and the like apply to it.[15] When knowledge arises, these and all other distinctions and differences disappear, for all are unreal and due to ignorance alone.

[14.] *Atah sri-krsna-namadi na bhaved grahyam indriyaih/sevonmukhe hi jihvadau svayam eva sphuranty adah. Bhakti-rasamrta-sindhu* 1.2.234. Quoted in *Bhagavad-gita As It Is*, p. 368.

[15.] George Thibaut, trans., *The Vedanta Sutras of Badarayana with the Commentary by Sankara*, Part I (New York: Dover Publications, 1962), p. 62.

Modern advocates of this position tend to combine a Sankarite metaphysics with recent types of social and cultural relativism, leading them indiscriminately to accept practically all forms of religious life as equally valid. For what reason is there to discriminate invidiously among illusions? Everything is embraced with open arms, but precisely because everything is ultimately rejected right across the board.

Unlike *jnana, bhakti* does not devalorize individuality, diversity, and relativity as such. Indeed, they are found here in this world because they exist in the origin. For *bhakti*, God, the individual souls, and the relations between God and the souls are all eternally, irreducibly, and ultimately real. God sustains ongoing, ever-developing loving relationships with innumerable souls, and in those various relationship God is disclosed in different ways, according to the nature of the relationship. "As they surrender to Me, I reward them accordingly": the "as" in this verse refers not just to differences in *degree* of surrender and revelation, but also to differences in *kind*. In other words, diversity and relativity in religion is not necessarily due to accidental material conditions; it comes from transcendence itself.

Personhood is a social condition; it is made of relationships. We come to be the persons we are out of our personal relations: each relation teases into manifestation an aspect of ourselves that would otherwise remain unknown. So it is with God, who engages in innumerable relationships. The relations we can sustain before we begin to sacrifice internal coherence are limited; but God can in principle combine unlimited self-integration with unlimited relations. Each relationship reveals more of the supreme personality of the Godhead.

In this way, the personalistic theology of *bhakti* recognizes positive spiritual value in religious diversity. To affirm genuine religious experiences wherever they do occur, it is hardly necessary to supersede devotion with speculation and a personal with an impersonal Absolute. We need not propagate ontologies of emptiness to be liberal, broad-minded, and tolerant. If the sectarian intolerance of some devotional communities is actually a consequence of their personalism, then it is owing to too little rather than too much of it.

ISKCON thus offers a vision of inter-religious unity and harmony on the platform of *bhakti*. There are, of course, other traditions like the nontheistic *advaita-vedanta* that also tend to systematically subordinate *bhakti* to *jnana* – most notably the Buddhist traditions. One may object that the view presented here is distinctly inimical to such traditions and is therefore not as liberal-minded as one might like. On the other hand, a view that systematically relegates God, the devotee, and their relationship to the realm of illusion might in turn be considered hostile to *bhakti*. Vaisnava theology, at any rate, accepts that the absolute truth has an impersonal feature as well as a personal feature, so the spiritual achievement of those engaged in various kinds of *jnana* is not written off as a delusion. It is only when people on the basis of such experience propagate philosophies hostile to the Supreme Person that ISKCON devotees raise objections.

Certainly, ISKCON's ecumenical theology of *bhakti* does not end all disagreements. But at the least it achieves this: It recognizes no real difference between *intra-* and *inter-*religious discussion, debate, or dialogue. We may disagree and argue, but still, it is in the family.

WORKS CITED

Bhaktivedanta Swami Prabhupada, A. C. *Bhagavad-gita As It Is.* Complete edition, revised and enlarged. Los Angeles: The Bhaktivedanta Book Trust, 1985.

_____, *Sri Caitanya-caritamrta of Krsnadasa Kaviraja Gosvami. Adi-lila*, vols. 1-3; *Madhya-lila*, vols. 1-9; *Antya-lila*, vols. 1-5, Los Angeles: The Bhaktivedanta Book Trust, 1974-1975.

_____, *Srimad-Bhagavatam.* Cantos 1-10. 30 vols. Los Angeles: The Bhaktivedanta Book Trust, 1972-1980.

Brooks, Charles R. *The Hare Krishnas in India.* Princeton: Princeton University Press, 1989.

Dasgupta, Surendranatha. *A History of Indian Philosophy*, vol. 4. Cambridge: Cambridge University Press, 1922. Reprint edition, Delhi: Motliai Banarsidass, 1975.

De, Sushil Kumar. *Early History of the Vaisnava Faith and Movement in Bengal.* 2nd ed. Calcutta; K. L. Mukhopadhyay, 1961.

Deadwyler, William. "The Contribution of *Bhagavata-dharma* Toward a 'Scientific Religion' and a 'Religious Science.'" In T. D. Singh, ed., *Synthesis of Science and Religion: Critical Essays and Dialogues.* San Francisco: The Bhaktivedanta Institute, 1987.

Frye, Northrop. *The Great Code: The Bible and Literature.* San Diego: Harcourt Brace Jovanovicn, 1981, 1982.

Gelberg, Steven J., ed., *Hare Krishna, Hare Krishna: Five Distinguished Scholars on the Krishna Movement in the West.* New York: Grove Press, 1982.

Goswami, Satsvarupa Dasa. *Srila Prabhupada-lilamrta: A Biography of His Divine Grace A. C. Bhaktivedanta Swami Prabhupada, Founder-Acarya of the International Society for Krishna Consciousness.* Vol. 1-6, Los Angeles: The Bhaktivedanta Book Trust, 1980-1983.

Kapoor, O. B. L. *The Philopsophy and Religion of Sri Caitanya: (The Philosophical Background of the Hare Krishna Movement).* New Delhi: Munshiram Manoharlal, 1977.

Manjumdar, A. R. *Caitanya His Life and Doctrine: A Study in Vaisnavism.* Chowpatty and Bombay: Bharatiya Vidya Bhavan, 1969.

Sankaracarya. *The Vedanta Sutras of Badarayana with the Commentary by Sankara.* Translated by George Thibaut. Sacred Books of the East, vols. 34, 38. Oxford: Clarendon Press 1890, 1896. Reprint ed., New York: Dover Publications, 1962.

Smart, Ninian. *Reasons and Faiths: An Investigation of Religious Discourse, Christian and Non-Christian.* New York: The Humanities Press, 1958.

Smith, Wilfred Cantwell. *The Meaning and End of Religion: A New Approach to the Religious Traditions of Mankind.* New York: The Macmillan Company, 1962, 1963.

_____,"The Modern West in the History of Religion." *Journal of the American Academy of Religion*, vol. 52, no. 1 (March, 1984), pp. 3-18.

MARXISM AND THE RELIGIOUS QUESTION

by

Zdenko Roter

with

Paul Mojzes

I

From the outset one must state clearly and unambiguously that it is simply impossible to provide a single answer as to how the Marxist tradition regarded and continues to regard other religious traditions and *what may be possibilities for the theoretical basis of a common program of action* of all people of good will, including Marxists and Christians, for a better and more just world, in which peace and cooperation between people and between states would prevail.

Namely, it is impossible to speak of a single Marxist tradition, of one Marxism, either as a political theory which aspires to change human relations, or as a political movement, or worldview (*Weltanschauung*), or as an ideology. It is not necessary to prove today, especially in view of the high level of development of mythical, philosophical, sociological, political, and theological studies, that we must speak of Marxisms, about a plurality of Marxisms, about many Marxist traditions, which are related only by a common name and an appeal to the work of Marx. Looking at it radically, from an extremist view, and especially taking into account the experiences of my country and land (Yugoslavia and Slovenia) one could claim, for instance, that there are more commonalities (theoretical and empirical) between "left wing" Christians and humanist Marxists than between the humanist Marxists and dogmatic Marxists.[1]

Methodologically it would be unsound to start from a presupposition about Marxism as a homogeneous theoretical and empirical system. Another very crucial methodological point is the necessity of differentiating between the Marxism as a theoretical reflection appearing in Western countries (including the U.S.A.), which is linked with the activity of Marxist-inspired political movements or intellectual constellations, and the Marxism which appears in the so-called socialist countries, especially in Eastern Europe, in which, until recently, the communist parties enjoyed a monopoly social and political position. Under the circumstances of a one party political system and functioning, Marxism develops into an official state ideology. One needs no great wisdom and analytical cleverness to see the *great differences* between Marxist understanding in a so-called Eurohumanist movement (the paradigm being the Communist Party of Italy) on the one hand and Marxism functioning as an official ideology, for instance in the Soviet Union. Due to the complete prevalence of the concept of a state and social power in a classical Jacobin-Bolshevik manner, Marxism *had to* function, so to say as a mandatory, privileged and necessarily *exclusivistically* conceived ideology.[2]

These *great differences* have now, for a long time, pointed to numerous questions and dilemmas. It is known that the pre-Vatican II integralist Catholic criticism of Marxism claimed that Marxists (Communists) are willing to cooperate and dialogue with Christians only when they are struggling for power, when they are in the opposition. As soon as they take

---

1.   Dogmatism is being used in the analysis of Marxist models as a metaphor for a model in which function supremely a certain number of Marx's, Engels' and Lenin's theorems as dogmas, as unquestioned truths.

2.   Of course, there are differences between East European socialist countries. In some of them, at least for a period of time, the liberal-democratic concept of holding power functioned also (e.g., Czechoslovakia in 1968, Yugoslavia in 1966-1972 and in Slovenia in 1988-1989), although, the determining factor of the system with the Communist Party as the leading force was never allowed to come into question. However, radical changes are under way now in Poland, Hungary, and parts of Yugoslavia.

over power they reject their former "allies" (including Christians) and establish an ideological dictatorship, which leads to persecutions of religion, believers, and religious organizations. I must admit that this criticism was quite effective and that it was based on significant sociological and historical evidence. Related to this on a theoretical level, one may raise a question whether the very essence, the very being of Marxism may contain a latent structure of exclusivism and absolute rejection of religion.

Such criticism and theoretical exploration overlooked something which was less well known in the Western world. During the entire period of the existence of Eastern European socialist states it was not only typical that there was a repressive Jacobin-Bolshevik dictatorship (also in regard to religion), but that there was also a protest, a resistance to such a dictatorship. What is essential for our subject is the permanent existence and renewal of a serious protest against the ruling, official understanding and practice of Marxism as well as its relationship toward religion *within* the Communist movement, *within* the Marxist-inspired intellectual groups and even *within* the ruling politocracies, i.e., oligarchic groups. One should not reduce these phenomena to the usual notions of dissidence. It is not possible to characterize them as occasional changes of emphasis and even less as only a power struggle among various groups and leaders. The case with Milovan Djilas in 1953 in Yugoslavia is in this respect very instructive. We may say that his was the first very serious intellectual Marxist-inspired theoretical rejection of what I called the Bolshevik-Jacobin structures.[3] Historical evidence about the political and cultural events after 1946 to the present in Poland, Czechoslovakia, Hungary, Yugoslavia, and East Germany allows us to look at the breadth, content, and extent of these protests within the Marxist-inspired movements. This evidence proves the possibility of a different, non-dogmatic, humanist interpretation of Marxism.

Another reason for insisting on the model of a conflict within Marxism is due to general theoretical considerations. On the one hand it proves the correspondence (mutual dependence, processes of integration)

---

3.   We are, of course, referring to the first phase of Milovan Djilas' dissent and his book, *The New Class*.

between latent manifestations of structures of a given ideology and the socio-political structures of a specific time and place (in this case the social space of socialist countries). On the other hand, historical and sociological evidence warns us of the fruitlessness of the concept of so-called authentic Marxism (and likewise authentic Christianity and Buddhism, etc.) and of returning to the original teaching, presupposing some unspoiled, clean teaching of the "prophets," and the subsequent departure or deviation of an erroneous teaching. This, of course, does not mean the rejection of recognizing some latent and manifest structures in the original teaching of an ideology or religion. But the futility of this concept is evident especially in the neglect of the processes of interaction between the social and spiritual spheres in a society.

Thirdly, at least from a sociological point of view, the *great temptation* of every ideology (not only Marxist) becomes evident when the followers of an ideology take power into their hands by appealing to their ideology. Thereby they wish to construct, for example, a Marxist society, a Christian society, a Muslim society, and so forth, namely, societies in which a concrete ideology would provide the required criteria for the functioning of all social spheres. The main temptation is that *no ruling ideology tolerates rivalry*, namely, the equal status of other ideologies. The relationship of ruling ideologies toward others ranges from explicit prohibition, to hidden represssive measures, to tolerance in the sense of temporary permissions to exist, provided the privileged status of the ruling point of view is unquestioned. Our discussions of the relationship between ideologies (and religions) should not overlook this.

Concerning the relationship between ideologies in socialist countries, the analysis of the events starting with the October Revolution in the Soviet Union and to the present must not overlook that in those countries there was an encounter, a conflict of *ideology*, of which the totalitarian interpretation was evident not only in Marxism. Totalitarianism was also characteristic of those ideologies which, with the so-called revolutionary changes, lost their formerly privileged totalitarian status (e.g., Russian Orthodoxy in the Soviet Union or Catholicism in Slovakia and Slovenia). This confirms the thesis of the great temptations of every ideology which takes power in an entire society.

II

Since the theoretical reflection about Marxism and the religious question is empirically based I am going to present the case of Yugoslavia – not only because I know it best, but also because Yugoslavia is a part (despite its particularities) of the socialist world, and hence it will be possible to generalize our findings. In 1948 Yugoslavia came into conflict with Stalin, but the so-called *Bolshevik syndrome* continues to burden it to the present day. Observations, analyses, and conclusions about Marxism and the religious question in Yugoslavia are possible and necessary on two levels.

The first level is *theoretical reflection*. The analysis of this reflection includes writings, theoretical studies, and elaborations about Marxism and the religious question at our universities, publishing ventures, and in professional literature. One might call this *academic Marxism*.

The second level must include the so-called *socio-political and ideological practice*, the contents and ways of functioning of Marxist theorems in all spheres of social life, from politics to economy, culture, nurture, education, and morality. This is the level of everyday life, namely, of real conditions and possibilities of human life both as individuals and as various social groups.

First one should point out that in Yugoslavia in respect to the relationship of Marxism to the religious question there was *development, change* and *evolution* which started with relatively firm, rigid, dogmatic theoretical positions of the Bolshevik-Leninist models of interpretation of Marxism and a narrow-minded practice of militant atheism from 1945 onward. By the 1960s it developed in the direction of a pluralism of theoretical searching. From the 1960s to the present it led to a relative (and mostly pragmatically inspired) democratization of the socio-political and ideological practice. Despite that evolution we must not overlook that to the present day the constitution and the laws provide for the Communist Party of Yugoslavia a guaranteed and secure privilege, the so-called avantgarde position, namely, to be the leading social determinant which is responsible "in toto" for social development.[4] Decisive is the fact that the Communist Party still proclaims Marxism as the theoretical basis of its program of social development.

Nevertheless, on *the level of theoretical reflection* within the limits of academic Marxism, the changes are great, qualitative and significant. In the first period (1945-1960) there was the absolute prevalence of the classical Bolshevik-Leninist dogmatic and traditionalist theories of religion. That means that in academic institutions Marxism of the Leninist-Stalinist type was being practiced. The historical materialist philosophical and sociological theory about society and religion was based upon the ontological and gnoseological *theory of reflections* (whose main proponent was Todor Pavlov).

The first characteristic of religion, is that it is a reflection (false, reversed and illusory, of course) of changes and experiences of people in their daily life, especially in the economy.

The second characteristic of religion is that in its essence it is a specific form of social consciousness, which in contrast to other forms of consciousness (culture, science, etc.) will wither under changed social conditions.

The third characteristic of religion deals with the *differentia specifica* of religion as a form among other forms of social consciousness. In distinction to science, art, culture, and morality, which are rational interpretations of the world, religion is in its essence an unscientific, irrational interpretation of the world and society. The essence of religion is mysticism.

The fourth characteristic of religion deals with the so-called social factors of production and maintenance of religion. It was held that religion existed because of the undeveloped economic basis and people's ignorance and negative emotions (fear, disappointment, etc.) as well as the negative social functions created for the needs of the ruling class (religion as the opium for the people). Supposedly, because of all of this, there is the need

---

4.   In the past few years even that claim was legitimately questioned. Currently in the Western parts of the country, especially in Solvenia, the predominant thesis became that of political pluralism, the discontinuation of a single party monopoly and the separation of the Communist Party from power.

for an indirect and direct struggle against religion (militant atheism). Even today one can find in academic circles the remnants of these theories.

However, at present the predominant trend within academic Marxism in Yugoslavia is the so-called *radical, historical humanism*, which established itself in philosophy, sociology and political sciences at the beginning of the 1960s and which affirmed itself as the dominant academic movement in all major Yugoslav academic centers (Zagreb, Ljubljana, Belgrade).

It was not by chance that in the period from 1960 to 1989 there was open and vehement conflicts of groups of Marxist-inspired philosophers and sociologists in these centers with politocractic structures (i.e., the political leadership), which attempted to destroy or at least marginalize precisely this radical humanistic orientation *much more so* than other theoretical orientations (from phenomenology, structuralism to Thomism). This explosion of Marxist humanistic orientation came after the publication of the theoretical works of the young Marx. Already in 1953 the Zagreb sociologist Rudi Supek in a polemic against Stalinism underlined the humanistic nature of the real, original Marxism. Such Marxism does not move on into the primary plane, the abstract laws of dialectics and the so-called objective laws of matter, but rather it stresses the dialectical subjectivity and historical development of the human being's conscious activity, namely, dialectics as the creator of history; the starting point of Marxist humanism is the category of *praxis* and this category is closely connected to the notion of alienation as the prime mover of *praxis*.

Religion should not be primarily seen as a form of social consciousness, but rather as a human appropriation of the world, as a manner and form of human production and of human self-creative praxis. Religion is simultaneously not only an expression and form of human alienation but also the active attempt to conquer human alienation. As a human, authentic praxis religion goes through historical and social changes as well as its own internal renewals. Therefore, the so-called struggle against religion is complete nonsense. Rather, dialogue is needed as a theoretical and socio-political approach to relationships between people.

The presupposition of such a dialogue is the recognition and activity of all people toward creating a universal and structurally social, political, cultural, and spiritual pluralism in society, socialist societies included. Naturally there are differences among various authors of this new orientation relative to the emphases and forms of elaboration of this philosophy of praxis, the meaning of the concept of alienation, and the evaluation of the meaning and interpretative possibilities of empirically based research of religious (and other cultural) phenomena. However, all these differences do not threaten their unanimity in respect of the need to reject the Leninist-Stalinist Marxist tradition on the one hand, and the search for radical socio-political and ideological praxis on the other hand. The changes and evolution on this empirical level are, nevertheless, much more modest and somehow limited due to numerous interests and institutional reasons. The question of the so-called *second-class citizenship of believers* remains, despite everything, a real and open issue to this day in *all* socialist countries.

III

In my opinion one may talk about Marx as a *historical humanist*, but not as an atheist. That is a much richer and more nuanced notion. It is true that historical humanism includes also a form of atheism as a faith in the creative possibilities of the human being. Surely, if the basis of Marxism is dialectical materialism, then from such a basis one can rightly conclude that atheism is its essential component. But for me and for my good colleague and the great Marxist-humanist, Dr. Esad Cimic, Marx was primarily a social philosopher. Hence, it is more useful to view his understanding of religion and atheism from the perspective of the philosophy of praxis. Hence, his beginning position was radical historical humanism within which we see the *human need for transcendence* as an absolute and universal human need. The need for transcending and the forms and contents of the realization of that need do not have to (but can) be religious. From a theological position, which is certainly legitimate, that which transcends (the great transcendence, according to Thomas Luckmann) is something radically different, outside of history, absolutely original and in principle unreachable by our thought. To the contrary, from a Marxist view-point, "*that*" is different, though still somewhat mysterious, unclear, foggy, yet nevertheless, temporal, and in many ways dependent upon the "this worldly" and in many respects open to deciphering. Human history is therefore also the history of different forms, manners, and contents of the realization of the universal human need for transcending. Pluralism of religious and non-religious humanisms is therefore fruitful both on the theoretical as well as on the practical level. The Marxist-inspired model of differentiating between religion *per se*, i.e., religion as a historical-social fact, and religion as an ontological and anthropological structure, which was recently proposed by Prof. Esad Cimic and which created much polemic and dialogue, is in my opinion not only fruitful but also corresponds to Marx's notions of religion. It opens new possibilities for dialogue and simultaneously represents the demand for radical changes in the socio-poitical, cultural, and spiritual realities of socialist countries. This radicalness is also reflected in the demand for the discontinuation of those socio-political, ideological, and cultural structures of that reality, which permits only pragmatically limited and perhaps also only temporary changes in regard to human liberties, and thereby also religious liberties in socialist countries.

Translated from Serbo-Croatian by
Paul Mojzes

ADDENDUM
by Paul Mojzes

When viewing Marxism as a whole one observes that the question of the relationship of Marxists to the "other" is fraught with ambiguity. Two clear alternatives have emerged, with many nuances in between these two alternatives. Viewed separately these alternatives show less ambiguity. Those who mix features of the two views, correspondingly cloud the picture.

The first alternative is the Bolshevik-Leninist-Stalinist interpretation of Marxism, which many also call "dogmatic" Marxism. They envision their own position as "scientific materialism" or *diamat*, an abbreviation for dialectical materialism. The proponents of this view have tended to be very intolerant of not only non-materialistic interpretations of the world but also of other materialistic interpretations which are not deemed to be dialectical and historical. They have tended to wage bitter struggles, even violent ones, not only against non-Marxist positions but even against other Marxist positions. Their Marxist opponents have labelled them for this reason "sectarian" Marxism (*sektastvo*) because they tended to eliminate from contention all views at variance with their own.

The reasons for their rigidity are complex but among the major factors is a certain understanding of science and of truth, as well as the historical context in which this view asserted itself successfully. "Science" and "scientific" has been understood in a simplified 19th-century manner, namely, that the universe is characterized by immutable laws of matter. These must first be understood and then harnessed by complying with them. Thus freedom means the freedom of those who know the true nature of scientific laws and who decide to abide by their determined character. Laws of nature are complemented by laws of society which are equally immutable and determinative. Only those who clearly understand the laws of social development are fit to guide society in the direction in which it is heading anyway. Of all social scientists only the Marxist social scientists have the full grasp of these laws and therefore are fit to be the vanguard, leading that class in society which alone is ultimately capable of being the powerful historical agent of change, namely, the proletariat. Such an understanding of science leads to a notion of Truth rather than truth or truths. Only those insights which are completely compatible with these discerned insights are true; the others are false, illusory, subjective, and as such have no inherent right to exist. In order to free people they have to be helped to liberate themselves from the illusory notions (among which the religious illusions are particularly persistent and hence need to be resolutely rejected) which have a reactionary character. All movements and forces in the world tend to be divided into "reactionary" and "progressive." The Bolshevik-Leninist-Stalinist concept sees Marxism as a progressive, all-embracing, total worldview, which answers all fundamental human questions. Hence it has no real need of other worldviews. Usually it accords the classics of Marxism (Marx, Engels, Lenin, Stalin, etc.) complete consistency with each other and a status of infallibility in nearly all questions. Issues are resolved by searching for a correct interpretation of the classics whose authors are often hailed as the greatest geniuses of humanity. The works of others are examined only as samples of erroneous views and approaches. This is not only the case in philosophy and social sciences, but also in literature, art, music, natural sciences, morality, and lifestyles. If mistakes are made by proponents of this view, the classics are never blamed; at fault must be the interpreters who deviated somewhere from the Truth.

The second alternative is humanistic Marxism. the humanistic Marxists envision themselves as agents for changing society from alienated to less alienated or unalienated forms in which both the individual and collective would find greater opportunities for creativity, freedom, and fulfillment. Humanistic Marxists tend to differ from each other as to how much and which parts of the Marxian corpus is most helpful in accomplishing the task of furthering the development of the human welfare (e.g., there are discussions about the "young Marx" and the "old Marx" and even "post-Marxism"). They do agree with each other that not all insights of the later Marxists or even Marx himself are equally valid (or valid at all); thus they insist on the need to up-date and revise some of the classical Marxist notions. At times they voluntarily embrace the term "revisionist" which from the perspective of dogmatic Marxists, is a "kiss of death," a term equivalent to "heresy" in religion.

Likewise the humanistic Marxists find many valuable insights in other movements, even in religious movements. They tend to be "open" (open-ended) in their thinking, not wishing to create a self-sufficient system of thought but willingly incorporate both traditional insights as well as many non-Marxist contemporary notions as complementing and enriching their own views. The Czech humanistic Marxist Milan Machovec, for instance, stated that a Marxist critic of Christianity should not fault Christians for following Jesus, but for not following him enough. He also maintained that the values promoted by Jesus are so important for subsequent European civilization that he would rather not live in a world without Jesus and the other great religious leaders. Many humanistic Marxists have vigorously sought to interact with other viewpoints, including religious ones, and have freely appropriate ideas which emerged in circles other than their own. They often reject the validity of maintaining that Marxists have better solutions to the world's problems than others, but they show appreciation for certain insights and approaches of Marx and the Marxist tradition, which, they feel, help the human species to come to grips with the real social conflicts and offer the possibility (though not certainty) that changes could be implemented in the direction of greater equality, participation, and self-determination of human beings as active shapers of history.

The "dogmatic" Marxists are generally not interested and even not capable of dialogue, just like the fundamentalist Christians or Muslims, pretty much for the same reasons. If they do participate in some processes which are given the title "dialogue" they are generally able to explain their views and to defend them, i.e., in participating for apologetic and sometimes tactical purposes, seeking practical cooperation in order to accomplish some desired goal which they are at present not capable of accomplishing themselves. These are, however, not genuine dialogues, but, rather, parallel monologues.

The "humanistic" Marxists, who are frequently in serious conflict with "dogmatic" Marxists, have engaged in dialogue, sought it, and sometimes pioneered it. They have often championed tolerance, human rights, civil liberties (including religious liberty) in the societies in which they live, often at considerable risk to their careers and, sometimes, even to their personal and family survival. Since traditionally the Bolshevik-Leninist-Stalinist Marxists held power in socialist societies and even within Communist parties in countries in which they did not hold political power, they monopolized power and tried to silence the "humanistic" Marxists. Politics always played an important, even crucial role, when it came to the question whether Marxists were to engage in dialogue with "the other." Currently (1989) the sociopolitical situation in many Marxist countries (but not in all) is conducive to tolerance and dialogue. Humanistic Marxists are struggling to keep it so.

One of the contributions of humanistic Marxists to our general understanding of dialogue and openness to the other is that such an attitude is not without conflict within one's own tradition. As one relates to the "other" one must be in conflict with the dogmatism within one's own tradition, perhaps within oneself, in order to be open rather than closed.

A MINNESOTA RESPONSE*

by

Patrick G. Henry

A group of scholars in Minnesota became involved in Global Education on Dialogue and Peace among Religions and Ideologies (GEO-DAPRI) because we wanted to help the project avoid the fate of so many academic enterprises that set out intending to do something for the general good and end up doing the standard academic thing in the standard academic way. GEO-DAPRI is too important, holds too much promise, to let it succumb to scholarly business-as-usual. We wanted the GEO-DAPRI authors to have their introductory conference among us in Minnesota so we could challenge them to see their task in a fresh light, jar them loose from the conventions of their disciplines and the routines, the habits into which they, like all scholars, like all people for that matter, tend to fall. We wanted the beginning of GEO-DAPRI to be, in the most basic sense, a *new* beginning. Scholarly help for a world being torn apart by religious and ideological conflict requires a new set of characteristics, or, at the very least, the deployment of the traditional characteristics in a new fashion. We conceived and organized our conference to suggest to the authors that there is a more excellent way, and the suggestion was made not just now and then, but by the structure of the conference itself.

---

* This chapter was drafted by Patrick Henry, Executive Director of the Institute for Ecumenical and Cultural Research, Collegeville, Minnesota, who was one of the Saint John's University representatives to the planning committee and a participant in the conference. It has been revised and refined in discussions with other planners and participants, including Pat Avery, Fred Lukermann, Mischa Penn, and John Sullivan of the University of Minnesota, Paul Martinson, David Preus, Paul Sponheim, and David Tiede of Luther Northwestern Theological Seminary, William Franklin, Robert Spaeth, and Sylvester Theisen of Saint John's University, and Michael Roan of Project Tandem, Inc.

Most academic conferences could take place anywhere. Hotel convention centers are as indistinguishable from one another as airports, and even when a conference is held at a university, the character of that particular university seldom has much effect on deliberations or outcomes. We decided that it would make a difference that our conference was being held in Minnesota, and that the special character of particular institutions would be highlighted, not masked in some high-sounding but specious homage to neutrality or objectivity. We would remind the GEO-DAPRI authors that their audiences are real people with parts and passions, commitments and points of view, not students in classrooms preparing for examinations or other scholars lying in wait for the missing footnote. Of course our goal was not an emotional binge, but our goal was to engage the intellect seriously and appropriately with less ordered dimensions of the common life.

Minnesota is certainly not the only fit setting for such a conference, but the state has a tradition of open politics and widespread active religious life that lends itself to thoughtful consideration of GEO-DAPRI issues. In Minnesota, as in most places, matters of religion and public policy can on occasion become heated, rancorous, divisive, but on balance a remarkable civility infuses debate. The civility is rooted in the state's history and culture, and does not reflect a religious indifference. Studies of religious life and attitudes in Minnesota reveal confusion and perplexity, to be sure, but there is conviction too, and the conviction does not preclude compassion.

One reason for the climate of tolerance is the influence of a variety of academic institutions with different sorts of commitments, and commitments that are not always easy to reconcile. Project Tandem, the nonsectarian, nonprofit corporation that focuses on promotion of the 1981 United Nations Declaration, suggested that the challenge posed to the GEO-DAPRI authors by their project – write in such a way as to change the behavior of individuals and groups – might generate a similar challenge to three distinctly different Minnesota educational institutions: Bring your different interests and goals to bear on a common enterprise. A Protestant seminary, Luther Northwestern, a Roman Catholic liberal arts college, Saint John's, and the University of Minnesota, aided throughout by Project Tandem, discovered in planning and guiding the GEO-DAPRI conference an unexpected expanse of common ground as well as new awareness of and appreciation for each institution's special character and unique role in the overall scheme of the state's intellectual and cultural life. Though we all had different reasons for it, we all agreed on this: we wanted the GEO-DAPRI project, these ten volumes on major religious and ideological traditions, to be something other than what most people would expect. We wanted to help GEO-DAPRI make a difference.

The Question

The question we posed to the GEO-DAPRI authors was, as noted in the Preface above, the following:

> *How does the tradition about which I am writing account for the fact that there are many other religious traditions whose adherents are as firmly committed to them as I am to mine?*

Besides asking for consideration of the way religious traditions themselves *account for* pluralism, and not just the way the traditions *deal with* it, the question also puts the academic lecturer in an unaccustomed spot by using the first person. It does not set up a parallel between "firmly committed adherents of other religious traditions" and "committed adherents of the tradition about which I am writing." The parallel is between "those" and "me" – as firmly committed to them as *I am to mine.*

A fine part of the GEO-DAPRI design is the general, though not entirely consistent, assignment to each tradition of one or more authors who is a committed adherent, and one who is a knowledgeable outsider. Triangulation on a tradition from two perspectives, inner and outer, can serve to deepen the picture. We in Minnesota, however, believed it important at this early stage of the GEO-DAPRI process to encourage the insider authors to acknowledge their involved status, not only their objectivity as scholars but also their commitment as adherents. If at the very beginning of their work together these authors were reminded, in an inescapable way, that the question of religious pluralism is not just an issue they study but also a part of their life in the world, the whole project would gain both in honesty and in intensity, and in its capacity to attract the attention of a global public mesmerized and distracted by religious conflict. Readers honor authors who know their stuff; readers love, and hence may be changed by, authors who not only know their stuff but reveal, either overtly or subtly, that they have lived their stuff as well.

Unsurprisingly, the degree to which the authors of the chapters in this book took the first person challenge varies widely, as does the range of issues they take up under the general rubric of "accounting for" others' beliefs. It is highly instructive to see how different the question itself sounds to adherents of different traditions. While there is a good deal of difference in perspective between Luther Northwestern, Saint John's, and the University of Minnesota, all are American and Western, two are explicitly Christian in their commitments and the third, while secular, is part of a culture deeply shaped by the religious tradition adhered to by the other two, so the question we devised, broad as it is, has a particular cast, a slant that rings odd in the ears of Asians and Africans. Perhaps we should have asked a prior question: "Does my tradition – do I – even attempt to account for others' beliefs? Does the concern of other traditions with such a question strike me as curiously obsessive?"

Whatever prior questions lurk, we asked what we did, and the remainder of this chapter will be a "Minnesota commentary" on the papers in the volume. Into the commentary will be woven some of the observations made in formal presentations by representatives of Luther Northwestern, Saint John's, and the University of Minnesota. It is important to note that in the April conference, as at all such gatherings, much of what really happened is not part of the scheduled proceedings at all, but was talk around the dinner table, chance conversations at coffee breaks, whom you sat by on the bus from one site to another. Cosmologists now suspect that about nine-tenths of the mass of the universe is in unobservable "dark matter." About the same percentage applies to the unrecorded substance of scholarly conferences. In some instances, where the formal talk by the GEO-DAPRI author skirted the personal engagement issue, the personal dimension of the question became apparent in one-on-one conversation or small group discussion.

Woven into the entire conference was an issue posed most directly by faculty at the University of Minnesota: if we acknowledge and value pluralism, how can we maintain a social and intellectual *via media* when there are such strong pulls toward either a thoroughgoing relativism that paralyzes action or a fanaticism that unleashes destructive action? Do judgments ("this opinion is better than that," "one view is truth and another is error") necessarily entail intolerance and discrimination? Can intellectual, moral, even religious commitments be isolated from their political consequences?

To get down to cases: does the missionary tradition and activity that is central to the purpose of Luther Northwestern Theological Seminary have a claim to adherence to the 1981 UN Declaration equal to that of the Hindu tradition which, according to Kana Mitra, has no interest at all in trying to make non-Hindus Hindus? Does Hindu indifference to the missionary enterprise itself–it can even be said that Hindus want to keep others out–seem problematical in light of the remark of one Christian participant in the conference, who said his Marxist partners in Christian-Marxist dialogue tell him, "We don't want you to agree with us, we want you to try to convert us–that way we can have a real discussion!" But this attitude itself is peculiarly culture-bound to the West, for as several scholars from Asia pointed out, Asians characteristically go to great lengths to avoid confrontation. What may be dismissed by a Westerner as a shallow, even insincere politeness may be, for the Asian, simply an expression of proper civil human relations. The Western scheme for ferreting out the truth through argument is not generically human.

The Tradition of Pluralism

The Minnesota conference made clear that pluralism is itself a tradition in the West, and not just a description of a complex current situation. Since Western culture has such pervasive influence throughout much of the world, nearly all other traditions must reckon with the tradition of pluralism. And "reckoning with pluralism" means more than just "foreign relations." It is also "domestic policy": How do adherents of a particular tradition manage their own sharp disagreements over how to deal with pluralism? Indeed, the Minnesota conference may have demonstrated that the question, How do we decide what is *within* our tradition? is more pressing than, How do we deal with/account for those outside? As Roter says explicitly, dialoguers are in a head-on collision with dogmatists. In virtually every tradition there is no single answer to the conference's governing question, about accounting for others' beliefs; many accounts are given, and often those competing accounts are seen as rooted in incompatible versions of the tradition's most fundamental beliefs.

The chapters in this volume display an exciting and daunting range of fundamental assumptions and arguments. According to Abimbola, for the Yoruba there simply is no problem of monotheism and polytheism that seems to obsess others. Deadwyler criticizes those who, by making a particular kind of philosophical theology the norm for dialogue, wipe pluralism out of consideration from the beginning. And language can confuse as easily as it can enlighten. Discussion in a conference session underlined the significance of a point made by Kabilsingh, that we must not too quickly assume that others mean by a word what we would mean by it were we using it. Buddhists are often characterized as "aetheist," but if Christians hear that term as though it carried the weight and nuance of the 19th and 20th century Western philosophical onslaught against classical Western theism, they will seriously misunderstand Buddhism. As Kabilsingh notes, God is put aside not as an error but as a distraction from more pressing concerns. The Christian may find it puzzling, even incomprehensible, that the question, of God can be thought anything less than the most urgent question of all, but the Buddhist is drastically misrepresented when dismissed simply as "aetheist." A case could be made, though probably not conclusively, that the Buddhist downgrading of the God question and the Christian elevating of it are both designed to serve a similar religious end. In any event, a too easy reliance on convenient labels for other traditions is a dangerous habit when we are trying to account for others' beliefs.

Pluralism: Listening Before Defining

Pluralism does not have a single, essential formulation. It is not an a priori description or definition of a state of affairs. The problem of pluralism *feels* different in the settings of the secular university, the Protestant seminary, and the Catholic liberal arts college. The involvement of the three Minnesota institutions in the conference, and their engagement with each other, underlies both our appreciation for the clarity of Paul Mojzes' outline of types of encounter between religions and our unease with its clarity. *The nature of pluralism requires that each group's depiction of pluralism be taken seriously.* The very notion of dialogue itself looks and sounds different from different perspectives. Mojzes notes that there is a variety of individuals in any tradition, but he does not carry his analysis far enough. We have discovered that on the question, How to account for other's beliefs? there is variety *within* individuals over time, and even at the same time. Certainly there are people who have very clear and distinct ideas about who "the other" is and why, but we suspect that equally numerous are those who are quite unsure what pluralism means for them, their beliefs, their attitudes, their behaviors. When this ambivalence is factored in to the analysis of "types of encounter," some of the clear distinctions Mojzes makes, such as between "co-existence" and "defeat of the enemy," appear too neat, too formulaic, and his description of the dynamics of "negotiation" appears too simplistic. Negotiation on these matters is a process not only between religions, but within adherents of those religions – how am I going to sort out, resolve, my own competing convictions about the relation of my religion to others' religions?

Point-Counterpoint
We turn now to a consideration of the individual chapters.

Judaism
Daniel Polish's essay demonstrates subtly and compellingly the reflexive nature of the question the conference posed. He notes that Jewish tradition, in uncompromisingly rejecting "idolatry," has failed to represent the reality of the self-understanding of those condemned as "idolaters." As Polish says, no one self-consciously worships "idols." But then he goes on to show how frequently Jewish self-understanding, especially the notions of chosenness and mission, has been distorted by others. Chosenness does not

mean a claim of superiority, mission does not inspire to proselytism. What Christians would mean by chosen, and what they mean by mission, are not what Jews mean by those terms.

Polish acknowledges, at least implicitly, that there are many Jewish points of view on these, as on nearly every question (even chosenness, he says, is not easily understood by Jews, and he implies that even those who have a clear interpretation of it realize they do not *easily* understand it), and he himself is presenting and advocating an attitude that warmly welcomes and widely accommodates others. We in Minnesota appreciate Polish's openness, but we believe the long-term interests of interreligious understanding will be even better served if more attention is given to the internal debates within a tradition about how to relate to others. We need to hear more about the Orthodox Jewish attitude, and how Reform Jews carry on debates with the Orthodox about, for example, the interpretation of the place of Christianity and Islam in the divine scheme.

One particularly instructive move Polish makes is to insist that the Jewish attitude toward others is not an isolated issue, but is an aspect of the organic thought of Jewish life; this allows him to talk about as fundamental an issue as revelation without appearing to evade the conference's question (though he makes the questionable assertion that divine revelation is a definitive constituent of religion; the Buddhists would object). A very attractive feature of Polish's essay is his frequent allusion to stories, to narratives that reveal attitudes (e.g., the account of God's rebuke of the angels for joining in the Israelites' song of triumph at the Red Sea, the concluding reference to a Kafka story, the image of the lighthouse). By their sensitive use of literary materials, Polish and Abimbola have set an example the other authors would be well advised to follow as they develop their volumes for the GEO-DAPRI project.

Christianity

The paper by Demetrios Constantelos has the advantage of a specific perspective – it does not pretend to be generically Christian, but is self-consciously and explicitly from the point of view of Greek Orthodox Christianity. The paper notes that Orthodox recognize the presence of forces both human and divine that enable them to accept change and seek reinterpretation. However, we in Minnesota wish this point had been the central theme of the essay, because it would have focused attention on crucial questions that are left unaddressed, most especially the question of authority.

For instance, Constantelos says that historical consciousness is crucial for the Orthodox, but history does not provide its own guidance; there has to be some principle or source of authority by which we know what in the past takes priority over what else in the past. Constantelos says that sometimes debate is justified, but does not tell us how to decide whether this or that debate is one of the justified ones. And if the faith is as sure and secure as he says it is, one wonders why there would be resistance to dialogue on the grounds that dialogue itself might weaken the faith. Who determines, and on what grounds, that the goals of two different religions are the same? We raise these questions not because we think the answers are clear, but precisely because we think they are the tough questions, the ones that need to be opened up if the GEO-DAPRI project is to break fresh ground in interreligious understanding.

There is need for adherents of religion A to understand adherents of religion B better. But there is equal need for adherents of religion A, as they think about their relations to adherents of religions B and C and D, to raise and face fundamental questions about themselves. If, as Constantelos argues, pneumatology is the basis for improving relations between the Orthodox and others, the Orthodox need also to consider the implications for their relations with others of their own increasing awareness that 1500 years of intra-Orthodox mutual anathematizing may have resulted from misunderstanding rather than from dogmatic clarity. And Constantelos's conventional attribution of Christianity's universalism to its classical Greek heritage and its exclusivism to its roots in Hebraic tradition needs to be challenged by Deadwyler's observation that philosophical theology masks its own kind of exclusivism that rules out pluralism.

Islam

Khalid Duran's account of Muslim attitudes toward non-Muslims begins with a forthright recognition of the power of historical experience, especially in a tradition's formative period, to shape decisively the way adherents will view outsiders. Whatever theological convergences might be found between Islam and Christianity, it remains permanently true that for the first three hundred years after Jesus Christians were politically and culturally marginalized, and only with the conversion of Constantine did the church rise to the top socially, while for the first three hundred years after Muhammad Islam held complete political sway. It has always been easy for Muslims to say a return to fervent faith will solve all current problems. The question, What caused our downfall? colors all Islamic evaluation of others. And Duran acknowledges that while academics make a disjunction between the caliphate and the theological system, such a distinction has had little practical effect among most Muslims.

In one way or another each essay in this book shows that understanding of others helps shape a tradition's understanding of itself, but in no other case is the connection so clear as in Duran's recognition that the relation to other religions is central to the question, What is authentic Islam? Partly as cause, partly as effect, of this fact, Muslims have a proclivity to consider religious biases as primarily responsible for any discrimination they suffer; they have a strong sense of being victimized because Muslim. We in Minnesota appreciate Duran's unflinching recognition of the social and political context of religious attitudes; his analysis is a model of fair, balanced treatment of one's own tradition. But perhaps he bends over too far – we would like to see more attention to the theological basis for the Muslim attitude toward others.

Hinduism

Kana Mitra's paper is especially instructive for us in Minnesota, since it alerts us to some of the hidden assumptions in our own questions. We are so conditioned by our centuries-long experience of highly articulated and self-conscious religious traditions, that it comes as a surprise to hear that Hinduism, frequently designated the oldest of the major religious traditions, has been thought of as a religion by its adherents only since the 19th century, and not because of any internally generated dynamic, but because of India's encounter with the West. Because religion is such a fundamental category of historical and social analysis for Westerners (even if its precise definition is subject to dispute), it requires a major effort of imagination to understand the implications of Mitra's argument – the question of "the other" simply does not work the same way for "Hinduism" as for the traditions we in the West are more familiar with.

As Mitra says, the Hindu attitude toward the non-Hindu is a specifically *modern* question, so history itself gives no particular guidance how to approach the question. And while Hinduism is now beginning to understand itself in terms imported from Western understanding of "religion," it is still rare for the Indian-born to regard non-Indian "converts" as Hindus. From Mitra's perspective, the history of "Hindu" exclusiveness is not part of the history of religion, but of social relations; it is based on the rules of noble society. Certainly there is among Western historians an increasing tendency to attribute to social and other factors events and developments in Western history (e.g., class warfare in the time of the Protestant Reformation) and even current events (e.g., the economic basis of the conflict in Northern Ireland); we in Minnesota wonder whether, conversely, there may be more "religion" in Indian history than Mitra's analysis suggests.

Further questions that arise from her paper are suggested by other chapters in the volume. She says that for Hindus the net of pluralism is cast very wide, but cannot include the denial of pluralism (in rough terms, the intolerant cannot be tolerated). But Kabilsingh says, or at least implies, that Buddhist tolerance is boundless, and Abimbola argues that for the Yoruba the exclusivist claims of the Christians and the Muslims become "second order" issues that do not preclude Yoruba tolerance of those traditions. We would like to see some discussion of this difference between Hinduism on the one hand and Buddhism and Yoruba religion on the other hand (or is it only an apparent difference?). Moreover, Mitra presents in a highly favorable light the Vedanta tradition, characterized by Ramakrishna's assertion that all the religious roads lead to one goal. But Deadwyler, as we have already noted, raises a sharp question about the practical implications of this

ostensibly open, welcoming view, a question that is intellectually compelling
in its own right and is energized by the experience of Deadwyler's own
tradition, the International Society of Krishna Consciousness, of being
rejected by other exponents of Hindu tradition.

Buddhism

Chatsumarn Kabilsingh's portrayal of Buddhism makes clear that the
tradition has been explicit in its address to the question of "the other" by
addressing issues intrinsic to Buddhism.   Buddhists have difficulty
understanding "authoritarian" religions because in theory no statement is to
be accepted by Buddhists on authority but only after being tested in one's
own experience; nevertheless, there has developed in some branches of
Buddhism a reliance on Bodhisattvas, enlightened ones who can show the
way, and there is a kind of authority that resides in the respect given to the
canon of Buddhist scriptures.   We in Minnesota find ourselves wondering,
however, whether anything non-Buddhist could even be imagined.   Is the
Buddhist net cast so wide that nothing is outside?   As Kabilsingh says, gods
present no problem, since even they are considered to be enmeshed in the
overarching realm of samsara.

Kabilsingh argues for the value of dialogue between religions, but we
wonder whether dialogue has much point if one of the traditions by its nature
can absorb every other tradition.   She notes that making converts is
irrelevant to Buddhism, but is that because Buddhists believe their
interpretation of who others are simply accounts for those others fully?   Do
Buddhists have a scheme that allows them in good conscience not to pay very
close attention to what others are saying?   We believe there are unexamined
implications in Kabilsingh's observation at the end of her essay, that in
Thailand being Thai and being Buddhist are almost equivalent terms – and
not just demographically equivalent, but culturally and even psychologically.
Is the tradition really quite so open as, in theory, it purports to be?

China

Julia Ching's essay begins with a startling observation: for much of
Chinese history the question, How do you regard outsiders?   would have

appeared meaningless, for the Chinese thought they inhabited the full extent of the world. As in the case of Hinduism, there is a fundamental question about the designation of traditions as "religions," with the terminology currently used having developed only recently, "representing a retrospective outlook on the results of historical developments." But while the identification of the "three religions" (Confucianism, Taoism, Buddhism) puts them all in the same category, Chinese are fully aware that Buddhism came from elsewhere, and "the insider/outsider dichotomy can be discerned in the interrelationships *between* China's three religions."

More than any of the other chapters in the book, Ching's demonstrates awareness of the way the question of "the other" can become not just one over against another, but a sense of inner division (or complementarity) in the self. In one of the discussion sessions Ching herself spoke of her own profound sense of dual citizenship in both the Christian and Confucian traditions, and implied both that the dual citizenship comes naturally to a Chinese, and that the dual citizenship also helps her understand similar experiences on the part of other religious persons. With a finely-tuned historical sense, Ching demonstrates how the appearance of a new "other," the Jesuit missionaries, sharpened distinctions already present in the Confucian community, leading to what some modern students of Confucianism believe is a serious imbalance in the tradition itself. And her historical sense informs also her recognition that in actual practice Taoism is virtually indistinguishable in some of its features from Confucianism and in others from Buddhism.

She highlights questions about "the other" that seem especially clear and compelling in the Chinese context: which is closer to the truth – the Buddhist conquest of China or the Chinese conquest of Buddhism? and what difference would it have made to the Christian mission in China had the Christians been more willing to adapt culturally? Ching's account of the practical adherence to all three traditions on the part of many people suggests a blurred line between "harmony" and "syncretism," but goes beyond even that question to suggest that the Western determination to figure out which of those it is may itself be a highly culture-bound concern. Ching says we can speak of Chinese religion in the singular with manifestations in the plural. In so doing, she is trying to mould traditional Western analytical terms to fit an Asian reality. She is of course in this chapter writing for a Western audience. We in Minnesota would be interested to know how she would try to make the dynamics of Western religion intelligible to a Chinese audience for whom the experience of "the religious other" comes from another universe.

Yoruba Religion

The most immediately striking feature of 'Wande Abimbola's chapter in the context of this volume is its attention (similar to Polish's) to stories, to traditional texts that make the point about Yoruba attitudes toward outsiders (e.g., that all human beings are kin) not in terms of formal argument but in the dynamics of the relations between characters in a tale. We would encourage all the GEO-DAPRI authors to take a clue from Abimbola and Polish, and look for anecdotes, episodes, songs, poems (and for rituals too, such as the kingship rituals that Abimbola notes are "occasions when the new religious pluralism, tolerance and peaceful relations among the several religions in Yoruba communities are openly acknowledged and demonstrated") that capture, sometimes indirectly, the shades and nuances of religious attitudes better than discursive argument. After all, people experience their lives not in seminars but in the middle of things.

Abimbola makes clear that how a tradition understands another tradition may depend not only on what the other proposes by way of belief and practice, but also on the way that tradition is first encountered. Islam, he notes, came on the scene gradually, not demanding a complete conversion immediately, whereas Christian missionaries required immediate destruction of traditional beliefs – in a traditional Yoruba verse, "It was all of a sudden that Christianity emerged." "Others" who appear "all of a sudden" may shape our response to them by the very manner of their appearing.

Krishna Consciousness

William Deadwyler's chapter, among all those in the volume, deals most directly with the question we posed for the Minnesota conference. He shows how the question of "the other" is experienced by the International

Society of Krishna Consciousness (ISKCON) both as internal to Hinduism and as external, in the dealings of Krishna Consciousness adherents with adherents of other traditions. He balance his general remarks with personal reminiscences and reflections. We particularly appreciate these features of his contribution to the conference, and also the challenge he presents to the opinion, common both among religionists and academics, that philosophical speculation is the realm of religious convergence and the particularity of piety and practice necessarily divides.

Deadwyler makes a forthright claim that there are positive spiritual values in religious diversity itself, but seems to contradict himself, implicitly at least, in proposing that ISKCON is not practicing a religion but is simply teaching *dharma*, and *dharma* is simply "the truth." His observation that treating "religion" as a separate sphere of life is a modern development would be seconded by some historians of culture, though not all; the observation resonates with Kana Mitra's point that "Hinduism" as a concept is a product of the 19th century. But by saying ISKCON is a complete alternative culture that has no place among the religions of modernity, Deadwyler appears to us to be asserting a privileged place for ISKCON even while he applauds religious diversity: if those in ISKCON do not see people outside ISKCON as "practicing another religion," are those in ISKCON really taking seriously those outside? This amounts to telling the outsider, "Your think you know what you are doing, but you are not really doing so; I know better than you do what you are doing." We wonder if anything can escape quite so completely from its contemporary context as Deadwyler says ISKCON does.

The dynamic of Enlightenment versus Counter-Enlightenment that Deadwyler sets up is suggestive, and may help explain a great deal that is going on in our culture. But the way in which the Counter-Enlightenment organizes and understands itself is decisively shaped by our formation in the Enlightenment tradition. We cannot leap back over the eighteenth century and pretend it did not happen.

Marxism

Roter begins his essay with a refreshing admission: it is impossible to give a single answer to the question about the Marxist attitude toward other traditions, because there is no such thing as a single Marxist tradition. Other chapters in the volume deal with their traditions' own ambivalences, but Roter is more forthright than any of the others. His open admission of difficulty is striking testimony to the ferment currently occurring in Marxist communities around the world, a ferment underlined in Mojzes's commentary on Roter's essay. (There is an interesting conversation lurking in these remarks of Roter's and Julia Ching's observation that it is Marxism that has most stridently introduced an insider [party members]/outsider [the rest of the population] mentality into China.) Indeed, Roter even speaks of a "permanent protest" built into Marxism, and argues strongly that it is fruitless to search for a so-called "authentic" Marxism (or, by extension, Buddhism or Christianity).

The social and spiritual spheres interact, according to Roter, and as a result tidy categories do not work. More clearly than anyone else in the volume, Roter illuminates the effect political power has on the extent to which a tradition is tolerant of others, and his statement is unequivocal: "no ruling ideology tolerates rivalry." Some of us in the West would want to debate that proposition, though the debate would probably get bogged down in efforts to define and delimit "ideology" and even "ruling." Still, Roter's way of dealing with the conference's question suggests to the other GEO-DAPRI authors that they pay more attention to the political context in which a tradition's understanding of "the other" is shaped. It is certainly striking that at a time when some adherents of ancient religious traditions are arguing that modernity has ruled out transcendence so religion must come to terms with and make a place for itself in a world devoid of any reference beyond itself, a committed Marxist speaks of the human need for transcendence and declares the struggle against religion to be complete nonsense.

It does seem to us that Roter, despite his disavowal of any effort to disentangle an "original" or "authentic" Marxism, is throughout his essay implicitly appealing to what Marx "really" meant against what he sees to be terrible distortions by the Soviet state. We do not find this surprising, and in fact wonder whether it is possible for any of the traditions discussed in this volume to avoid debates over what is "original" and "authentic."

Conclusion

As we conclude our comments, both appreciative and critical, on the chapters in this volume, we Minnesotans register our astonishment that a project such as GEO-DAPRI, and our conference that inaugurated it, have happened. We are accustomed to scholarly gatherings, and dialogue has become a way of life for many religious people. But in the coming together of experts in so many traditions, under the rubric of the 1981 United Nations Declaration, to consider how scholarship can further the aims of that document, and in their coming together at the invitation of three such disparate institutions as Luther Northwestern Theological Seminary, Saint John's University, and the University of Minnesota, with all their differences in atmosphere, context, history, mission, there was a sense of fresh winds blowing in new directions. To be at the conference was to feel oneself in unfamiliar, though not alien, territory. Many of us marveled: "This is going on! This is really happening, right now, here in this place!" It takes something way out of the ordinary to get a rise like that out of jaded academics.

We hope our contribution to the discussion, both during the days of the conference in April 1989 and in our comments in this chapter, will prove useful to the GEO-DAPRI authors as they move forward in composing their books. We believe this present volume, which opens up the enriching and potentially explosive question of how religious traditions account for "the other," can itself serve the purposes of the 1981 United Nations Declaration, by reminding readers that interreligious relations are not abstract theories, but are the stuff of people living together in a challenging world.

The GEO-DAPRI Conference had its own integrity, but our working together on the issues raised by the subject has opened for us new horizons for exploration and cooperation. We Minnesotans intend to continue the discussion, and we hope others, perhaps from institutions unlike the three we represent, will join the conversation.

We will explore further what "toleration" means. One of the local speakers at our conference asked the disturbing question, "Can you remember a time when you were 'tolerated'?" suggesting that from one point of view, toleration is a form of control, inextricably linked to issues of power and dependence.

We will consider in more detail the problems and possibilities inherent in the notion of *hospitality* as an alternative to *tolerance*. The monastic tradition is especially well practiced in the arts and skills of welcoming outsiders: the "other" is first of all the "guest." And as one of our local speakers noted, "Listening is the fundamental attitude of the monk." But the question was also raised: Will male monastics be able ungrudgingly to look to women monastics for guidance, really to *listen* to them? And is there a danger that hospitality will subtly nudge the outsider to "fit in"? Academic institutions with clearly articulated religious identities are ready-made laboratories for experiments in reckoning with pluralism.

We will continue to advocate, for ourselves and anyone else concerned to promote understanding across religious lines, the "turn to the concrete"–the use of stories, narratives, poetry, ritual, to probe and illustrate the actual lived experience of religion. Everyone, especially academics, needs to be reminded repeatedly that we live not in abstract categories, but in the middle of things. Indeed, "in the middle" might be the most succinct expression for where our Minnesota group finds itself. We look for a *via media*, but our image for that place is not a narrow fence upon which we balance in constant trepidation that we will fall to one side or the other, thoroughgoing relativism or fanaticism. Rather, we take our bearing from another of our local speakers, who suggested we are in a salt water marsh, where there is constant motion, teeming life, and an ever-shifting boundary between sea and land. Our task is not to figure out where we are, but to notice what is gong on all around us. Like all scholars, we will analyze, theorize, speculate, muse, concoct, but the distinctions in our points of view will remind us always to return to the actual situation. Anecdotes may loom larger for us than dogmatically-stated axioms.

Finally, we will try to be guided by one of the most eloquent statements made during the conference. It came from an undergraduate who had been asked to comment on the papers presented at Saint John's. "Be simple," he challenged all of us. This was not directly a critique of the papers; he expressed great appreciation for them. It was, rather, a profound plea from someone in the next generation that we bequeath to them a story as unencumbered with our own disciplinary preoccupations as we can make it. The student has no illusions that the world is easy to describe or live in. He knows scholarship is hard work. But he suspects the fruit of hard work is, or at least can be, a simplicity won through an honest engagement with complexity. Among the many and noble ideals enunciated in academic coats of arms—*truth*, *light*, *wisdom*, to name a few—*Be Simple* deserves an honored place.

AUTHORS

'Wanda Abimbola (Yoruba) studied at University College, Ibadan, Nigeria, received a BA at the University of London, an MA from Northwestern University and a Ph.D. from the University of Lagos. He has taught at the universities of Ibadan, Lagos, Ife, Indiana and Amherst College. He was the Vice-Chancellor of Obafemi Awolowo University, Ile-Ife, Nigeria from 1983 to 1989, and at present is Fulbright Visiting Scholar at Amherst College. His books include: *Sixteen Great Poems of Ifa* (1975), *Yoruba Oral Tradition* (1976), *Ifa Divination Poetry* (1977) and *Ifa: An Exposition of Ifa Literary Corpus* (1977).

Julia Ching (Confucian and Catholic) is Professor of Religious Studies and East Asian Studies at the University of Toronto. She has also taught in Australia (Canberra), the USA (Columbia and Yale), Germany (TÜbingen) and Taiwan (Tsing Hua). She is the author of eight books, including most recently, *Probing China's Soul: Religion, Politics, Protest* (New York: Harper and Row, 1990). Born in China and educated in Hong Kong and the West, she has constantly striven to advance the mutual appreciation and understanding of East and West. Among her honors and distinctions is her recent election as a Fellow of the Roual Society of Canada.

Demetrios J. Constantelos (Greek Orthodox, Charles Cooper Townsend Sr. Distinguished Professor of History and Religious Studies at Stockton State College, Pomona, NJ, is a graduate of Holy Cross Greek Orthodox Theological School, (B.A.Th.), Princeton Theological Seminar (Th.M.), Rutgers University (M.A, Ph.D.). He is the author of *Byzantine Philanthropy and Social Welfare* (1968), *Understanding the Greek Orthodox Church* (1982); editor of *Orthodox Theology and Diaconia* (1981); and author of many studies, articles, and reviews published in over thirty journals. His latest work is *Society, Poverty and Philanthropy in the Late Medieval Greek World (1204-1453)* (in press).

William H. Deadwyler, III (Krishna Consciousness) received a Ph.D. in religion from Temple University, Philadelphia, PA in 1980 with a dissertation on Hartshorne's notion of God. He has taught religion on the university level for several years and published a number of scholarly articles in the field. In 1971 he became the President of the International Society for Krishna Consciousness (ISKCON) of Philadelphia; in 1986 the Initiating Guru of ISKCON; in 1987 a Governing Body Commissioner of ISKCON; and in 1988 the Chairman of the Governing Body Commission of ISKCON.

Khalid Duran (Muslim), educated in Spain, Pakistan and Germany (political science and sociology at the universities of Bonn and Berlin), became Associate Professor at the Islamic Research Institute in Pakistan, and taught at Islamabad University and the Pakistani National Institute of Modern Languages. From 1978 to 1986 he was research scholar at the Deutsches Orient-Institut in Hamburg, was Visiting Professor of Islamics at Temple University (1987) and American University (1988), and currently at the University of California, Irvine. His books include *Islam and politischer Extremismus: Einführung und Dokumentation* (1986).

Patrick G. Henry (Protestant) is Executive Director of the Institute for Ecumenical and Cultural Research in Collegeville, Minnesota. Following undergraduate work in history and English at Harvard, theology at Oxford as a Marshall Scholar, and doctoral study with Jaroslav Pelikan at Yale, he taught in the Religion Department at Swarthmore College in Pennsylvania from 1967 to 1984. His publications include *New Directions in New Testament Study* (1979) and, with Donald K. Swearer, *For the Sake of the World: The Spirit of Buddhist and Christian Monasticism* (1989).

Chatsumarn Kabilsingh (Buddhist) received an M.A. in religion from McMaster University, Canada, and a Ph.D. in religion from Magadh University, India in 1982. Since 1973 she has been professor at Thammasat University, Bangkok, Thailand. Her many books published in Thai include: *Essence of Buddhism: Theravada-Mahayana* (1975), *History of Buddhism in Thailand* (1981), *Buddhism in China* (1982), *Women in Buddhism* (1985), *Buddhist Women in Foreign Lands* (1989). Her English books include: *A Comparative Study of Buddhist Nuns' Monastic Rules* (1984), *A Cry from the Forest* (1987).

Kana Mitra (Hindu) received an M.A. in philosophy from Calcutta University in 1956 and a Ph.D. in religion from Temple University, Philadelphia, PA in 1980. She taught for over ten years at Calcutta University and more than fifteen years at several universities in the U.S. At present she teaches at LaSalle and Villanova universities. She has published a number of scholarly articles and the book: *Catholicism-Hinduism: Vedantic Investigation of Raimundo Panikkar's Attempt at Bridge Building* (1987). She is an Associate Editor of the *Journal of Ecumenical Studies.*

Paul Mojzes (United Methodist), a native of Yugoslavia, was educated at Belgrade University, Florida Southern College and Boston University, where he received his Th.D. He is Co-Editor of the *Journal of Ecumenical Studies*, Editor of the *Occasional Papers on Religion in Eastern Europe* and Professor of Religious Studies at Rosemont College, Rosemont, PA. He is author of many articles on religion in Eastern Europe and Christian-Marxist dialogue. His books include *Varieties of Christian-Marxist Dialogue* (1978), *Christian-Marxist Dialogue in Eastern Europe* (1981), *Christian-Marxist Encounter: Is Atheism Essential to Marxism?* (1985).

Daniel Polish (Jewish) recieved a M.A.H.L. and rabbinic ordination at Hebrew Union College in Cincinnati, and a Ph.D. in the History of Religion from Harvard University. He was Associate Executivwe Vice President of the Synagogue Council of America, the umbrella agency for the Reform, Conservative and Orthodox movements in the United States. He has taught at Tufts University, the University of Maryland and the Los Angeles School of the Hebrew Union College. He has published many articles and co-edited *The Religious Basis for Social Policy in the Jewish and Catholic Traditions* and *The Liturgical Foundations for Social Policy in the Jewish and Catholic Traditions.*

Zdenko Roter (Marxist) is a professor and Dean of the School of Sociology, Political Science, and Journalism of University of Ljubljana, Yugoslavia. He received his education at the universities of Ljubljana and Sarajevo, with a speciality in the sociology of religion. He is the author of numerous studies, including three books in the field of sociology of religion, and edited the journal *Theoria in praksa*. Currently he is leading a team of sociologists studying public opinion in Slovenia. Several of his articles on Christian-Marxist dialogue, human rights and religious freedom were published in the *Journal of Ecumenical Studies* and *Occasional Papers on Religion in Eastern Europe.*

Leonard Swidler (Catholic) has an STL in Catholic Theology, University of Tübingen and a Ph.D. in history and philosophy, University of Wisconsin. Professor of Catholic Thought and Interreligious Dialogue at Temple University since 1966, he is author or editor of over 40 books and Co-founder (1964) and Editor of the *Journal of Ecumenical Studies*. His books include: *Dialogue for Reunion* (1962), *The Ecumenical Vanguard* (1965), *Jewish-Christian Dialogues* (1966), *Buddhism Made Plain* (co-author, 1984), *Toward a Universal Theology of Religion* (1987), *A Jewish-Christian Dialogue on Jesus and Paul* (1990), *After the Absolute: The Dialogical Future of Religious Reflection (1990).*